RECONCEPTUALIZING LIBRARIES

Reconceptualizing Libraries brings together cases and models developed by experts in the information and learning sciences to explore the potential for libraries to adapt and transform in the wake of new technologies for connected learning and discovery. Chapter authors explore the ways that the increased interest in the design research methods, digital media emphases, and technological infrastructure of the learning sciences can foster new collaborations and formats for education within physical library spaces. Models and case studies from a variety of library contexts demonstrate how library professionals can act as change agents and design partners and how patrons can engage with these evolving experiences. This is a timely and innovative volume for understanding how physical libraries can incorporate and thrive as educational resources using new developments in technology and in the learning sciences.

Victor R. Lee is Associate Professor of Instructional Technology and Learning Sciences at Utah State University, USA.

Abigail L. Phillips is Assistant Professor in the School of Information Studies at the University of Wisconsin-Milwaukee, USA.

RECONCEPTUALIZING LIBRARIES

Perspectives from the Information and Learning Sciences

Edited by Victor R. Lee and Abigail L. Phillips

Routledge
Taylor & Francis Group

NEW YORK AND LONDON

First published 2019
by Routledge
711 Third Avenue, New York, NY 10017

and by Routledge
2 Park Square, Milton Park, Abingdon, Oxon, OX14 4RN

Routledge is an imprint of the Taylor & Francis Group, an informa business

Library of Congress Cataloging-in-Publication Data
Names: Lee, Victor R., editor. | Phillips, Abigail L., editor.
Title: Reconceptualizing libraries : perspectives from the information and
    learning sciences / edited by Victor R. Lee and Abigail L. Phillips.
Description: New York, NY : Routledge, 2019. | Includes bibliographical
    references.
Identifiers: LCCN 2018017067 (print) | LCCN 2018037145 (ebook) |
    ISBN 9781315143422 (eBook) | ISBN 9781138309555 | ISBN
    9781138309555 (hardback) | ISBN 9781138309562 (paperback) |
    ISBN 9781315143422 (ebk)
Subjects: LCSH: Libraries and education. | Libraries and community. |
    Libraries—Information technology.
Classification: LCC Z718 (ebook) | LCC Z718 .R43 2019 (print) |
    DDC 025.5—dc23
LC record available at https://lccn.loc.gov/2018017067

ISBN: 978-1-138-30955-5 (hbk)
ISBN: 978-1-138-30956-2 (pbk)
ISBN: 978-1-315-14342-2 (ebk)

Typeset in Bembo
by Apex CoVantage, LLC

Victor: For my kids, who always find something interesting at the library

Abigail: For my Dad

CONTENTS

ABOUT THE EDITORS

Victor R. Lee is Associate Professor of Instructional Technology and Learning Sciences at Utah State University. He is past recipient of the National Science Foundation CAREER Award, the Jan Hawkins Award from the American Educational Research Association, and a National Academy of Education/Spencer Foundation Postdoctoral Fellowship. Lee's previous book, *Learning Technologies and the Body: Implementation and Integration in Formal and Informal Learning Environments*, was published by Routledge in 2015. Current research involves wearable technologies, the quantified self, maker education, and STEM education both in and out of school settings. He received his Ph.D. from Northwestern University.

Abigail L. Phillips is an Assistant Professor in the School of Information Studies at the University of Wisconsin-Milwaukee. Prior to entering academia, Phillips worked as a librarian in a small, rural public library, where her interest in librarianship practices and young adults emerged. Current research involves digital youth, cyberbullying, digital citizenship, empathy, rural libraries, librarianship practices, making in the library, and neurodiversity. She received her Ph.D. from Florida State University.

CONTRIBUTORS

June Abbas is Professor in the School of Library and Information Studies at the University of Oklahoma, United States of America.

Barrie Adleberg is the Creative Director of Digital Learning at Connected Sparks, United States of America.

Micah Altman is the director of research for Massachusetts Institute of Technology Libraries, United States of America.

Megan Bang is an Associate Professor in the College of Education at the University of Washington Seattle, United States of America.

Philip Bell is a Professor and Shauna C. Larson Chair in Learning Sciences in the College of Education at the University of Washington Seattle, United States of America.

Elizabeth Bonsignore is Assistant Research Scientist at the University of Maryland, College Park, United States of America.

Ashley Braun is a Children's Services Librarian at Seattle Public Libraries, United States of America.

Josephina Chang-Order is a Ph.D. student in the School of Education at the University of Colorado Boulder, United States of America.

Tamara Clegg is an Associate Professor in the College of Information Studies and College of Education at University of Maryland, United States of America.

Lenese Colson is a Ph.D. Student in the School of Information at Florida State University, United States of America.

Richard Lee Davis is a Ph.D. student in the Graduate School of Education at Stanford University, United States of America.

Laura Gogia is a principal with Bandwidth Strategies, Inc., United States of America.

Derek Hansen is Associate Professor in the Information Technology Program at Brigham Young University, United States of America.

Diana Hellyar is a reference librarian at University of Hartford, United States of America.

Faye R. Jones is Senior Research Associate, Information Use Management & Policy Institute, Florida State University, United States of America.

Yasmin Kafai is the Lori and Michael Milken President's Distinguished Professor at the University of Pennsylvania, United States of America.

Sue Kimmel is Associate Professor in the Department of STEM Education and Professional Studies at Old Dominion University, United States of America.

Kyungwon Koh is an Associate Professor in the School of Information Sciences at the University of Illinois, United States of America.

Kari Kraus is Associate Professor in the Department of English at University of Maryland, College Park, United States of America.

Rekha Kuver is the Youth and Family Services Manager for Seattle Public Libraries, United States of America.

Victor R. Lee is Associate Professor of Instructional Technology and Learning Sciences at Utah State University, United States of America.

Kung Jin Lee is a Ph.D. student in the Information School at the University of Washington, United States of America.

Chris Leeder is a research associate in the School of Communication and Information at Rutgers University, United States of America.

Marcia A. Mardis is an Associate Professor in the School of Information at Florida State University, United States of America.

INTRODUCTION

Victor R. Lee and Abigail L. Phillips

Throughout the United States, libraries are facing pressures to change. After all, one can just run a Google search, turn to Wikipedia, or query friends on Facebook to see what information is available and recommended. New technological infrastructures and big data algorithms seem to render library services moot, as books and other publications are being suggested to us based on what we had purchased, read, or even glanced at before. For a large part of the population, it seems that printed books have become blasé. And while libraries and library personnel have long advocated for awareness that they are informational and educational institutions and professionals, the role that libraries serve in providing learning opportunities is often overlooked by the general public. Many do not realize that libraries are regularly providing instruction, exhibits, seminars, and programs for their communities. Many do not notice that many libraries in many different locales are seeking out ways to expand and improve upon how they support learning and information discovery. Many do not realize the kinds of partnerships that are being undertaken with researchers and designers to enhance the library experience. Given that, what prominent, concrete images do we have that best exemplify the efforts to change the popular image of what is happening in the physical library? How can we spotlight the changing roles of the people who are tirelessly doing and reinventing the work involved in making libraries into vibrant, community-relevant learning spaces?

Those questions motivated the preparation of this edited book. We (Lee and Phillips, the editors of this volume) were each beginning to wonder about these within our two respective academic communities. Lee was trained in the learning sciences and has been involved in projects studying and designing for learning in a range of settings for many years and with many populations. Phillips was a former librarian who was trained in information sciences and had been studying modern-day librarianship practices and young adult services in libraries. Funding opportunities and professional networks brought them together as colleagues in Logan, Utah, and the conversations that led to this book began.

In preparing this book, we had recognized that there were emerging success cases and new models for library-based learning that were being developed by experts in the information and learning sciences, and some dialogue between the fields was beginning. As a field, the learning sciences was expanding beyond its sociocultural and cognitively oriented design work with technology and activities in classrooms and museums and into more seriously examining a range of other settings for learning. Libraries were among those settings. The library and information sciences had been broadening its emphasis areas beyond information storage, archival, search, and retrieval and had been taking increased interest in the design research methods and digital media emphasis of the learning sciences. Documented success cases such as the *YOUMedia* program in Chicago and substantial research and development investment from organizations like the MacArthur Foundation's *Digital Media and Learning* program have motivated calls for more dialogue and collaboration between information and learning scientists. Connected learning, as a perspective on how to envision twenty-first-century, digitally enhanced, interest-driven learning, was establishing a unifying viewpoint. Leading organizations, such as the Association for Information Science and Technology, saw the arrival of a new special interest group in the area of information and learning sciences. A major conference at the International Society of the Learning Sciences saw a symposium that examined how libraries were increasingly important sites for designing computer-supported collaborative learning. Universities were beginning to hire across field boundaries, and faculty were obtaining joint appointments across information schools and schools of education. At the time of this book's preparation, a new peer-reviewed academic journal, *Information and Learning Sciences*, is set to premiere and become a venue for research at the intersection between the two fields. It seemed that this book, which would compile the research in these fields as it related to libraries, was timely and appropriate for helping to advance this dialogue.

Thus, we, the editors, began the months of work needed to identify who had been doing new research or design at this intersection of the information and learning sciences. It was through good fortune and enthusiastic response that we were able to find a number of outstanding scholars and projects that are represented in the pages that follow. As this book was being prepared, we learned about even more projects that were being conceived or had just gotten underway, and it is with some regret that the timing of this book's preparation and the launch of these new efforts were not aligned. It is our expectation that those other projects that did not get featured in this volume will later garner attention and also promote dialogue. What is included in this book, like all academic compendia, is a product of the time at which it was prepared. Moreover, at the time that we began to organize and compile this book, the intersection between information

Crystle Martin is the Director of Library and Learning Resources at El Camino College, United States of America.

Vera Michalchik is the Learning Officer for Measurement, Evaluation, and Learning at the Gordon and Betty Moore Foundation, United States of America.

Laura Pasquini is Lecturer with the Department of Learning Technologies at the University of North Texas, United States of America.

William R. Penuel is a Professor in the School of Education at the University of Colorado Boulder, United States of America.

Abigail L. Phillips is an Assistant Professor in the School of Information Studies at the University of Wisconsin–Milwaukee, United States of America.

Shana Pribesh is an Associate Professor of Research and Statistical Methods in the Educational Foundations and Leadership Department at Old Dominion University, United States of America.

Mimi Recker is Professor of Instructional Technology and Learning Sciences at Utah State University, United States of America.

Rebecca Reynolds is an Associate Professor in the School of Communication and Information at Rutgers University, United States of America.

Barbara Schultz-Jones is Associate Professor in the Department of Information Science at the University of North Texas, United States of America.

K-Fai Steele is Program Associate at the National Writing Project, United States of America.

Mega Subramaniam is Associate Professor in the College of Information Studies at University of Maryland, United States of America.

Orkan Telhan is Associate Professor of Fine Arts, Emerging Design Practices at University of Pennsylvania, United States of America.

Amy Twito is the Informal Learning Manager at Seattle Public Libraries, United States of America.

Carrie Tzou is Associate Professor in the School of Educational Studies at University of Washington-Bothel, United States of America.

Renee Walsh is a STEM librarian in the Department of Research Services at University of Connecticut Library, United States of America.

Rebekah Willett is Associate Professor in the Information School at University of Wisconsin–Madison, United States of America.

Jason Yip is Assistant Professor in the Information School at the University of Washington, United States of America.

Beth Yoke is Executive Director of the Young Adults Library Services Association (YALSA), United States of America.

ACKNOWLEDGMENTS

The idea for a book was developed from conversations that were made possible because of funding that was provided by Utah State University to allow Abigail Phillips to relocate to Utah and spend substantial time working with Victor Lee as he began to more heavily extend his learning sciences work to library settings. We are grateful that both Crystle Martin and Marcia Mardis were involved in making that match so that this collaboration was possible. Once Abigail had arrived, we were also grateful to the Institute of Museum and Library Services, from whom funding for a research grant was awarded (RE-31-16-0013-16) that provided an immediate context and stable group of research team members who helped us to see a need for such a volume. That research team included Mimi Recker and, at various times, Jennifer Hansen, Whitney Lewis, Kylie Williamson, Kenzie Sheppard, Kourtney Schut, Matthew Havertz, Aubrey Rogowski, and Liang Hu. In some form or another, as we all worked together to examine the literature, identify interesting crossover work, and attempt to bridge the information and learning sciences in our own activities, conversations and comments from these individuals helped push our thinking forward and also helped us recognize that a book like this one could be of value for others who were undertaking this kind of interdisciplinary work that we were seeing emerge.

At Routledge, we are grateful to Dan Schwartz, our managing editor. Dan has been an enthusiast about this book from some of our earliest tentative conversations and continuously accommodating and supportive in light of unexpected emergencies that we encountered along the way that were both related to and separate from the preparation of this book.

In a volume like this one, gratitude goes out to the various contributing authors, as they did much of the hard work of initial writing, while our jobs involved providing reviews, feedback, and suggestions and doing a lot of wrangling. The initial interest of various authors for such a volume to come into existence was also a driver in the preparation of this book. Special thanks go to Diana Hellyar and Elizabeth Bonsignore for being willing to step in with short notice, but we believe this book is far stronger for having them as a part of it.

Thanks go to our respective families who have been supportive, patient, and encouraging while we each worked long evenings to get this book assembled above and beyond what we would do as part of our "day jobs."

Finally, this book would not be possible without the tremendous work that is being done five, six, and even seven days a week across the country at libraries of varying sizes and in various settings, whether they are schools, cities, universities, or other organizations. As editors, we saw that all the work described in each chapter relied upon the partnership, interest, and involvement of these hardworking individuals who are seeking new ways to innovate and partner with members of their communities in order to provide access to high-quality information experiences. We would be remiss were we not to acknowledge first and foremost the various librarians and library personnel whose stories and wisdom are shared in the pages that follow.

INTRODUCTION

Victor R. Lee and Abigail L. Phillips

Throughout the United States, libraries are facing pressures to change. After all, one can just run a Google search, turn to Wikipedia, or query friends on Facebook to see what information is available and recommended. New technological infrastructures and big data algorithms seem to render library services moot, as books and other publications are being suggested to us based on what we had purchased, read, or even glanced at before. For a large part of the population, it seems that printed books have become blasé. And while libraries and library personnel have long advocated for awareness that they are informational and educational institutions and professionals, the role that libraries serve in providing learning opportunities is often overlooked by the general public. Many do not realize that libraries are regularly providing instruction, exhibits, seminars, and programs for their communities. Many do not notice that many libraries in many different locales are seeking out ways to expand and improve upon how they support learning and information discovery. Many do not realize the kinds of partnerships that are being undertaken with researchers and designers to enhance the library experience. Given that, what prominent, concrete images do we have that best exemplify the efforts to change the popular image of what is happening in the physical library? How can we spotlight the changing roles of the people who are tirelessly doing and reinventing the work involved in making libraries into vibrant, community-relevant learning spaces?

Those questions motivated the preparation of this edited book. We (Lee and Phillips, the editors of this volume) were each beginning to wonder about these within our two respective academic communities. Lee was trained in the learning sciences and has been involved in projects studying and designing for learning in a range of settings for many years and with many populations. Phillips was a former librarian who was trained in information sciences and had been studying modern-day librarianship practices and young adult services in libraries. Funding opportunities and professional networks brought them together as colleagues in Logan, Utah, and the conversations that led to this book began.

In preparing this book, we had recognized that there were emerging success cases and new models for library-based learning that were being developed by experts in the information and learning sciences, and some dialogue between the fields was beginning. As a field, the learning sciences was expanding beyond its sociocultural and cognitively oriented design work with technology and activities in classrooms and museums and into more seriously examining a range of other settings for learning. Libraries were among those settings. The library and information sciences had been broadening its emphasis areas beyond information storage, archival, search, and retrieval and had been taking increased interest in the design research methods and digital media emphasis of the learning sciences. Documented success cases such as the *YOUMedia* program in Chicago and substantial research and development investment from organizations like the MacArthur Foundation's *Digital Media and Learning* program have motivated calls for more dialogue and collaboration between information and learning scientists. Connected learning, as a perspective on how to envision twenty-first-century, digitally enhanced, interest-driven learning, was establishing a unifying viewpoint. Leading organizations, such as the Association for Information Science and Technology, saw the arrival of a new special interest group in the area of information and learning sciences. A major conference at the International Society of the Learning Sciences saw a symposium that examined how libraries were increasingly important sites for designing computer-supported collaborative learning. Universities were beginning to hire across field boundaries, and faculty were obtaining joint appointments across information schools and schools of education. At the time of this book's preparation, a new peer-reviewed academic journal, *Information and Learning Sciences*, is set to premiere and become a venue for research at the intersection between the two fields. It seemed that this book, which would compile the research in these fields as it related to libraries, was timely and appropriate for helping to advance this dialogue.

Thus, we, the editors, began the months of work needed to identify who had been doing new research or design at this intersection of the information and learning sciences. It was through good fortune and enthusiastic response that we were able to find a number of outstanding scholars and projects that are represented in the pages that follow. As this book was being prepared, we learned about even more projects that were being conceived or had just gotten underway, and it is with some regret that the timing of this book's preparation and the launch of these new efforts were not aligned. It is our expectation that those other projects that did not get featured in this volume will later garner attention and also promote dialogue. What is included in this book, like all academic compendia, is a product of the time at which it was prepared. Moreover, at the time that we began to organize and compile this book, the intersection between information and learning sciences was predominantly oriented toward teens and youth as the target learner population, although the potential and imperative to design for lifelong learning is clearly there. That means that public and school libraries are heavily represented in this book, whereas academic libraries and digital libraries, both of which are doing innovative work, are not featured. Similarly, the maker movement, with its emphasis on creation of digital artifacts such as computer games or circuitry, was also a major topical focus. That also meant that maker-oriented activities and spaces are especially prominent in the projects that are described.

Given the collection that we had curated, we have organized the book into four major sections, described in what follows.

Part I. Reconceptualizing Libraries and Communities

Libraries are information and learning spaces from and for their immediate communities, whether those communities are schools, neighborhoods, or cities. The two chapters in this section reconsider how libraries and communities interact. The first (Chapter 1), by Victor R. Lee, recognizes that much of the research and futurist discourse has begun to imagine what we would have in the "smart and connected communities" of the future. While much of this talk has been oriented toward new efficiencies that new social and technological systems could enable to improve the use of energy, land use, transportation, and safety, Lee argues that libraries should be an essential part of how smart and connected communities support learning. The second chapter in this section (Chapter 2), by Kyungwon Koh, June Abbas, and Rebekah Willett, sets the stage for much of the work around making and makerspaces that comes in later chapters. They discuss the appearance of makerspaces in libraries and what social role they play with respect to the communities that they serve. Their chapter is situated in the current concerns and directions encouraged by the American Library Association and includes case studies of library makerspaces from Norman, Oklahoma, and Madison, Wisconsin. Koh, Abbas, and Willett also talk about implications for the preparation of library and information science educators and researchers. The combination of these two chapters provides a broad view of how we could begin to think about libraries as they expand and change their services.

Part II. Reconceptualizing Library Experiences

The second section includes four chapters that emphasize new experiences for library patrons. The first chapter in this section (Chapter 3), from Yasmin Kafai, Orkan Telhan, Richard Lee Davis, K-Fai Steele, and Barrie Adleberg, describes a project based out of the Free Library system in Philadelphia. The project involved a new way of integrating the maker movement into libraries by encouraging the design and development of interactive murals at different neighborhood branches of the Free Library. In their chapter, Kafai and colleagues describe some of the motivation of this work and share some of the factors they had observed that led to different ways in which the murals were accessed and used to express the concerns of local youth. The next chapter (Chapter 4), by Carrie Tzou, Philip Bell, Megan Bang, Rekha Kuver, Amy Twito, and Ashley Braun, describes a community-based design partnership organized around STEAM (science, technology, engineering, arts, and mathematics) learning experiences with families in the Seattle area. The specific program they describe, called TechTales, sought to broaden the institutional focus of informal learning to include spaces such as libraries and involved processes of participatory design research that led to and continually helped refine this technology-enhanced family storytelling experience. Tzou and colleagues also distill lessons learned about how to make university researcher and public library partnerships productive and jointly oriented toward meaningful, shared goals.

Chapter 5, contributed by Elizabeth Bonsignore, Derek Hansen, and Kari Kraus, describes the practice of alternate reality gaming, which blends imagined game worlds with physical spaces. In Bonsignore and her coauthors' chapter, they describe efforts undertaken at libraries in Maryland where teens and a teen librarian undertook the challenging task of creating alternate-reality games at the library. This chapter offers a new perspective on the kinds of gaming that are possible at libraries and is instructive for those who aspire to a comparable undertaking at other library sites. Related to this theme of mixing realities, Diana Hellyar, Renee Walsh, and Micah Altman contribute a chapter on virtual, mixed, and augmented reality (Chapter 6). The authors provide some background on the resurgent interest in virtual, mixed, and augmented reality and offer a conceptual model for how these can be integrated into library interactions, whether those are related to information search or entirely new forms of visualized information. Hellyar and colleagues draw from relevant research to suggest what appears promising and where we should exercise caution as we integrate these technologies into libraries and the activities that libraries support.

Part III. Reconceptualizing Librarianship

Besides the relationship to communities and the kinds of experiences they offer for patrons, the roles and responsibilities of librarians and library professionals are also rapidly changing. This section focuses on some of those changes as observed in research from both learning and information sciences. Leading this section is a chapter by Crystle Martin (Chapter 7). In her chapter, Martin reports on partnered design experiences with librarians in Southern California who were implementing STEM programs for underserved youth using the Scratch programming environment. The main audience is researchers who wish to work with librarians and helps to make clear the types of considerations one should make about how to support librarians in realizing and creating creative programming experiences. The next chapter (Chapter 8), written by Tamara Clegg and Mega Subramaniam, argues that librarians are being looked upon to serve as mentors for youth. This is a contrast to the model of "librarian as expert" that is what many enact after their graduate training in library and information sciences (LIS). In their chapter, they pay particular attention to the different modes of mentorship that are required now in libraries and how youth interests can and should be made into a central focus in librarianship.

Abigail Phillips, Victor R. Lee, and Mimi Recker provide a chapter (Chapter 9) that draws on research done on libraries in small towns in Utah. From two cases of innovative librarians in these communities, they argue that these small towns can be loci of innovative practice, and a productive model for thinking about librarianship is to think of modern-day librarians as "experience engineers." They identify some common attributes of the two case librarians and provide examples of novel programs and services that these librarians had offered. The last chapter of this section, by Rebecca Reynolds and Chris Leeder, is a synthetic chapter on school librarianship and its importance in school success. One important role school librarians play is in promoting and supporting inquiry and partnering with other educators. A key takeaway of their chapter is that efforts to increase school performance should intentionally involve school librarians.

Part IV. Reconceptualizing Library Research

The last major section of the book focuses on research done on and in partnership with libraries by those in the information and learning sciences. While the other chapters certainly touch upon this, the chapters in this section maintain a dominant focus on the kinds of work that can be done to inform how to jointly work on supporting and enhancing the potential of libraries to support learning. Jason Yip and Kung Jin Lee lead with a chapter on participatory design with libraries (Chapter 11). They draw upon traditions from human–computer interaction and describe codesign work using the participatory design methodology with the KidsTeam at University of Washington. This approach was implemented over multiple sessions, partnering youth with Seattle Public Library librarians, and the reflection that Yip and Lee provide includes sound advice and acknowledgment of challenges that remain to successfully maintain participatory codesign relationships but points toward an adoption of new design-thinking processes with libraries.

The next chapter (Chapter 12), contributed by Marcia A. Mardis, Faye R. Jones, Lenese Colson, Shana Pribesh, Sue Kimmel, Barbara Schultz-Jones, Laura Pasquini, and Laura Gogia reports on work from an ongoing Mixed Research Synthesis, a review method that originates from nursing and social work research. Mardis and colleagues used this method to distill the research on school libraries in order to identify hypotheses that could examine causal relationships in small-scale research–practice partnerships with libraries. Finally, continuing also with the theme of research–practice partnerships, William R. Penuel, Josephina Chang-Order, and Vera Michalchik reflect further on the nature of such work by sharing experiences from a partnership with the University of Colorado Boulder and Anythink Libraries (Chapter 13). Anythink had sought to embrace connected learning and worked with the research team to identify problems of practice that could be addressed by research and also involve youth as researchers themselves. Theirs is a compelling case of how the connected learning approach could be replicated and evaluated in sites beyond those that represented the original success cases.

Closing

Finally, this book was fortunate to have a contribution that is part reflective and part future oriented from Beth Yoke, the executive director of the Young Adult Library Services Association (YALSA) of the American Library Association. Yoke has directly been involved in questions of research and practice in her role and was especially well positioned to prepare some closing remarks for the volume. While her thoughts and call to action are potent as they are, it is ultimately our hope that this entire collection of writings, including Yoke's contribution, accomplishes the goals that motivated the preparation of this book. Namely, we hope that this set of chapters and contributions continues to propel a dialog that is taking place between the fields of information and learning sciences and provides a current portrait of the kinds of models of relationships, experiences, librarianship, and research that lie ahead as more people become involved in the work of reconceptualizing libraries for the twenty-first century.

PART I

Reconceptualizing Libraries and Communities

1

LIBRARIES WILL BE ESSENTIAL TO THE SMART AND CONNECTED COMMUNITIES OF THE FUTURE

Victor R. Lee

Unquestionably, the current state of computing with handheld devices, digitally enhanced household objects, distributed miniaturized sensors, massive-scale knowledge sharing, big data, and enhanced artificial intelligence algorithms is advancing a transformation across how we work, play, and live. We have seen how this transformation has radically altered how we seek entertainment, connect with friends, and access modes of transportation. The extension of these changes is a move toward "smart and connected communities," a futuristic vision of the locales in which we live that leverages these technological advances to improve how collections of people in the same geographic area can exist in the designed and natural environment. For example, a smart community of the future may have an energy grid system that utilizes technology to identify ways that we can better harness sustainable energy sources and increase efficiencies by making suggestions for residents based on usage analytics. Or perhaps our food supply chain can be made more efficient and more responsible environmentally by forecasting food needs over time and agricultural recommendations that can be simultaneously nutritious for the end consumer and profitable for farmers and ranchers who are involved in food production. These are just some of the possibilities that we might imagine in which the means we have and are developing to obtain data, detect trends, and allocate resources could help make the large-scale sociotechnical system that constitutes a city or community more responsive and aligned to our concerns, needs, and values.

If the calls of funding agencies—both public and private—are any indication of this enthusiasm and optimism for smart and connected communities, then we should expect this to be a continuing emphasis for research, development, and public discourse for many years to come. I write this chapter as someone who has had the good fortune to be involved in some early conversations, as one of several participants in a multiday Innovation Lab in Menlo Park, California, with researchers and leaders from across the country to discuss the possibilities for designing and researching Smart and Connected Communities for Learning (Roschelle, 2016), and as someone whose work as a learning scientist has, in recent years, involved productive relationships with libraries as sites for learning. As a researcher, I am enthusiastic about the efforts underway to make investments in improving how communities and technology can jointly support learning. Some of these involve, for instance, tracking of utilization of STEM education programs in large urban spaces (Quigley et al., 2016) and providing youth with opportunities to develop their own countermaps of the cities in which they live (Taylor, 2017). These types of projects hold a great deal of promise for improving learning in cities and communities, and the findings of these projects over time are ones that will likely attract attention and interest for many in the learning sciences and community leadership.

However, at the same time, this budding area of research and development has yet to tap into the opportunities offered by our physical libraries. Libraries should play an essential role in the smart and connected communities of the future. Arguably, libraries already play an essential role in our current communities and are already instrumental in keeping us smart and connected thus far. The path forward toward a new sense of smart and connected will build upon and involve the resources and infrastructure that libraries offer today yet augment it with new sociotechnical arrangements and tools.

On the Extant Importance of Libraries

As a citizen and an academic, I have a robust appreciation of libraries. A fair amount of the work I do as a university professor that involves research, writing, and teaching involves trips to libraries. As a parent, the library represents a special trip for my family to see what is being newly displayed, examine various media, and run into friendly and familiar faces. When I have library fines, I personally have few qualms about paying them because I know that the cents or dollars that I owe for forgetting my agreement to return materials on time should ultimately go to maintaining collections and supporting my library in whatever form the hardworking people whom I encounter there see fit. This appreciation and respect for libraries does not make me an expert on libraries, though. I feel it is incumbent upon me to acknowledge that my formal training is not in the library and information sciences, and my professional experience—some educational research collaborations notwithstanding—does not come from partaking in the professional day-to-day work of a librarian, library director, or library technician. As such, this section will offer my position on the importance of libraries to communities. Yet to a veteran librarian or a scholar of libraries, I expect that what I have to say here may lack the nuance that is involved in current discourses about libraries.

However, my observations and engagements with libraries in recent years have elevated the following features that make libraries important to their communities along with some observations that point toward important negotiations for the future for libraries to be leveraged as a key locale for smart and connected communities.

Libraries Provide Democratic Access

By and large, libraries are accessible to anyone in the community. At a school, any teacher, student, staff person, or administrator is welcome to visit the library. In a community library, whether one is fluent in English, comes from a high or low socioeconomic status, is young or aged, is textually or computationally literate, is neurotypical or represents some aspect of neurodiversity, or whether someone even has a permanent home address are all of little concern. All can come to the library so long as they are willing to abide by the rules of the space respectfully. There are not many places of learning that can boast such status. Many museums require admission (as their funds are limited and pieced together from various sources), K–12 schools are largely populated by students and staff, community colleges and universities require admission and tuition for courses, and courses that can help with professional advancement often require some payment in order to obtain the certification that is ultimately sought. As we look at the digital age as enabling truly lifelong learning (e.g., Collins & Halverson, 2009), libraries are one of the best spaces for anyone to have access to information. While the internet has made more information available than at any other time in human history, it still requires access to a device that can render web content and connectivity that often requires payment for service. Libraries provide internet access, whether through their Wi-Fi networks or through workstations that people can use. Public librarians spend hours helping those who do not know how to use the internet or operate a computer access the information that they need online. People of all ages use the library, whether it's parents with young children, other adults, teens, or seniors.

That diversity of patronage represents a broad range of local expertise. At the same time, that diversity raises considerations of how different population segments can be best served. Different populations gravitate to the library for different reasons, and the desires each has can be in conflict. Those seeking a warm place to be may have different interests then those who are looking for a quiet place to study, who may yet have different interests from those who want to gather and play games. A challenge continually exists with respect to serving the various interests and keeping the library open and available for all interested parties who deserve access.

Libraries Provide Space

Not to be overlooked is the physical space that libraries provide. Libraries are warm indoor spaces when for some individuals there may be no other options. By design, many libraries offer study rooms or meeting rooms available by reservation or the library can be arranged to serve as a meeting space in its entirety after hours. In my experience across the various cities I have lived or visited, it is not uncommon to find community organizations gathering in the library for a meeting. Some libraries have auditoriums to support guest lectures and presentations for larger volumes of attendees. The space between shelves offers small private spaces, sometimes with their own separate seating or study carrels. Long tables and chairs are common in libraries and can be used as a surface upon which to read, set up a laptop, study for school, fill out paperwork, or play a tabletop game. Some libraries are providing media viewing and production spaces, and versions of those may emphasize digital maker activities, while others exist as a teen space for young people to gather and hang out. Such space is a valuable resource that is not always recognized as part of the value libraries provide.

Similar to the democratic access that libraries offer, however, a challenge exists around how the norms guiding the usage of such space will be negotiated. For example, a teen hang-out space that may involve chatter and gameplay may not be conducive to quiet reading. Similarly, a room that has expensive media creation equipment may be available with the best of intentions, but if it is kept out of view or under lock and key, its potential may not be realized. Also, libraries offer space to the public, which limits the ability for any individual party or group to make strong claims to any set of resources.

Libraries House Information Experts

Librarians are professionals in the area of information search, retrieval, and storage and thus are one of the primary resources for those seeking information about particular topics or current issues. As things stand now, American society is recognizing just how important it is to be able to discriminate between accurate and trustworthy information on the one hand and information that is intentionally designed to mislead on the other. Librarians have long been and should continue to be some of our most important allies in this ongoing work. A large part of their work involves promoting information literacy and helping interested patrons in navigating the reams of information that are available within print archives. This work has extended into digital information realms, with digital librarians and cybrarians becoming prominent figures who will lead the way (Johnson, 2011).

Granted, this is a lot to ask of already busy professionals. Much of the work within a library ultimately extends beyond information expertise. However, my contention is that those who utilize these services profit greatly from it, and the more awareness and the more actively we use and ask for these services, the more we will acknowledge how important they are for our own individual learning and for our societal benefit. What I see as a challenge for the future is how the expertise in information management can be leveraged and mobilized while so many other demands are being made of library professionals. Librarians are experts on the information around many things, but we must be careful not to expect them to be experts about the information around all things.

Libraries and Their Communities Are Mutually Constitutive

Whether the community being served is a large metropolis, a small neighborhood, a university campus, or an elementary school, the community is reflected in its library, and the library is reflected in its community. Libraries develop the unique portions of their collections based on what is produced in the community that they serve, making a trip to any library an opportunity to learn about the tastes of the local population and the history and priorities of its immediate community. This is also reflected in exhibition space, which libraries provide. The work of local artisans and community organizations appears in display cases and on walls. The work of students appears at school libraries, and as discussed elsewhere in this book, the distinctive character of a city and a neighborhood—complete with artistic styles and local concerns—appears at the library (Kafai et al., this volume). The local events and activities are hanging on bulletin boards and are expressed in the suggestions and recommendations of the personnel employed at the library. City council minutes, maps, local historical documents, and collections of local benefactors reside in the walls of the library. These collections also mean that the library is a place for the community to know what is happening and what issues are of local concern. The library is a public space for a civic debate or a local elected candidate forum. They are an investment in shared knowledge for people who will enter, and they represent the embodiment of what a community wanted or thought was worth preserving for others to discover in the future.

It itself, the library community dynamic is impressive. There are not many organizations or institutions that we can consistently rely upon that will both preserve and create the history of the people who use it. In this era of big box stores and chains, it can be hard to see the distinct character of a community. Yet the library is deeply rooted in its community and vice versa. It contains knowledge and connects information to people and people to people. If one asks how communities have already been smart and connected, libraries would have to be part of the answer. Cultivating those connections within a community is arguably one of the main reasons why we have and value libraries to this day.

Looking Forward Toward Future Smartness and Connectedness That Involves Libraries

If libraries have already served as vehicles for enriching our understandings and connecting us to information and other people, but the pervasiveness and advances of digital technology are radically altering the sociotechnical landscape, then what role, if any, should physical libraries play? That is the underlying question driving this chapter. Here, I share a few imaginings of potential futures for libraries in the next generation of smart and connected communities. At a minimum, my expectation is that libraries will continue to preserve the valuable collections that they have and expand their digital presence further—not so that people no longer need to go to the library but so that people have a means to access some of what the library offers when they are not already physically there. Yet beyond that, there is much that we can do.

One potential is to leverage the access to costly resources and the ability to add to existing collections along with the information expertise possessed by librarians to enhance opportunities for individual and collective learning of patrons. Jennifer Kahn, a professor at the University of Miami, has demonstrated how this could be possible by way of her dissertation research conducted at Vanderbilt University (Kahn, 2017). In her work, she partnered with a major urban public library that had license access to expensive software and provided both space and laptops for high school–aged youth to explore migration patterns and their own families' "geobiographies." These youth met repeatedly at the library and were supported by Kahn, her colleagues, and the public librarians in the creation of digital narrative records that were made into permanent parts of their special collection as archives of what had been learned. It was a research and design project that involved using special collections migration data, visualization software, and after-hours meeting groups that later involved not just the youth but also their family members. These youth and families together reconstructed how and why their families and the groups with which they affiliated converged in the locales where they lived, adding to their individual understandings of their placement in their communities and also adding to a knowledge repository about the community for others.

Another option is to further the efforts of libraries to diversify the kinds of information materials that they make available to patrons. For example, many libraries offer "backpack programs" whereby individuals can check out full kits with supportive guide materials so that they and others in their household can jointly explore and learn a new topic given a set of curated resources (Tzou et al., this volume). Some of the efforts underway for smart and connected communities rely upon sensors obtaining large pools of data from different places in order to enable new kinds of discoveries to get made. In some endeavors, this would involve individuals, homes, and families providing sensor data. However, the ability for any individual or household to have the immediate resources to equip such sensors is dependent on many factors. Libraries, however, could become sensor lending hubs where families can borrow and return various sensors and equipment that can help collect data that enables a community to be smarter and more responsive to the needs of the many. Mobile air quality sensors or wearable fitness trackers that can accompany an individual regardless of their financial means have the potential of better capturing an accurate image of what life is like within a community and what regions and populations could be better served.

Perhaps libraries can become a sort of "home base" for those who are mobile and pursuing activities such as place-based learning or augmented reality gameplay (e.g., Bonsignore, this volume). A vision that was described and that I am now seeing explored from my time at the Smart and Connected Communities for Learning Innovation Lab that I had mentioned in the introduction was place-based learning in the city. Using mobile devices, a city and its history and concerns can be explored when those places are encountered. The library can be its starting point and a place to access mobile devices for loan to pursue such explorations. That can be the service provided for residents or visitors. Perhaps locals can also have access, through the library, to technology that enables them to digitally add new sights one can encounter and annotate community spaces with personal histories or stories.

Finally, what if libraries became major regional data visualization centers for their communities? Libraries are already key sites for local data to be archived and, with some added support and technological resources, could one day become places where dynamic visualizations of population demographics over time, material circulation statistics, municipal service data, GIS maps of the region, and many other features of the community could be accessed. New forms of visualization, whether they are massive displays or virtual and augmented reality (Hellyar et al., this volume) are moving from science fiction to plausible next-generation realities. Should libraries continue to be repositories of information and spaces where that information can be discovered and inspected, this extension of library as local visualization center could be a reality. The information expertise of the future librarian may thus evolve to involve guiding visitors in the work of data cleaning and visualization rendering along with instruction on how to interpret visualizations. While it is potentially ambitious work to undertake, the expectation that our society must develop both computational and data literacy in the digital age coupled with the democratic access and continual efforts from librarians to be providers of information expertise make this possibility one worth considering.

These ideas are just a beginning. The smart and connected cities of the future have yet to be fully articulated or even imagined. They may look like the images we have seen in science fiction, or they may look simply like a more efficient version of today. Yet it is hard to imagine the next generation of smart and connected cities, no matter how impressive the virtual reality systems we are to develop, that do not have physical spaces that we traverse and explore. What we can ultimately do is leverage and value the spaces that we have already and explore the possibilities to make those into hubs for our learning, socializing, working, and playing. Certainly some parts of those spaces will change, but the fundamental idea of a place that mediates our relationship to an abundance of information that all can access and is continually shaping and shaped by our communal values and experiences is one that seems worthy of retaining as we look toward the future. It may be that building on the idea of a library and exploring new sociotechnical opportunities and arrangements that can reside there may be one of the best ways for us, as residents and citizens, to be smart and connected in the digital age.

References

Collins, A., & Halverson, R. (2009). *Rethinking Education in the Age of Technology: The Digital Revolution and Schooling in America*. New York, NY: Teachers College Press.

Johnson, M. (2011). *This Book Is Overdue! How Librarians and Cybrarians Can Save Us All*. New York, NY: Harper Perennial.

Kahn, J. B. (2017). *At the Intersection of Self and Society: Learning, Storytelling, and Modeling with Big Data*. Unpublished Doctoral Dissertation. Nashville, TN: Vanderbilt University.

Quigley, D., Dibie, O., Sultan, A., Horne, K. V., Penuel, W. R., Sumner, T., . . . Pinkard, N. (2016). Equity of learning opportunities in the Chicago city of learning program. In T. Barnes, M. Chi, & M. Feng (Eds.), *Proceedings of the 9th International Conference on Educational Data Mining* (pp. 618–619). Raleigh, NC: International Educational Data Mining Society.

Roschelle, J. (2016). Innovation Lab maps the future of learning in smart and connected communities. *Computing Research News, 28*(6), 9–10.

Taylor, K. H. (2017). Learning along lines: Locative literacies for reading and writing the city. *Journal of the Learning Sciences, 26*(4), 533–574. doi:10.1080/10508406.2017.1307198

2

MAKERSPACES IN LIBRARIES

Social Roles and Community Engagement

Kyungwon Koh, June Abbas, and Rebekah Willett

Introduction

The maker movement—a community of people who tinker, create, and share personally meaningful projects—is increasingly prevalent in contemporary libraries, offering people an opportunity to access technologies, interact with mentors and peers, and engage in creative projects. Since the first public library makerspace in the U.S. opened at the Fayetteville Free Library in New York in 2011, makerspaces in libraries continue to develop across the country (Good & Doctorow, 2013). A growing number of libraries now offer a dedicated space for creation or programs to promote making. The American Library Association (ALA) Center for the Future of Libraries (2014) identifies the maker movement as one of the key trends in contemporary libraries. However, there is little consensus about the social roles that library makerspaces assume in the contemporary society.

Community is a central concept to both librarianship and the maker movement (ALA, 2004; Remold, Fusco, Vogt, & Leones, 2016); successful makerspaces recognize community engagement is key (Koh & Abbas, 2016). The term *community*, however, is being used in different ways across the literature, often without defining the concept. This chapter discusses how libraries promote active community engagement through makerspaces and what roles library makerspaces play in today's society, addressing the following overarching questions:

1. What social roles do makerspaces in a library assume in the contemporary knowledge society?
2. How might we conceptualize "community" in relation to library makerspaces?
3. What are the implications for educators and researchers to promote community engagement and social roles in and through library makerspaces?

This chapter first outlines theoretical perspectives on libraries and community and then addresses each of these questions with reference to professional and scholarly literature and empirical data from research projects.

Perspectives to Conceptualize Library Makerspaces

Different perspectives on libraries and community describe the library as a place for community members to create and learn. Historical research shows that libraries have long promoted making experiences and a sense of community (Good & Doctorow, 2013; Wiegand, 2015a). The following is a brief overview of selected perspectives that inform researchers and practitioners regarding the social role of library makerspaces and the meaning of community in the context of library makerspaces.

Library as Place

The public space that libraries provide is one of the central values of libraries in the life of their users, suggesting libraries as public places that promote and maintain community (Buschman, Leckie, Wiegand, & Bertot, 2007). Historical analysis of American public libraries shows the role of libraries is more than providing useful information and reading materials. A variety of meaningful experiences occur in library spaces, giving millions of individuals a sense of belonging (Wiegand, 2015a, 2015b). History shows libraries have continuously adapted to serve the needs of their communities, and a library makerspace is an exemplar of library as place in this contemporary, technology-rich society. Frequently a makerspace is defined as a community of people who gather to create, learn, and socialize rather than as a physical space. Beyond the tools and programs they provide, library makerspaces play a role of public place determined by meaningful participation experienced by community members. A few concepts are useful in discussing the role of library makerspace as place. The notion of "public sphere" explains the social space, in which individuals come together to discuss freely different opinions and public affairs and communicate to develop collective solutions (Habermas, 2014). Library makerspaces can also be considered as "third space"—one of the core settings of informal public life—places of escape from the home (first place) and work setting (second place)—characterized by its leisurely and inclusive nature (Oldenburg, 1997). Similarly, "affinity space" indicates a social place—virtual or physical—where informal learning occurs while people voluntarily participate based on a shared interest (Gee, 2005).

New Librarianship

Lankes (2015) suggests the mission of librarians is "to improve society through facilitating knowledge creation in their communities" (p. 17). Community engagement is the core of librarianship, as he defines a library as "a mandated and facilitated space supported by the community, stewarded by librarians, and dedicated to knowledge creation" (p. 96). Lankes's view on new librarianship, which focuses on communities and knowledge over collections and buildings, supports integrating the maker movement into librarianship, because a maker-space is essentially a community place for learning and creation. His definition of "knowledge creation" is based on constructivism, in which knowledge is created by an individual and through conversations, whether internal or social discourses. To facilitate conversations, librarians connect people around common activities or interests, for example a group of people who gather to quilt, knit, sew, craft, or build more complicated fabrication projects. Librarians also facilitate people's learning and knowledge creation through providing access, knowledge, environment, and motivation.

Radical Change Theory

According to the theory, "Radical Change" indicates fundamental changes in this digital age, departing from the usual or traditional in information resources or behaviors, although still grounded in the foundational meanings (Dresang, 1999, 2013; Koh, 2015). Makerspaces look radically different from a traditional library space; yet they are rooted in the core of librarianship—resources, inquiry, creativity, and discovery that follow patrons' passion and interests. The theory explains that contemporary information resources and human behaviors represent three core characteristics—*connectivity*, *interactivity*, and *access*, which are frequently observed in library makerspaces. As community learning centers, makerspaces provide *access* to a range of resources and technology as well as a place to *connect* with other community members. The way people learn and create in a makerspace is *interactive;* it is dynamic, user-initiated, nonlinear, and not always sequential.

Communities of Practice

Emphasizing the social nature of making and makerspaces, Halverson and Sheri-dan (2014) write, "*makerspaces* are the communities of practice that are constructed in a physical place that is set aside for a group of people to make as a core part of their practice" (p. 502, original emphasis). Communities of practice are a widely used concept in library and information studies, with projects aiming to develop learning communities in various contexts, facilitate collaboration and knowledge sharing, and strengthen the role of libraries in communities. Communities of practice are also of interest to researchers conceptualizing social aspects of learn-ing. Lave and Wenger (1991) developed the theory of communities of practice by studying ways learning occurred amongst groups of people who were involved in a common activity that centered on a particular area of knowledge. Their theory takes account of the development of practices as well as ways relationships and identities are fostered in connection to the community. According to Lave and

Wenger, as learners become involved in the practices of a community, they take on particular identities associated with that community.

The Social Roles of Library Makerspaces

The earlier perspectives explain that making in libraries is not new but rooted in the fundamentals of libraries, suggesting libraries are appropriate community places for integrating the maker movement. This section discusses social roles library makerspaces may assume in today's society, based on the ALA (American Library Association) core values of librarianship and existing literature on the maker movement in libraries and education.

Among the social roles libraries play, library makerspaces promote *knowledge creation, access, learning,* and *equity and diversity* with and through their *community.* Grounded in the core values of librarianship, these concepts are further pronounced in library makerspaces and require a new understanding of the role of libraries in the contemporary knowledge society. Above all, library makerspaces represent a shifting role of libraries as an institution for *knowledge creation.* The ALA Center for the Future of Libraries explains "libraries, traditionally collecting institutions that provide access to materials created by others, may now adopt new functions, providing communities with opportunities to create or cocreate content for an individual's own use, for use by the community, or for inclusion in the library collection" (2014, n.p.). Library makerspaces support the creation of knowledge by providing community members *access* to a range of resources, technologies, programs, experts, and peers.

While access has been one of the core values of librarianship, a traditional view of access is limited to providing existing resources, predominantly in print formats. In reconceptualizing libraries as an institution to facilitate learning and creation, a library collection is not restricted to books and other written materials, because people learn from a range of resources (e.g., arts, fiction, or entertainment sources) through different ways, such as hands-on experiences. Envisioning library makerspaces includes not only providing access to existing knowledge and fabrication resources but also making community expertise and knowledge produced by their members available to the world, what Lankes (2015) calls "two-way access," or access as two-way conversations between the community members and the world. By doing so, libraries play a role of "platforms and publishers of the community as much as . . . consumers of publications" (Lankes, 2015, p. 45). More work is needed, however, to advance theories and practices on how librarians can document and preserve maker processes and products developed by community members and how to make community knowledge and expertise available to people outside specific maker communities.

The maker movement assumes people learn by making, which has roots in learning theories of constructivism, constructionism, or experiential learning; and makerspaces are considered learning environments (Peppler, Halverson, & Kafai, 2016). Therefore, makerspaces in libraries manifest library as a community *learning* center. Libraries have long been places to learn and advance knowledge. Since American public libraries emerged as part of the public education movement in the nineteenth century, librarians have supplemented the public education system in different ways—whether through cataloging learning resources or offering information literacy instruction, reference services, and spaces for study and meetings (Lankes, 2015; Wiegand, 2015a). What and how people learn in a library makerspace, however, may look different from learning often observed in the dominant formal education system (i.e., direct instruction, specified curriculum, standards, and assessments).

The Maker Education Initiative—a national nonprofit organization that promotes maker-centered education—affirms their focus on the *process* of learning, recognizing a diversity of approaches (Maker Education Initiative, n.d.). Literature suggests the desired outcomes of learning in a makerspace include maker empowerment, self-efficacy, and twenty-first-century skills, such as creativity, inquiry, computational thinking, critical thinking, and social skills (Clapp, Ross, Ryan, & Tishman, 2017; Dubriwny, Pritchett, Hardesty, & Hellman, 2016). People may acquire those qualities without recognizing that learning occurs, and learning in a library makerspace may not always be explicit. Therefore, the role of librarians working in a library makerspace requires more carefully designed learning facilitation. For example, the Exploratorium Tinkering Studio develops dimensions of learning (engagement, initiative and intentionality, social scaffolding, and development of understanding) and suggests educators can promote these learning dimensions through three facilitators: sparking interest, sustaining participation, and deepening understanding (Gutwill, Hido, & Sindorf, 2015).

To facilitate learning, it is critical for librarians in makerspaces to establish and maintain partnerships and connect with people and organizations across the community. ALA affirms the value of education and lifelong learning through coalitions and partnerships in the community, stating

> ALA promotes the creation, maintenance, and enhancement of a learning society, encouraging its members to work with educators, government officials, and organizations in coalitions to initiate and support comprehensive efforts to ensure that school, public, academic, and special libraries in every community cooperate to provide lifelong learning services to all.
>
> *(ALA, 2013)*

Makerspaces embedded in libraries inherit this heavy emphasis on engaging communities and building networks.

Library makerspaces hold their promise for *equity and diversity*. Libraries have the potential to democratize and diversify the maker movement by making a range of resources, tools, and processes more readily available to community members, which otherwise would not have been available to them, at little or no cost. Equity is one of the core values of librarianship; as ALA states, "all information resources that are provided directly or indirectly by the library, regardless of technology, format, or methods of delivery, should be readily, equally, and equitably accessible to all users" (2004, n.p.). Further, ensuring equity and diversity in a makerspace is not limited to equal access to certain tools and programs. The initial maker movement that emerged from independent organizations has been criticized for its white-male-dominant culture. The majority of makers consisted of men and boys, and the range of making activities was somewhat narrow, including primarily electronics, robotics, and vehicles. As makerspaces spread to nonprofit organizations such as libraries, schools, and museums, the maker landscape has been expanding, engaging people who may not self-identify as makers, including children, women, and families, in a variety of making activities (Halverson & Sheridan, 2014). Makerspaces in libraries regularly embrace low-tech and artistic projects and result in broadening the maker horizons from STEM to STEAM (science, technology, engineering, art, and math), with the addition of art. More efforts are needed, however, to place equity at the center of making and support maker learning for all (Vossoughi, Hooper, & Escudé, 2016), such as embracing the culture of individual community members from diverse backgrounds, beyond a narrow set of tools and activities (e.g., 3D printing, robotics, and electronics). Diversity efforts should also extend to providing makerspaces that are accessible to differently abled individuals of all ages (Brady et al., 2014).

Finally, the roles and values discussed here are not separate practices in reality, and library makerspaces perform these roles *with and through their community*. The concept of community, however, needs to be clarified, and it is to this concept we now turn.

Conceptualizing Community in Relation to Library Makerspaces

According to the Oxford American Dictionary (OAD), the term *community* is defined as:

1. a group of people living in the same place or having a particular characteristic in common.
2. a group of fellowship with others, as a result of sharing common attitudes, interests, and goals.

In this chapter we use the term *community* to refer to both meanings. Community is a group of people whom libraries serve; a library itself is an integral part of their community. Community also refers to a sense of belonging and support.

Across the literature about library makerspaces, the term *community* reflects these two definitions: library makerspaces have the potential to serve local communities, engage with wider communities, include communities of interest, foster a sense of community, and develop new communities of practice. In these varying uses, community sometimes refers to the geographic area—for example, working with people from the neighborhood surrounding a local library or developing partnerships with organizations within a larger geographic community, as in the OAD's first definition. Other times community refers to a sense of solidarity and/or to a specific group of people with a shared common goal and identity, regardless of geographic location, as in the OAD's second definition.

Geographic Community Makerspaces

Most often, advice about developing makerspaces and related programming in public libraries refers to geographically based definitions of community. Many guidelines emphasize the role of the local community and suggest ways to develop community connections as part of a library maker program (e.g., Burke, 2014; Hamilton & Schmidt, 2015; Remold et al., 2016; Willingham & de Boer, 2015). Advice includes drawing on community experts, developing partnerships, gathering information from community members about their needs and wants, and designing specifically for the local community.

A common response to concerns about how to skill up librarians in order to run a makerspace is to turn to the community to find experts whose skills can be employed in the library, thus building a program on a base of volunteers to complement the skill sets of librarians. In addition to individual experts, advice to librarians includes finding groups in the community, for example, hobby associations, who might be interested in assisting with makerspace programming. There is a broad spectrum of volunteer and paid positions in public library makerspaces, including different tiers of volunteers, paid experts, and artists in residence. Some libraries have systems in place to ensure goals of community experts and the library are both being met through makerspace programming, such as carefully structured planning processes that require community experts to apply to makerspace programs and to identify goals and objectives for themselves and for participants. In these geographically based conceptions of community, libraries are seen as community places for the cocreation of knowledge, as in Lankes's discussion of new librarianship. However, there are also portable library makerspace programs that move to spaces such as community centers, schools, and parks. These align with Dresang's ideas about connecting with a variety of communities and providing access in a myriad of ways. The following case study illustrates how a makerspace program can be designed to meet the needs and interests of a specific geographic community and draw on the resources within that geographic area.

Case Study 1 Meteorology Makers' Club at Irving Middle School Library in Norman, Oklahoma

The Meteorology Makers' Club began at the Washington Irving Middle School Library in Norman, OK, in fall 2014. In collaboration with the University of Oklahoma School of Library and Information Studies, Norman Public Schools, and the Oklahoma Climatological Survey, the project team was comprised of a middle school librarian, a science teacher, a school library supervisor, a meteorologist, a library and information studies (LIS) professor, and graduate research assistants. The middle school is located in a mid-sized suburban community in Norman, Oklahoma, a geographic region where tornadic activity is predominant and is also the home of internationally acclaimed weather facilities and meteorologists. Meteorology is a relevant and authentic theme for young Oklahomans, who are faced with severe weather such as tornados and hail in everyday life. For example, one eighth-grade boy, who experienced the devastating tornado in Moore in 2013, applied for the club because he wanted to study meteorology and share what he learned with his family and friends to help them predict the weather and storms. Students felt personally connected to different weather issues and had insights into the scientific and social ramifications of weather.

The goal of this program was to promote students' STEM interest, knowledge, and skills, with particular emphasis on meteorology and technology, as well as twenty-first-century skills, such as inquiry, critical thinking, creativity, collaboration, and digital information literacy skills. Ultimately, the program aimed to provide a supportive and creative social environment that enhanced students' sense of agency by increasing their capacity to learn and create. Club activities varied, including skill building (e.g., 3D design, video editing, graphic design, and music production), learning basic meteorology concepts through presentations and experiments, field trips, creating different weather-related projects, and the Makers' Club Fair at the end.

As the school library offers a welcoming environment for all, the Makers' club attracted and engaged even students who are not particularly interested in STEM, meteorology, or making. A seventh-grade girl, who did not identify herself as a "sciencey" student, came to the club and decided to create weather goddesses as her making project. She drew six weather goddesses, each personifying a weather-related phenomenon; scientific principles behind wind, rain, snow, tornado, hurricane, and lightning were creatively expressed in her art project. Students with different interests collaborated to record forecast videos, edit the videos, create music for the forecast, and perform as forecasters. Each student used their personal experiences and talents to inform their projects.

As a result, the final projects addressed a variety of meteorology-related topics including a kid-friendly weather website, forecasts, severe weather survival guides, scientific demonstrations on soil moisture and pH for gardening, 3D design/prototypes of storm shelters for pets, and 3D hail models of different shapes and sizes and their relative effects. At the end of the semester the library hosted a Makers' Club Fair to showcase student creations to community members. Students shared their successes, challenges, and collaborative efforts with guests, which included their families, teachers, school administrators and board members, university professors, and local librarians. Students expressed genuine excitement and pride over their accomplishments, conveying a desire to see their efforts sustained and developed in the future. The Makers' Club Fair reflected the extent to which young people are aware of community needs and resources and are integrated into their communities. Students sought to meet needs they self-identified in order to improve lives beyond their own. Partnering with local agencies and institutions also made students more aware of community needs and able to feel more like a part of the community. This case study shows that the library can play a leadership role in community partnerships to promote students' learning and making opportunities.

Makerspaces as Communities

Library makerspaces are also discussed in terms of developing a sense of community both within the library and in the geographic community. The broader makerspace movement is founded on a model of shared skills and knowledge within a community of makers, and the development of a community of learners is a key component of individual makerspaces. However, advice concerning library makerspaces rarely refers to this type of community development, that is, the development of a sense of community within a makerspace. In contrast, in literature about the broader makerspace movement (e.g., Anderson, 2012; Hatch, 2014), discussion of geographic communities is not often the focus; rather, community is conceived of in terms of communities of practice. As described in the introductory section of this chapter, the theory of communities of practice (CoP) considers the roles of experts and novices in the community and ways that identities related to the community are defined and modeled. The following case study illustrates ways a library system's consideration of geographic community works hand in hand with the development of a sense of community to provide a feeling of belonging and support. The case study also describes an example of a CoP that developed through the library's makerspace program.

Case Study 2   The Bubbler at Madison Public Library in Madison, Wisconsin

Madison Public Library's makerspace program, the Bubbler, spans across nine libraries as well as various community spaces and has a focus on people, community connections, and skill sharing. For example, the program includes an artist-in-residence program to which local artists or makers can apply with the understanding that the program involves training the artist to work with members of the public in a variety of settings. For their artist-in-residence program, the library specifically recruits Latino and African-American artists to work with teens on projects such as music production, photography, and murals. The Bubbler also includes expert-led programs for children and adults in areas such as sewing, cooking, screen printing, animation, and video production. In the broad description of the program provided here, community might be seen in terms of a geographic area; people from the community of Madison participate in the Bubbler in different ways. However, the emphasis on skill sharing and diversity implies that community is more than the square miles of the city. A community consists of people; and people have diverse interests, needs, and identities.

There is evidence that some regularly offered Bubbler programs are creating a sense of group identity and belonging around the Bubbler, that is, a sense of community. For example, a Bubbler program called Making Justice involves work with court-involved teens in three different locations. The teen services librarian leading Making Justice, Jesse Vieau, reports that teens in these programs are asking when Bubbler programs are running, they refer to themselves as "group" when in Bubbler sessions, and they use "Bubbler" as a verb (e.g., "we are Bubbler-ing today"). The library supports Jesse Vieau's prioritization of going into community spaces to offer programs rather than running programs at a library. This consideration of the geographic location of makerspace programming works hand in hand with the development of a sense of community. One of the mantras for all Madison Public Library (MPL) programming is "there's no one-size-fits-all program." When a program is being offered, there are questions about what might work in a specific community space and what adjustments might need to be made. For Making Justice programming with teens in the Juvenile Detention Center, a Juvenile Shelter Home, and a court-mandated neighborhood intervention program, Bubbler staff ask what these teens need and what will work in these different settings.

One example of the way the needs of a specific community were considered was a Making Justice program run by a seamstress who was an artist in residence at the Juvenile Shelter Home. One of the requirements of the artist-in-residence program is to meet with Bubbler staff and other stakeholders (in this case the Shelter Home teacher employed by the school district) to identify needs of potential Bubbler participants and to work out goals of the Bubbler program on offer. From these discussions, the artist in residence developed two sewing projects—string backpacks and pillows. The backpacks met a need for teens to have something to keep their belongings in, and the pillows responded to an emotional need for teens to have something of their own in their rooms. The artist-in-residence brought in fabrics featuring bright graphic designs, for example, comic book illustrations. The program was popular, and the Shelter Home teacher noted that teens particularly responded to having something of their own that was "soft" and "comforting" that they could take with them. Some teens also took pride and pleasure in making a pillow or backpack for a loved one. This program exemplifies the strength of working with a specific geographic community to develop a program, and it indicates the intricacies of developing an understanding of that community as a group in order to run a successful making project.

A second example from the wider Bubbler program is a cartography group. This example provides evidence of the development of CoP in which members come together to engage in a common making activity that centers on a particular area of knowledge and in doing so take on the identity of that community. The focus of the cartography group is on exploring open-source software and helping each other learn and solve issues with software such as QGIS, CartoDB, OpenStreetMap, and Leaflet. One member described the cartography profession as "the wild frontier," saying 80% of skills he uses he learned himself. Others conferred that they were self-taught (beyond their graduate degrees), and that at the moment, there are no guides or models for "best practice." Established by three women after getting their MA in cartography, the group was started to keep dialog going after completing their degree, to extend the community, "to have fun brainstorming ways to solve problems," to share information in an ever-changing field, and to supplement their MA training. Monthly meetings involve exploring specific software and sharing information about resources (conferences, books, professional journals, web groups, online tutorials), career advice, and general knowledge about the state of the field. The group chose to meet at the library specifically because they wanted to invite members of the profession or hobbyists to join them; and as one founding member said, because "it feels like a neutral space, it is not intimidating." They noted that another Madison cartography group meets in a brewpub and is focused more on career advice than on skill sharing.

The library supports the cartography group by providing a space and laptops loaded with free software with which the group would like to work. Group members and visitors include established professionals who are known within the field as well as novices who have related degrees (such as geography) and are looking to upgrade their technology skills and knowledge. This group exemplifies the role of the public library makerspace program in supporting a CoP; cartographers who have a common goal are sharing skills, knowledge, and technologies as part of their process of taking on the identity of the profession. In providing a space and resources for this group, MPL's Bubbler program aligns with the three other theoretical perspectives outlined in the introduction: applying Weigand's notion of library as place, we can see MPL as important for facilitating the group's knowledge sharing in a "neutral" space; the group exemplifies the facets of Lankes's new librarianship by focusing on knowledge sharing and creation within the wider Madison community of cartographers; and the group is aimed at connecting cartographers and providing access to social and technical resources, as described in Dresang's Radical Change theory.

Implications for Educators and Researchers

The earlier discussion and case studies suggest important implications for LIS educators and researchers related to the social roles of the makerspace and library to their community and the ways that makerspaces conceptualize community. This section summarizes the main points presented about the social roles of library makerspaces, community, and community engagement and provides some suggestions to LIS educators and researchers about how to effectively promote community engagement and social roles when teaching future practitioners of makerspaces and researchers who seek to understand this emerging area of practice.

Social Roles

The literature on makerspaces and the case studies outlined suggest that library makerspaces are fulfilling many traditional social roles but are also reconceptualizing these roles. Library makerspaces promote *knowledge creation, access, learning,* and *equity and diversity.* The case studies provide evidence of the importance of these roles but also how they are shifting. For instance, in library makerspaces knowledge creation is the process of making that can be shared with others, as opposed to libraries only providing access to print and digital resources that facilitate knowledge creation. New knowledge is created and shared with others through the products produced in the maker programs; makers are no longer just consumers of knowledge but producers of knowledge. Ideally, library makerspaces need to make the new knowledge produced by community members accessible and available to communities outside of the makerspace, as suggested by Lankes's *two-way* access concept.

Equitable access to technology and resources is a vital function of libraries, but within library makerspaces we need to rethink what access means. Is it simply providing access to the tools of making (for example, sewing machines, 3D printers, video recording software), or does access also include the facilitated learning experiences and access to the expert mentors in the maker programming? In the Meteorology Club example, the maker program facilitated student knowledge creation through interest-driven programming and also provided access to resources and experts in meteorology that students would not have had access to without the maker program. Access also speaks to the expanding roles of library makerspaces. For example, the Chicago Public Library's Maker Lab saw one of the roles of the library as an on-ramp to meeting other groups with similar interests (Urban Libraries Council, 2015). The cartography group is another example of this expanded role. The library makerspace not only supported the group with a place to meet and software to learn and use, the makerspace also provided access to mentors and others who could add to the professional development of the group. The issue, however, is that library makerspaces are all unique, and although they might develop around the perceived needs of their community, mostly they are based on the resources available to them (e.g., community experts, funding, resources, skills, and interests of library professionals, etc.). Without an understanding of the overall goals of the makerspace and the roles it provides to the geographic community, the makerspace is in danger of being underutilized or just a cool place to go at the library.

One of the library's primary societal roles has always been to provide resources to support and facilitate learning. That learning has traditionally taken place in programming, such as storytimes, book talks, book groups, craft sessions, information, and digital literacy sessions, to name a few. Learning within the makerspace has expanded the role of learning within libraries. Learning within the makerspace takes many forms, whether it is achieved through long-term, facilitated, interest-driven sessions or less formal one-off sessions that provide access to expert mentors, artists in residence, or maker tools and technologies. To fulfill this enhanced role, librarians have had to reconceptualize how they think about and provide learning, which requires training in facilitating learning in its many forms. One of the most often mentioned skills managers desired as an information professional working in a makerspace as reported in Koh and Abbas (2015) was the ability to teach (to facilitate informal learning, to develop user-centered programs). Being able to develop interest-driven, informal programming and to facilitate these sessions is essential to learning within a makerspace. Further, knowing which making tools to use to support programming is an important skill but a skill information professionals felt they needed to learn more about (Abbas & Koh, 2015).

Library makerspaces have the potential to "level the playing field" by providing programming to more diverse audiences than those who traditionally use makerspaces in other venues. Libraries have potential to democratize and diversify the maker movement by making resources, tools, and processes more readily available to *all* community members, regardless of ethnicity, race, age, gender, or ability. Providing equitable access to a diverse audience is one of the primary societal roles of libraries. Makerspaces fulfill this role through programming based on community needs. Understanding users, their needs, and their cultures (being culturally competent) is a desired competency for expert mentors and information professionals working in makerspaces (Abbas & Koh, 2015; Koh & Abbas, 2015). Barton, Tan, and Greenberg (2017) emphasize that makerspace programming should be shaped by the culture of the community and that notions of community should be broken down to include anyone interested in making.

LIS educators should emphasize that the social roles of libraries are changing, especially within library makerspaces. LIS students need to understand the social roles that libraries and library makerspaces provide but also how maker programming supports these roles. LIS education should reemphasize the professional and societal roles, as promulgated by ALA, which libraries have within their communities. Library makerspaces have the unique opportunity to foster new ways of thinking about community engagement, learning, and ensuring equitable access for a diverse audience. Makerspace programs should be inclusive programs based on the needs of participants and the community and developed by participants, facilitated by librarians. Mentors with cultural competency provide meaningful learning experiences based on community demographics and cultural understandings. Therefore, LIS courses should include methods to develop culturally competent programming. Methods to conduct community needs assessments and develop community-centered programming should be taught. LIS programs should also include theory and practices associated with connected, interest-driven learning in which participants direct their own learning and the library professional serves as a guide or mentor.

Further, LIS programs should teach students about socially responsible decision making. Librarians managing a makerspace should have a clear understanding of the role the makerspace plays in the community and have clear goals in place to ensure the makerspace's sustainability and success. Teaching students how to conduct strategic planning that includes setting specific goals and envisions the makerspace's place within the larger organization and community are essential skills students need to learn.

Teaching these qualities can be achieved through independent courses focusing on makerspaces, or the knowledge and skill sets may be embedded across different courses. In any case, LIS educators who teach future makerspace professionals must be aware of theories underlying learning through making—for example, constructionism, communities of practice, and the development of particular mindsets (see Willett, 2017). These pedagogical theories and implications for programming might be taught directly to professionals interested in facilitating library makerspaces. In addition, LIS educators might consider ways their classrooms reflect characteristics of maker learning environments, such as flexible, open, accessible, and technology-rich learning environments, with hands-on, student-driven initiatives and possibilities for the development of communities of practice.

More research is needed to investigate the social role of library makerspaces. Efforts to develop an interdisciplinary field of research, such as the *Makeology* series by Peppler, Halverson, and Kafai (2016), is promising, and research from library and information studies has potential to make a unique contribution to the field, owing to the critical roles that libraries assume regarding access, equity, and diversity and as community anchors for learning and knowledge creation. We suggest researchers studying the social roles of makerspaces expand on and develop the theoretical perspectives introduced in this chapter in order to contribute to theory building and the advancement of scholarship of library makerspaces and the maker movement more generally.

Community

As indicated by the literature on makerspaces and the case studies outlined earlier, makerspaces may define community in several ways (e.g., as part of a larger geographic community, a group with common interests and norms—CoP, as belonging to the library maker group), or the makerspace may have no clear definition of community. In fact, competing definitions or understandings of the goals of the library makerspace may exist. For example, the makerspace may have been developed to fulfill the social roles of the library, to promote *equitable access* to its members by providing a space for community members to engage in making with new technologies, or as a way to learn new skills for job advancement. The makerspace may have a less defined purpose, as a place where people with common interests and norms can meet and share knowledge as a CoP. Alternatively, the makerspace may have a more defined purpose such as providing user-centered informal learning experiences. Whether a library thinks about community as geographically based, community within the makerspace, or as a CoP, understanding the demographics, culture, and life stories of the geographic community or the participants in a maker program should guide development of the makerspace and "interest-powered" making programming (Barton, Tan, & Greenberg, 2017; Koh & Abbas, 2015).

Participants of the library makerspace may also have a different idea of what community means to them. In the Meteorology Club study, students felt ownership over the maker program, and it was noted they also felt that they belonged to the larger community. Students directed their own learning experiences, guided by the experts who contributed to the maker experience and built community within the maker group, as well as providing the maker program as a service to the larger community. Also as illustrated in the case studies, the library makerspace provided a public space for cartography group members to meet and gain access to social and technological resources. The library's role in this case was to support the group in their activities (sharing resources and skills, supplementing their training, building community).

LIS educators should emphasize to students, who are future makerspace professionals, the importance of community within makerspaces but also to teach students the varying ways that community may be present in a makerspace. When developing a new makerspace, or if simply providing making programming, the library should have a clear idea of how they conceptualize community within the makerspace and/or making programming and the goals they have for building community, supporting CoPs, and/or providing the makerspace as a service to the geographic community. Students also need to be made aware that makerspaces may have competing definitions of community and that each definition may shape the outcomes of the makerspace or making programming.

LIS students need to understand the role that community and community members may play in the makerspace. Library makerspaces are supported not just by participants who come to make but by community organizations, media and technology experts, and many volunteers as outlined earlier. Each have a role to play in the makerspace, which may vary depending on the expertise or the level of commitment of the volunteers. Establishing, managing, and maintaining these partnerships is critical to the success of a makerspace. One of the competencies determined to be essential by managers and librarians in makerspaces as reported by Koh and Abbas (2016) was community engagement. LIS educators should include skills and strategies for building, managing, and maintaining these partnerships in classes on makerspaces and/or library community engagement.

Students also need to understand that the makerspace should have clear goals in mind for community engagement. Community engagement may include building and maintaining partnerships with organizations in the community that can support the makerspace in various ways (e.g., providing expert mentors or collaborating and sharing resources). A library may also see the makerspace as a way to engage with new community members who typically do not use the library and/or to support participants' activities in their own CoPs. Further, the library may equate community engagement as a way to garner support for increasing participation and sustaining or funding a makerspace (Koh & Abbas, 2016). Students should learn to develop strategies for engaging with the various members and groups of the community.

LIS courses that engage future makerspace professionals must be model learning environments for engaging communities and cultivating a sense of community among the learners. Ideally, courses include partnerships and collaborations with libraries and makerspaces. Field trips to various types of makerspaces that serve different user groups (e.g., makerspaces in academic, public, school, special libraries, nonprofit organizations, museums, and more) can teach students that there is no one-size-fits-all makerspace. Inviting mentors, experts, librarians, and other professionals to the class allows LIS students to be exposed to a range of topics and skill sets, which may not be accomplished by a single LIS instructor. Internships, fieldwork, and service learning are all great opportunities to teach students *with* community. Furthermore, educators must utilize strategies for creating a sense of a learning community in class. The experience of developing a community of practice during their preservice training is vital for LIS students who will be cultivating a learning community in their library makerspace. Therefore, LIS instructors should play the role of a connector to community resources and a facilitator or guide for a learning community.

Researchers who study library makerspaces need to be aware of the potentially competing perspectives of community within the makerspace. As outlined, makerspace developers or participants may have differing perspectives of how they view community or may not have considered how they are defining community. Therefore, included in research should be methods or processes that document and take account of different stakeholders' understandings and definitions of community. In addition, researchers need to be aware of their own perspectives of community as they study library makerspaces and not impose their own ideas of community on the makerspace when studying how community is present in a library makerspace. The role of community and how community is built in the makerspace should be further explored. Conducting research *with* community, beyond research *on* community, may advance both scholarly and practical fields of makerspace. Librarians who facilitate makerspaces are often being pulled in many directions: developing new programs, building various community connections, raising funds, and so on. Researchers can support librarians by working with them to create and develop makerspaces that align with goals and tenets of their libraries and communities. Several promising research approaches exist to engage community through innovative research, such as research–practice partnerships (RPPs) (Coburn & Penuel, 2016, p. 48), design-based research (McKenney & Reeves, 2012), and participatory action research (Mirra, Garcia, Morrell, 2015).

Conclusion

The growing maker movement in librarianship is an important phenomenon in reconceptualizing libraries, not only because makerspaces are equipped with cutting-edge technologies but also because they retain and reinvigorate the core values and roles of librarianship. Theoretical perspectives and historical analyses show the history, culture, and values of librarianship are revived in library makerspaces. Instead of viewing a makerspace as a new fad or as a separate space disconnected from the rest of the library, this chapter suggests library makerspaces represent a transformative role for libraries in the contemporary knowledge society, as libraries continuously adapt to serve the needs of their communities. The name, "makerspace," and tools they offer vary across the institutions and are likely to change over time; however, the roles that library makerspaces assume, to facilitate knowledge creation, access, learning, and equity and diversity, will remain critical in order to sustain and promote their local communities. Further, these roles must continue to be examined, negotiated, advanced, and refined by the members of the profession and their communities.

This chapter particularly focuses on the concept of community and its differing meanings. Community may refer to a geographically based local community, a group of people who share the same interests, or a sense of belonging. With real-world examples of library makerspaces, the chapter discusses the significance of library makerspaces being grounded in their local communities as well as supporting a sense of community among the participants. A review of literature on community and makerspaces reveals that the library profession has strengths regarding ways to engage local community and develop community connections. Meanwhile, literature from the broader makerspace movement emphasizes the development of a community of makers and learners—that is, a sense of community that supports one another—in physical and online spaces. Both provide valuable perspectives, and researchers and professionals in library makerspaces can learn from cross-disciplinary conversations to contribute to the community and the larger maker movement.

Acknowledgment

The case studies presented in this chapter, the Meteorology Makers' Club at the Irving Middle School Library [grant number: RE-07-14-0048014] and the Bubbler at Madison Public Library [LG-06-14-0174-14], are made possible in part through funding from the Institute of Museum and Library Services.

References

Abbas, J., & Koh, K. (2015). Future of library and museum services supporting teen learning: Perceptions of professionals in learning labs and makerspaces. *Journal of Research on Libraries & Young Adults, 6*. Retrieved from www.yalsa.ala.org/jrlya/2015/11/future-of-library-and-museum-services-supporting-teen-learning-perceptions-of-professionals-in-learning-labs-and-makerspaces/

American Library Association. (2004). *Core Values of Librarianship.* Retrieved from www.ala.org/advocacy/intfreedom/corevalues

American Library Association. (2013). *ALA Policy Manual.* Retrieved from www.ala.org/aboutala/governance/policymanual/updatedpolicymanual/section1/1mission

American Library Association (ALA) Center for the Future of Libraries. (2014, September 15). *Maker Movement.* Retrieved from www.ala.org/transforminglibraries/future/trends/makers

Anderson, C. (2012). *Makers: The New Industrial Revolution.* New York, NY: Random House.

Barton, A. C., Tan, E., & Greenberg, D. (2017). The Makerspace Movement: Sites of possibilities for equitable opportunities to engage underrepresented youth in STEM. *Teachers College Record, 119*(June), 1–44.

Brady, T., Salas, C., Nuriddin, A., Rodgers, W., & Subramaniam, M. (2014). MakeAbility: Creating accessible makerspace events in a public library. *Public Library Quarterly, 33*(4), 330–347, doi:10.1080/01616846.2014.970425

Burke, J. (2014). *Makerspaces: A Practical Guide for Librarians.* New York, NY: Rowman & Littlefield.

Buschman, J., Leckie, G. J., Wiegand, W. A., & Bertot, J. C. (2007). *The Library as Place: History, Community, and Culture.* Westport, CT: Libraries Unlimited.

Clapp, E. P., Ross, J., Ryan, J. O., & Tishman, S. (2017). *Maker-centered Learning: Empowering Young People to Shape Their Worlds.* San Francisco, CA: Jossey-Bass.

Coburn, C. E., & Penuel, W. R. (2016). Research-practice partnerships in education: Outcomes, dynamics, and open questions. *Educational Researcher, 45*(1), 48–54.

Dresang, E. T. (1999). *Radical Change: Books for Youth in a Digital Age.* New York, NY: H.W. Wilson Company.

Dresang, E. T. (2013). Digital age libraries and youth: Learning labs, literacy leaders, radical resources. In J. Beheshti & J. A. Large (Eds.), *The Information Behavior of a New Generation: Children and Teens in the 21st Century* (pp. 93–116). Lanham, MD: Scarecrow Press.

Dubriwny, N., Pritchett, N., Hardesty, M., & Hellman, C. M. (2016). Impact of Fab Lab Tulsa on student self-efficacy toward STEM education. *Journal of STEM Education: Innovations and Research, 17*(2), 21–25.

Gee, J. P. (2005). Semiotic social spaces and affinity spaces. In D. Barton & K. Tusting (Eds.), *Beyond Communities of Practice: Language Power and Social Context* (pp. 214–232). Cambridge, NY: Cambridge University Press.

Good, T., & Doctorow, C. (2013). Manufacturing maker spaces. *American Libraries, 44*(1-2), 44–49.

Gutwill, J. P., Hido, N., & Sindorf, L. (2015). Research to practice: Observing learning in tinkering activities. *Curator: The Museum Journal, 58*(2), 151–168. doi:https://doi.org/10.1111/cura.12105

Habermas, J. (2014). *The Structural Transformation of the Public Sphere: An Inquiry into a Category of Bourgeois Society.* Cambridge, UK: Polity.

Halverson, E., & Sheridan, K. (2014). The Maker Movement in education. *Harvard Educational Review, 84*(4), 495–504.

Hamilton, M., & Schmidt, D. H. (2015). *Make It Here: Inciting Creativity and Innovation in Your Library*. Denver, CO: Libraries Unlimited.

Hatch, M. (2014). *The Maker Movement Manifesto*. New York, NY: McGraw-Hill.

Koh, K. (2015). Radical change theory: Framework for empowering digital youth. *Journal of Research on Libraries and Young Adults, 5*. Retrieved from www.yalsa.ala.org/jrlya/2015/01/radical-change-theory-framework-for-empowering-digital-youth/

Koh, K., & Abbas, J. (2015). Competencies for information professionals in learning labs and makerspaces. *Journal for Education of Library and Information Science, 56*(2), 114–129.

Koh, K., & Abbas, J. (2016). Competencies needed to provide teen library services of the future: Survey of professionals in learning labs and makerspaces. *Journal of Research on Libraries and Young Adults, 7*(2). Retrieved from http://tinyurl.com/competencies16

Lankes, R. D. (2015). *The New Librarianship: Field Guide*. Cambridge, MA: MIT Press.

Lave, J., & Wenger, E. (1991). *Situated Learning: Legitimate Peripheral Participation*. Cambridge, UK: Cambridge University Press.

MacKenney, S. E., & Reeves, T. C. (2012). *Conducting Educational Design Research*. London: Routledge.

Maker Education Initiative. (n.d.). *Maker Education Initiative*. Retrieved from www.makered.org/

Mirra, N., Garcia, A., & Morrell, E. (2015). *Doing Youth Participatory Action Research: Transforming Inquiry with Researchers, Educators, and Students*. New York, NY: Routledge.

Oldenburg, R. (1997). *The Great Good Place: Cafes, Coffee Shops, Community Centers, Beauty Parlors, General Stores, Bars, Hangouts, and How They Get You Through the Day*. New York, NY: Marlowe.

Peppler, K., Halverson, E., & Kafai, Y. B. (2016). *Makeology: Makerspaces as Learning Environments* (Vol. 1). New York, NY: Routledge.

Remold, J., Fusco, J., Vogt, K. A., & Leones, T. (2016). *Communities for Maker Educators: A Study of the Communities and Resources That Connect Educators Engaged in Making*. Menlo Park, CA: SRI International. Retrieved from www.sri.com/sites/default/files/brochures/makereducatorcommunities.pdf

Urban Libraries Council. (2015). *Making a Diverse Maker Community in Chicago*. Retrieved from www.urbanlibraries.org/making-a-diverse-maker-community-in-chicago-innovation-1231.php?page_id=420

Vossoughi, S., Hooper, P. K., & Escude, M. (2016). Making through the lens of culture and power: Toward transformative visions for educational equity. *Harvard Educational Review, 86*(2), 206–232.

Wiegand, W. A. (2015a). *Part of Our Lives: A People's History of the American Public Library*. New York, NY: Oxford University Press.

Wiegand, W. A. (2015b). 'Tunnel vision and blind spots' reconsidered: Part of our lives (2015) as a test case. *The Library Quarterly: Information, Community, Policy, 85*(4), 347–370. doi:https://doi.org/10.1086/682731

Willett, R. (2017). Learning through making in public libraries: Theories, practices, and tensions. *Learning, Media and Technology*. Retrieved from http://dx.doi.org.ezproxy.library.wisc.edu/10.1080/17439884.2017.1369107

Willingham, T., & de Boer, J. (2015). *Makerspaces in Libraries*. New York, NY: Rowman & Littlefield.

PART II

Reconceptualizing Library Experiences

3

MAKING CONNECTED MESSAGES

Designing Community-Relevant Murals With Youth in Public Libraries

Yasmin Kafai, Orkan Telhan, Richard Lee Davis, K-Fai Steele, and Barrie Adleberg

Introduction

Maker activities already popular in fabrication spaces, children's museums, science centers, community organizations, and maker fairs (Honey & Kanter, 2013; Peppler, Halverson, & Kafai, 2016a and 2016b), are moving into public libraries (Lee et al., 2017; Lui, 2016). In support of their mission to provide access to information and resources to the general public, public libraries have embraced maker activities as a new mission to provide access to technologies and new competencies for their young and old patrons. Many central and local library branches now offer 3D printers for producing designs, recording studios for mixing music, wireless hotspots and laptops that patrons can check out, as well as computers and informal classes for introducing programming, and more. In addition, they organize workshops and mentors to support patrons in completing their projects (reference chapters in this book).

However, most maker activities in public library locations and library-based workshops have focused on individual personally relevant designs such as robots, toys, and clothing. While these designs are often created with support of others and shared with others, they leave aside the potentially rich applications of community-relevant designs that could not only engage local participants but also connect them to global audiences. Community-relevant designs can introduce new genres of maker activities that are concerned not only about teaching a particular skill set but also about fostering a sense of connection. For instance, quilt designs engage a circle of makers into creating a collective project—the quilt—and celebrating events such as weddings, while murals found in many cities often depict historical events or memorials and consist of messages, images, or scenes built by individuals or groups who intend to preserve the spirit of the community (Golden & Updike, 2014).

It is within this larger landscape of participatory public murals that we situate our design of an interactive community mural, called *Connected Messages*. The context and content of the public, participatory, and interactive display drew on Philadelphia's identity as the "City of Brotherly Love and Sisterly Affection" and Lady Gaga's "Born Brave" bus tour in 2013. *Connected Messages* provided a summer project opportunity for youth in the city of Philadelphia to both create and share ideas with their community in the form of mural displays as well as through the web, communicating their messages of concern and safety as well as love and acceptance across the city and around the world using Free Library branches as makerspaces. This approach brings together community outreach efforts of engaging youth in designing interactive murals with themes relevant to their lives and uses low-cost networking technologies of connecting local groups with global audiences. We describe the design of an interactive community mural that functions like a public display, which can be remotely programmed through an online interface. The implementation of *Connected Messages* murals was supported by maker mentors: part-time library staff who did not fit the typical mold of a librarian. Instead of possessing a Master's of library and information science (MLIS), as is typically required for most professional librarian positions in the United States, the mentors were local artists, tinkerers, recent college graduates, and musicians. *Connected Messages* spanned five Free Library branches in Philadelphia and reached more than 1,000 youth. In the discussion, we review key dimensions expanding youth and mentor participation in community-relevant designs.

Background

The design and implementation of *Connected Messages* builds upon prior work on developing murals and providing mentor support in community efforts. The idea of designing and digitally augmenting community murals is not a new one; it has involved the development of digital murals for connecting online and offline worlds and DIY low-cost efforts. But our adaption of mural design as a community maker activity showcases how making, which often takes place in communal settings and provides support and expertise to individual makers, can also be used for making a collaborative artifact that brings together makers across a city. In what follows, we discuss various platforms and modalities of community murals that served as inspiration for *Connected Messages*.

Traditional community murals, such as the types found on the walls of buildings, are designed to be fixed representations. They often depict historical events and consist of messages, images, or scenes built by individuals who intend to preserve the spirit of the community. Most traditional public murals embrace a do-it-together mentality (Jenkins, 2009), fostering a sense of ownership by encouraging the community to realize its public image together. For instance, the city of Philadelphia has a rich tradition of community displays and murals. It is home to the *Mural Arts* Program, a thirty-year organization which has populated the city with more than 3,600 murals that are the visual product of each community's grass-roots discussion of identity and history (Golden & Updike, 2014). The murals' design and execution are led by a professional artist, of which more than 300 are employed yearly by the Mural Arts Program (for examples, see www.muralarts. org). These murals capture the richness and diversity of different neighborhoods, communicate civic and social messages, and connect individuals and the supporting institutions with a sense of belonging to the community.

Traditional murals are static in nature, and they do not capture change in communities. Digital displays such as large-scale permanent projections and media facades have the potential to allow communities to express themselves in more dynamic ways because they allow real-time participation and bridge the personal and the local with online communities. Efforts here range from the pioneering work by Brignull and Rogers's (2003) *Opionizer* that let participants voice and share their ideas to Peltonen and colleagues' (2007) *CityWall* projects that let children display their designs. More education-oriented efforts have also taken advantage of interactive displays, such as Hsi and Eisenberg's (2012) *Math on a Sphere* project, which provided children with a programming language to create and share designs for spherical displays in public science centers, or Lamberty and colleagues' (2011) *DigiQuilts* that help students build designs that engaged with mathematical challenges and shared their outcomes using large screens.

Other public displays have gone multimodal, as in the case of Detken and colleagues' (2009) prototype of a tangible public display that combines physical interaction with an online search to improve the use of public libraries among youth. Their *Search Wall* allows youth to browse and select book titles using different physical representations such as cubes, baskets, puppets, or knobs. Here, book search becomes a social activity as kids can search with their parents, siblings, or friends and see each other's selection on the wall display at the same time. In a similar vein, Brignull and colleagues (2004) created *Dynamo* to see how interactions in physical space change when a display system is introduced. The system established a sense of communal awareness through sharing a wide variety of personal content—such as photos, music, and video clips—through displays embedded inside the common room of a high school. However, these digital public displays, while inviting contributions and interactions, often lack the sense of intimacy, community voice, and identity that traditional murals possess.

We also wanted to increase interaction in public displays by allowing an exchange of different kinds of messages. We compared research that explored the sharing of existing messages such as Instagram photos or Tweets with projects that allow participants to create custom messages that are specifically designed to be shared through the public display. Successful examples here include the use of plasma screens networked in office environment to function like digital bulletin boards and let local and remote workers connect by sharing multimedia messages (Churchil, Nelson, & Denoue, 2003) or the use of displays for sharing of photos collected via Instagram, Twitter, or Weibo. More unusual and creative forms of content are also reported to be successful in stimulating interaction with public displays. Kim and colleagues (2009) developed *Bubble Letters*, a game played by creating virtual messages on a public display by blowing bubbles into a custom physical interface. These examples highlight the importance of the communicative function of the messages and suggest that when children create specific messages for the interaction and deliberately communicate with each other, they extend the mode of interaction beyond a simple sense of sharing and building awareness.

In designing the infrastructure and implementation of *Connected Messages*, we combined the community-empowering nature of murals with the dynamic qualities of digital displays into a low-cost platform for a community-created interactive digital mural. Our interactive community mural was designed for three interaction modalities that allowed site-specific, remote, and offline-only interactions to happen at the same time. In the context of public participatory and interactive displays, that meant: (1) allowing for creative expression in multiple ways by providing various readily available materials such as paper, markers, and LEDs; (2) making displays accessible to large numbers of participants by using cheap materials; and (3) facilitating local and global participation by connecting it to the web. We emphasized the DIY approach by using everyday materials and combining drawings with digitally mediated content. In addition, the display itself was not a large-scale or spherical computer screen but rather a simple 4 feet-by-4 feet foam board augmented with copper tape connected and controlled through the internet.

Furthermore, we wanted to support a broad group of library patrons across library user groups and library departments in creating a dialog around community and identity while also capturing the richness and diversity of neighborhoods across Philadelphia. Here we focused our attention on maker mentors, a new staffing position at the Free Library that was enhanced through professional development from two national movements around content creation and making in after-school/out-of-school environments: the Maker Ed Initiative and the YOUMedia Learning Labs Network. The use of mentors or facilitators with youth in community centers and spaces has a long tradition, often combining social work, arts education, and community activism (Kafai, Peppler, & Chapman, 2009). Maker mentors are not typical library staff; none of them possessed MLIS degrees that are typically required for professional positions in libraries. The position was part time and seasonal (20 hours/week for the duration of the summer). The maker mentor position builds on the mentorship models developed by the Digital Youth Network (DYN) and YOUMedia Chicago at the Chicago Public Library. In both of these programs, the mentors were adults chosen for their arts expertise and for their ability to connect with youth (Larson et al., 2013).

Mentors can adopt different roles in their interactions with patrons ranging from guidance to mediation to acting as confidants (Strobel, Kirshner, O'Donoghue, & McLaughlin, 2008). Mentorship also involves amplifying youths' voices in regard to library administration and stakeholders. For example, when youths' concerns and needs are taken into account in the design of library programs, those programs become more authentic and relevant to the youth in the community (Steele, 2013). In YOUMedia, the mentors wear many hats, acting as role models and connectors to outside resources and offering guidance; but what remains constant in their work is a commitment to letting youth take charge. By adopting this role, the mentors develop trusting, meaningful relationships with the youth who frequent the space. These relationships are built on shared interests, identity, and respect. Youth may be initially attracted to the technology, but they stay for the relationships they build with other patrons and mentors. Giving youth in these learning spaces multiple pathways to engaging with learning allows them to engage at their own pace and at their own desire to participate. This creates a social environment in which participation is not mandatory, and hanging out is allowed and encouraged (Ito et al., 2009). This is in opposition to traditional library services for youth, in which youth are only allowed to be present when participating in structured programs such as book clubs.

The maker mentor model adopted as part of the *Connected Messages* project was inspired by the YOUMedia/DYN model in that the mentors were chosen for their ability to connect with youth and for their creative backgrounds. What differed was that the maker mentors were also chosen for their experience and involvement with the maker movement. In addition to being artists, two of the five mentors were already familiar with the maker movement and had experience working with digital fabrication (e.g., laser cutters, 3D printers) and computer programming. The other three mentors were eager to learn more about digital fabrication and to engage youth in projects that combined artistic practices with the more high-tech media and tools. In examining youths' agency and maker mentors' support of youth in accessing, participating in, and expressing their ideas and concerns about their communities, we addressed the following research questions: What impacts youth participation in and expression of community themes at different sites? How can mentors support youths' voices, making, and technical learning in the context of community-relevant designs?

Context

Public Library Makerspaces

The project began during the summer of 2013 as part of an international initiative by the Digital Media and Learning Competition and was hosted at the Free Library of Philadelphia (FLP). The Free Library is a major urban library system, serving 1.5 million people within the city of Philadelphia through forty-nine branch libraries, three regional libraries, a Central Library, the Regional Library for the Blind and Physically Handicapped, and the Rosenbach Museum. Although the library offers some paid programs such as author events, there are also programs that specifically target underserved populations, including immigrants, youth in especially impoverished neighborhoods, and young children. In a city where nearly 33% of children live below the poverty level and more than 50% of public schools lack on-site libraries, the Free Library is one of the largest free after-school programs for Philadelphia students.

Five branches of the Free Library were identified and selected as hosts for each of the five *Connected Messages* boards, engaging local youth ages 6 to 19 years old in communities across the city. The participating branches were distributed across North and West Philadelphia in socioeconomically disadvantaged neighborhoods with predominantly African-American (61.61%) and Hispanic (32.5%) members and fewer than 2% of adults employed in professional, scientific, and technical services. The communities participating in the project were decimated by poverty, with 65% of households earning less than $25,000. In Philadelphia as a whole, more than 40% of households lack internet access. The high-need context in these neighborhoods proved to be a constant theme influencing maker programming, specifically around the design and implementation of *Connected Messages*.

Physical Board and Online Portal

The *Connected Messages* platform consisted of the following components: (1) boards for displaying and connecting messages created by participants, (2) tiles created by participants with images, designs and an LED, and (3) a website that displayed a virtual representation of the mural and allowed the LEDs to be controlled. These boards and materials were installed in five participating library branches around Philadelphia. Each "blank" *Connected Messages* board (see Figure 3.1) consisted of a 4 × 4-foot piece of foam board purchased at a local art supply store, strips of adhesive copper tape laid out in an overlapping grid, an Electric Imp hardware module, a 16 × 8 LED matrix controller, and a 4G modem that connected the board to the internet. The Electric Imp and 4G modem turned the board into an internet-connected device—in other words, anyone with a computer and an internet connection can interact with it. These materials were chosen because of their low cost (the total cost for a board was US$300) and because of their relative simplicity. The board could be constructed in a short amount of time using little more than scissors, a soldering iron, and wire strippers and was designed so the underlying hardware was part of the aesthetic design. In other words, anyone could examine the board to see how it worked.

Each board had room for an 8 × 8 grid of 5-inch-square cardboard boxes with clear lids (sixty-four boxes in total per board). Participants decorated the lids using colored markers and installed a single white LED in the box using two conductive copper traces. When these traces were connected to 3.3 volts, the LED inside the box would turn on and illuminate the design on the lid. Once the box was pinned to the copper-tape grid on the board, the LEDs in the boxes could be turned on and off from the main website. When an entire board was populated with boxes,

FIGURE 3.1   Foam board with copper traces (upper left), Electric Imp and a modem (upper right), back of tile boxes with copper connectors (lower left), and tile boxes with designs on board (lower right).

it also functioned as an 8 × 8 display that could display running messages typed into a text box on the board's web page (see Figure 3.2).

The website connected.ecrafting.org provided a local and global access point to control and display messages on the foam board. Each library location had its own page on the site that represented the boxes on the physical mural. Whenever a new box was added to the board, a mentor would upload an image, title, text explaining the design, and (optionally) a video of the creator explaining the motivation for the design. All of this information could be accessed by clicking on the virtual box on the website. Clicking the on/off toggle button on each virtual box turned the physical LED inside the box on and off. When an entire board was populated with boxes, it also functioned as an 8 × 8 display that could display running messages typed into a text box on the board's web page (see Figure 3.3).

Maker Mentors

The mural activities were led by five mentors, a team that consisted of two women and three men, ages 21 to 31, working artists and undergraduate students with backgrounds ranging from chemistry to industrial design and engineering. The mentors were part of a Maker Ed Initiative grant to lead workshops in

FIGURE 3.2 *Connected Messages*: Letter "R" scrolling (left) and selected lights on (right).

electronics, arts, and crafting. They were hired for this part-time summer position and trained for three weeks on materials, projects, and theoretical frameworks to making. Then they were assigned to each of the five library branches, where they shadowed other library staff to get to know the program, participants, other staff, and patrons. The workshops were often youth driven, depending on the interests of participants. Mentors guided youth as they developed themes and designed the message tiles, sometimes in workshop-type settings, other times in informal drop-in environments. In addition, members from the research team helped with the technical setup. One researcher visited all sites, observed activities, and later interviewed mentors about their experiences.

FIGURE 3.2   (Continued)

Making and Mentoring of Community Murals

We set up the project during the summer of 2013 in five Free Library locations in neighborhoods across North and West Philadelphia. At the end of the summer, the activities culminated with a celebration in the Central Library location that brought together all five boards plus a blank one, which visitors of the Celebration could complete with their own messages. More than fifty youth presenters and more than 100 additional attendees gathered in the lobby of the Central Library to display their messages of community. Participants had the opportunity to share the meaning behind their tiles, as well as the technological

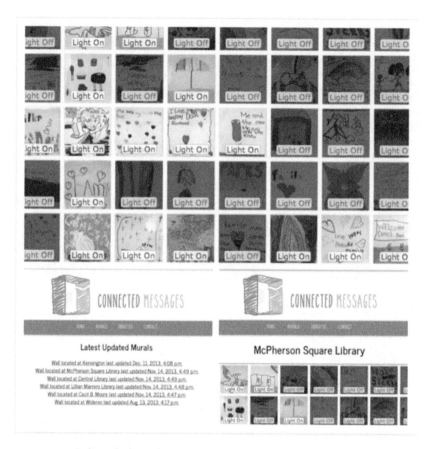

FIGURE 3.3 Online platform for *Connected Messages.*

knowledge they accumulated over the summer by helping attendees create their own postcards. One of the boards was also connected to the internet, and visitors could type in a message and see it scroll across the LEDs. Furthermore, *Connected Messages* became an award-winning exhibit at the 2013 World Maker Faire that took place a few weeks later in New York City. Our observations focused on youth maker and mentor activities in library branches and debriefing interviews conducted with mentors.

Making the Mural Elements

A total of 1,036 total youth participants, between ages 6 and 19 years, participated in *Connected Messages* activities, their daily participation fluctuating from three to thirty participants. Youth and mentors at each location developed a theme for their board based on conversations relating to the themes (e.g., bravery, kindness, acceptance, antibullying) of Lady Gaga's Born Brave bus tour, which visited Philadelphia in March 2013. The most striking differences were found in themes for the boxes adopted in each library branch. While all of them started from Lady Gaga tour themes, the mentors realized in order to imbue a true sense of ownership in the project, the making had to be personalized. One library location—embedded within a nonprofit whose mission is to reduce the recidivism of adjudicated African-American youth—created boxes that addressed recent school closings versus new prison construction, their perspectives on the Trayvon Martin trial, and choosing positivity and creative outlets over perpetuating violence. As the mentor explained, "[The participants] took each problem as an interesting challenge and made it their own. It was easier to scaffold their learning to the point where I could be almost completely hands-off during their making."

At one library branch, the mural served as an opportunity for improvisational storytelling:

> The first day it ended up going through these inside jokes that we had . . . one was about 'uncle,' and there was another one about 'grandpa' . . . And it was kind of a joke that spread between the whole clique of boys that I had during my second [workshop] . . . And basically they would keep on saying like, Uncle is dead, Uncle is dead . . . And they would always talk about grandpa and grandma and come up with this fantasyland of grandpa and grandma's house and stuff like that . . . We're starting *Connected Messages*, and one of the kids draws a headstone and it says RIP Uncle. And another kid draws a face and he calls it Grandpa . . . and we stood in front of the *Connected Messages* form and we lined up chairs and we had each kid say a eulogy about uncle.

The mural—a shared project—allowed for these young people involved in its creation to develop a shared and collaborative comic storyline. The technical aspects of box creation were seamless with the storytelling aspect, with both aspects building off of each other to become something larger than simply the individual parts.

Another library location, the Village Hot Spot, had thirteen participants aged 4 to 13 years, of which there were four girls (not repeat participants) and nine boys (many of whom came repeatedly). One of the four girls assisted the mentor, BK. Several of the participants got to the point where they were able to scan their designs to a thumb drive and process them for the website. As the mentor explained:

> Jonathan [a regular participant; pseudonyms used] is 13 and he could just pick it up anything and run. For Mica, who is 9, he has like the school system grilled into this head by his grandma, so he's like, "am I the best student," and he needed more oversight and guidance. I needed to tell him what we needed to do and work on. Amir was kind of in between that—he

could be working on anything and he'd be fine. I would say the coolest part is the breakthrough—when we had to do documentation for it—they would all work on Mozilla, the web-maker thing, and they would help piece together the html and the website.

Drew, like other mentors, noted that youth engagement increased with the global connectivity element, "once it was all put together getting to go on the website, they were just like really enthusiastic about that. Even the kids who looked like really jaded about that—like, oh this is stupid, but I'm gonna make one. But then once it was made, they were the ones borrowing a laptop from the library, turning it on and off." As another group activity, Drew guided youth as they decorated the mural with googly eyes and puffy paint.

Accessing Making Within Local Library Branches

The local branches also differed substantially in terms of participation, access, and completion of the community mural designs and illustrated some of the challenges in implementing such maker projects within different sites. In one library branch located in North Philadelphia, the mural board was displayed on the library main floor. Mentor Drew explained that this display was especially intentional, because by displaying it prominently, he was able to generate more curiosity and interest by the library community and staff. The project was "something that they can be proud of and see and that will last." Other branches had the board displayed in an area on the wall next to the computer lab, which is used heavily by community members, their families, and peers. In contrast, at another branch, the mural board was locked in a conference room and children were only able to populate it with shadow boxes when the maker corps member came three times a week. There were few repeat participants, but the teen librarian noticed that once summer camp had ended, there was a dramatic spike in participation. But many finished boxes were left unmounted; the maker mentor started mounting the boxes herself in the end.

While location of the mural boards played a significant role in how patrons had access to making, engaging youth of different ages also proved to be a challenge. In a North Philadelphia library branch, children aged 7 to 15 populated the board. While the board was completed within a week, there were problems with regular youth participation, as well as reluctance by older youth to participate in a project whose intended participants included youth younger than them. Other branches had fewer problems with engaging youth in making the mural. As one mentor noted,

I was able to get such a wide range of kids, like age groups too, to participate, even some of the real troublemakers . . . I was able to get them to make some boxes, and they really liked it too. So everyone got to build some boxes. I don't think there was anyone who was left out who I saw on a regular basis. Everyone got to be involved with [Connected Messages].

Reflections of Maker Mentors

At the completion of *Connected Messages*, we interviewed the five mentors about their experiences in supporting learning, production, expression of community voice, and their own learning. Overall, mentors guided the youth at their sites through a mentorship approach fueled directly by the main tenets of connected learning, which is interest driven, peer supported, and academically oriented (Ito et al., 2013). Several mentors recalled that youth described their neighborhoods of North and West Philadelphia in a way that echoed census statistics on drug abuse, violence, and low education: "It was a bit sad to hear their initial responses of *not safe, no good*." In response, mentors often shifted the conversation to a more asset-based approach that focused on positive aspects. "One of them wanted to make a box about recycling, not because the community is all that trash-conscious, but because it's something he wanted to say he feels is important to making a community healthy." By challenging a negative dominant narrative and supporting curiosity, youth were able to expose personal stories about their communities. One mentor described that the process became organic: "I quickly learned that kid input and project driving needed to be a priority of mine . . . Informal exploration time allowed me to connect with my kids a bit more." Mentors wanted to lead a project with youth input rather than define the outcomes.

In addition to supporting youth voices, mentors also encouraged them to explore different approaches in making. As one mentor stated, "I liked the idea of working with kids and getting to encourage creativity and getting them to see and try out projects that they would normally not have the opportunity to try out in their daily lives." Some mentors supported the artistic process: "Drawing and painting is all creative problem solving, and seeing things in a different way, trying to break them down to simpler problems than seeing it all as a whole. If you can step up and get closer and see the smaller parts, it makes it much more tangible to someone who is uncomfortable with their own skills." Another mentor described his teaching style as informal:

> They took each project or problem as an interesting challenge and made it their own. It was easier to scaffold their learning to the point where I could be almost completely hands-off during their making. This creeped into the majority of my kids near the end as they saw the final products of their collaborative efforts on *Connected Messages*. They began to be creative and express themselves through our documentation and in the end got into heated debates over who could present our work to the community . . . Surprisingly, at the end, kids were fighting over controlling *Connected Messages*.

In terms of academic support, mounting the boxes on the board introduced youth to a basic understanding of simple circuits. A mentor explained,

> I think the majority understood the idea of positive/negative, the leads on the board all meant positive/negative and how that had to operate. But as far as how it was actually transmitted and how you'd be controlling it from the computer, I don't think they quite understood . . . Once they were all finished, they'd hit the road and didn't really even ask how it was going to work. They were just like cool, I made this box, it's gonna light up, awesome.

In an attempt to spark more interest in the technology that provided the backbone of the connectivity, a mentor disassembled the board: "I took off the barcode box [showed them the hardware] just so they could see what was under the hood." In future iterations of the project, mentors agreed that exposure to back-end hardware construction would be a great impetus for deeper learning: "I think it would be cool if they were actually part of [constructing the hardware]."

Discussion

Connected Messages combined drawings with digitally mediated content and allowed for site-specific, remote, and offline-only interaction modalities at the same time. We utilized a maker-oriented approach and provided each participant the basic components to build a message box that would become the building block for expressing ideas about community and composing a larger public display. In the following sections, we discuss key themes relevant to the design of community-relevant murals.

A Construction Kit for Community-Relevant Making

In this project, we focused on making that combined a community-relevant with a personally relevant approach. We utilized a construction kit approach and provided each participant the basic components to build a "pixel." These materials would include cheap everyday materials such as a cardboard box, drawing materials, an LED, copper tape, and so on. Our anchoring theme was "reprogrammability." The idea was to have a public display that can combine individualized representations such as drawings, paintings with pixels, which can be grouped to form displays that can be reprogrammed by everyone. Based on our reprogrammability theme, we saw relevance emerging in various ways: drawing individual messages (single boxes), seeing the meaning of drawings in relation to each other (multiple tiles), eventually creating meaning as a group image by the entire board (parts aligning to make a whole), creating messages that can be sent remotely to different boards in different branches (reprogramming meaning from a global context). When these objectives are combined, they allowed us to demonstrate the workings of a digital mural. We observed that this framework can create a relatively enduring interaction model and has the potential for creating strong engagement within the community. The murals that are developed over the course of this research capture both the personality and richness of the experience of the participants and their capacity to connect with each other across different neighborhoods in Philadelphia with a relatively cheap display technology.

Supporting Making in Public Libraries

Central library staff and several mentors articulated that building relationship with participants is both a success in and of itself and a foundation for other positive outcomes. Mentors developed a rapport with participants, building a sense of belonging and welcome, particularly among young makers. For example, when youth entered makerspaces in the local branches, mentors recognized each by name, and youth were comfortable with mentors. In one instance, a participant offered to share his snacks with mentors at the beginning of a session. In interviews, librarians mentioned the positive relationships between mentors and the youth and adults they worked with. We found that a starter theme facilitated dialog and group discussion and let the kids ask questions about each other's tiles. We also found that letting youth build the physical mural fostered their participating and expressing of community ideas and concerns. In this process, message boxes began to gain secondary meanings based on their neighboring tiles and more importantly started to embrace a more collective role of combining individual efforts with a group sensibility. This also succeeded in drawing in participants and establishing an audience, which has been a key issue for many communal displays (Agamanolis, 2003). An important measure of engagement was that the program allowed patrons in five different library branches to engage in a dialog based on their selected themes.

Providing Access to Technical Expertise

It was, however, less obvious how to engage members in the making of the technical back end of the board and website. The technical material engaged youth in building a basic circuit to power up an LED and turn it into a pixel by showing how to control it (single), bring pixels next to each other to learn about seriality (multiple), align pixels on the board in terms of rows and columns to build a display, control pixels one by one and in group using the web interface, and make scrolling messages, where the programming of the LEDs over time (turning them on/off at particular speeds) can create the illusion of movement, showing how messages can extend limits of the rectangular boards.

In redesigning our approach, materials, and processes used in *Connected Messages*, one challenge for us is to design an interaction process that unfolds from simple to complex in multiple stages that are parallel to the learning objectives. We could definitely engage youth more in the process of laying out the boards, introduction to soldering and materials, and give them more time to play with/ see what other sites are doing (engage in peer production, peer learning via the internet). The *Math on a Sphere* project in which youth wrote basic programs in LOGO to see the output displayed on a giant, public sphere (Hsi & Eisenberg, 2012) provides an example of how this could be introduced. We could provide an interface through which participants could write simple programs to send or receive requests to control the mural. Furthermore, we could engage youth in learning how to write word filters that screen out offensive terms.

Connected Messages was inspired from the rich tradition of murals in the city of Philadelphia that communicate the local histories and the social and cultural diversity of different kinds of communal spaces, from parks and walkways to interiors of schools, museums, and libraries. Making murals—online and offline—is a rich tradition that can bring together members of different communities. Our constructionist model of building displays out of reprogrammable elements has great potential not only for teaching complex technological subjects but also for providing socially and culturally meaningful experiences.

Acknowledgments

This work was supported by a grant (#1238172) from the National Science Foundation to Yasmin Kafai, Orkan Telhan, and Karen Elinich. Any opinions, findings, and conclusions or recommendations expressed in this paper are those of the authors and do not necessarily reflect the views of the National Science Foundation or the University of Pennsylvania. The authors wish to thank the Free Library of Philadelphia and the MakerCorps members of the Maker Jawn initiative.

References

Agamanolis, S. (2003). Designing displays for human connectedness. In K. O'Hara, M. Perry, E. Churchill, & D. Russell (Eds.), *Public and Situated Displays* (pp. 309–334). Dordrecht, Netherlands: Kluwer.

Brignull, H., & Rogers, Y. (2003). Enticing people to interact with large public displays in public spaces. In *Proceedings of INTERACT* (Vol. 3, pp. 17–24).

Brignull, H., Izadi, S., Fitzpatrick, G., Rogers, Y., & Rodden, T. (2004). The introduction of a shared interactive surface into a communal space. In *Proceedings of the Conference on Computer Supported Cooperative Work* (pp. 49–58). New York, NY: ACM.

Churchil, E. F., Nelson, L., & Denoue, L. (2003). Multimedia fliers: Information sharing with digital community bulletin boards. In M. Huysman, E. Wenger, & V. Wulf (Eds.), *Communities and Technologies* (pp. 97–117). Dordrecht, Netherlands: Kluwer.

Detken, K., Martinez, C., & Schrader, A. (2009). The search wall: Tangible information searching for children in public libraries. In *Proceedings of the International Conference on Tangible and Embedded Interaction* (pp. 289–296). New York, NY: ACM.

Golden, J., & Updike, D. (2014). *Philadelphia Mural Arts @ 30*. Philadelphia, PA: Temple University Press.

Honey, M., & Kanter, D. E. (eds.). (2013). *Design, Make, Play: Growing the Next Generation of STEM Innovators*. New York, NY: Routledge.

Hsi, S., & Eisenberg, M. (2012). Math on a sphere: Using public displays to support children's creativity and computational thinking on 3D surfaces. In *Proceedings of the 11th International Conference on Interaction Design and Children* (pp. 248–251). New York, NY: ACM.

Ito, M., Baumer, S., Bittanti, M., Cody, R., Stephenson, B. H., Horst, H. A., . . . others. (2009). *Hanging out, Messing Around, and Geeking out: Kids Living and Learning with New Media*. Cambridge, MA: MIT Press.

Ito, M., Gutiérrez, K., Livingstone, S., Penuel, B., Rhodes, J., Salen, K., Schor, J., Sefton-Green, J., & Watkins, S. C. (2013). *Connected Learning: An Agenda for Research and Design*. Irvine, CA: Digital Media and Learning Research Hub.

Jenkins, H. (2010). Do-it-ourselves. In M. Knobel & C. Lankshear (Eds.), *DIY Media* (pp. 231–254). New York, NY: Peter Lang.

Kafai, Y. B., Peppler, K. A., & Chapman, R. (eds.). (2009). *The Computer Clubhouse: Constructionism and Creativity in Youth Communities*. New York, NY: Teachers College Press.

Kim, J., Jung, D., Lee, K., Jin, Y., & Yeo, W. S. (2009, June). Bubble letters: A child-centric interface for virtual and real world experience. In *Proceedings of the 8th International Conference on Interaction Design and Children* (pp. 206–209). New York, NY: ACM.

Lamberty, K. K., Adams, S., Biatek, J., Froiland, K., & Lapham, J. (2011, June). Using a large display in the periphery to support children learning through design. In *Proceedings of the International Conference on Interaction Design and Children* (pp. 62–71). New York, NY: ACM.

Larson, K., Ito, M., Brown, E., Hawkins, M., Pinkard, N., & Sebring, P. (2013). *Safe Space and Shared Interests: YOUMedia Chicago as a Laboratory for Connected Learning*. Cambridge, MA: MIT Press.

Lee, V. R., Lewis, W., Searle, K. A., Recker, M., Hansen, J., & Phillips, A. L. (2017). Supporting interactive youth maker programs in public and school libraries: Design hypotheses and first implementations. In P. Blikstein & D. Abrahamson (Eds.), *Proceedings of International Conference on Interaction Design for Children* (pp. 310–315). New York, NY: ACM.

Lui, D. (2016). *Situating Educational Makerspaces: Enacting the Maker 'Ideal' Within Diverse Contexts in Public Libraries*. Unpublished Dissertation. University of Pennsylvania. Philadelphia, PA.

Peltonen, P., Salovaara, A., Jacucci, G., Ilmonen, T., Ardito, C., Saarikko, P., & Batra, V. (2007). Extending large-scale event participation with user-created mobile media on a public display. In *Proceedings of the International Conference on Mobile and Ubiquitous Multimedia* (pp. 131–138). New York, NY: ACM.

Peppler, K. A., Halverson, E., & Kafai, Y. B. (eds.). (2016a). *Makeology: Makerspaces as Learning Environments (Volume 1)*. New York, NY: Routledge.

Peppler, K. A., Halverson, E., & Kafai, Y. B. (eds.). (2016b). *Makeology: Makers as Learners (Volume 2)*. New York, NY: Routledge.

Steele, K.-F. (2013). 'What we think actually matters?': Teen participatory design and action research at the free library of Philadelphia. *Young Adult Library Services, 11*(4), 12.

Strobel, K., Kirshner, B. E. N., O'Donoghue, J., & McLaughlin, M. (2008). Qualities that attract urban youth to after-school settings and promote continued participation. *Teachers College Record, 110*(8), 1677–1705.

4

BUILDING EXPANSIVE FAMILY STEAM PROGRAMMING THROUGH PARTICIPATORY DESIGN RESEARCH

Carrie Tzou, Philip Bell, Megan Bang, Rekha Kuver, Amy Twito, and Ashley Braun

Introduction

Tell the story of an important event that happened in your family. Tell a story of a place that is important to your family. With these prompts, TechTales—a multi-institutional design-based research initiative—invites families to transform their family stories into scenes within vivid dioramas. Families engage in narrative-based design work over the course of five nights and fifteen hours and learn how to bring their stories to life by programming robotics components (LEDs, motors, sensors) with Scratch. Unlike robotics teams or programming workshops designed mainly for youth where the technology is the focus, TechTales begins and ends with families' stories, with those stories centering the intergenerational engineering work and providing the impetus for deep agency with the technology. In Figure 4.1, the Pony family depicted their daughter's first lightning storm on a trip to their traditional homelands. LEDs in the cloud above the family home flicker to depict lightning as the family members' hair stands on end.

In Figure 4.2, a family tells a story about Eagle relatives visiting during a family RV trip. Motors attached to dowels turn a roll of paper depicting the scenery racing by as the family looks out of the moving RV window and sees the eagle relatives flying outside the window. In designing their box, this family made decisions about perspective taking and solved problems around how to construct the moving scenery as they combined the technology with traditional and family storytelling.

Across thirteen iterations of TechTales, more than sixty-five families have told a wide and rich range of stories deeply rooted in place and reflecting their lives, identities, and desires. Stories are deeply personal, and families recognize the projects as memory-building endeavors—that is, as families build their stories, they

FIGURE 4.1   A family participating in TechTales depicts the daughter's first experience seeing a lightning storm using robotic components.

retell and reimagine them and, in so doing, solidify them as family memories. Stories have included stargazing out the window of a cabin at "family camp," racing goats on a family reunion trip to Ethiopia, an epic family move from Arizona to Washington, and becoming a family on "adoption day."

This chapter describes a participatory design research (PDR) (Bang & Vossoughi, 2016) project that brings learning scientists into collaboration with public librarians, informal science education staff, and staff from Native American–serving community organizations who are jointly focused on designing family-centered and culturally expansive STEAM (science, technology, engineering, art,

FIGURE 4.2 Using crafting materials, motors, and other technologies, another family tells the story of their RV trip.

math) learning experiences with nondominant communities. We realized that, as a team, in order to design a program that itself "desettled" (Bang, Warren, Rosebery, & Medin, 2012) dominant relationships between humans and technologies, we needed to organize ourselves toward equity making in our own design processes. This meant taking seriously the need to "create . . . new openings for reciprocity" between design partners, accountability between each other and to community partners, and "de-settling of normative hierarchies of power" that typically can occur between university–community partnerships (Bang & Vossoughi,

2016, p. 174). Therefore, in this account of launching an equity-focused, multiorganizational PDR initiative, we turn our attention to the cultural situatedness of our design process in an attempt to understand the ways that "identities, power, and discourse are a part of and therefore integral to" (Zavala, 2016) the process itself.

We engage in PDR in the context of a design-based implementation research (DBIR) approach (Penuel, Fishman, Cheng, & Sabelli, 2011) by designing for innovation in learning within the context of the routines and structures associated with partner institutions—a university, a large urban public library system, a science center, and a community organization. We focus on developing innovative learning experiences for and with families while building institutional capacity for the enactment of those experiences within a growing network of individuals within partner institutions. Working from these perspectives, we specifically highlight (a) the importance of role remediation and porosity within the partnership, (b) the ways in which working toward "more just forms of partnering" (Bang & Vossoughi, 2016) allowed for the emergence of new identities, expertise, and agency to take shape in the design space, (c) the need to examine what it means to coordinate new initiatives within existing institutional structures and underlying images of and responsibilities related to professional activity (Bell, 2016), and (d) rethinking what it means to design within a library system that has a deepening equity agenda designed to coordinate library work away from stationary branches and in closer partnership with community members. We highlight how a PDR form of DBIR in library contexts both supports and constrains the development of an intervention that supports equity-focused family STEAM collaboration and learning, the professional learning of librarians and community leaders as facilitators, and the development and management of a productive, sustainable partnership.

Decentralizing Informal Science Education to Include Libraries

One goal of TechTales is to provide a model for decentralizing informal science education. While makerspaces in libraries represent a growing STEM initiative within libraries (Moorefield-Lang, 2015), many questions remain about how best to provide librarians and other library staff with the resources, professional development, and disciplinary expertise necessary to deeply engage learners with science phenomena and engineering design practices. As one of our library partners put it, there is "this fear of new technology, and fear of not having a coding or computer science background." However, informal STEM learning and teaching expertise lives in other community organizations such as science centers and universities.

In contrast to the wide swath of the population that tends to use libraries, however, science centers and museums experience a less diverse population audience, with only 9% of "core visitors" to museums being minorities (CFM, 2008). Of course, the use of museums (of which science centers are an instance) is dependent on multiple, complex factors, such as historical patterns of race-based exclusion, socioeconomic factors, level of education of users, age, and the presence of museums in community networks (Farrell & Medvedeva, 2010). One underlying challenge for museums is how to remain relevant to the increasingly diverse audiences they seek to serve. The role of mutually beneficial, community-centered partnerships has been established as a productive strategy for diversifying museum visitors and shifting to more culturally relevant forms of pedagogy (Bell, Lewenstein, Shouse, & Feder, 2009). Connecting the informal science education expertise within a science center with libraries, community organizations, and university teams—which already serve a diverse and geographically diffuse population in terms of age, socioeconomic status, and race and ethnicity—is a logical strategy for attempting to address this challenge.

Libraries as Vital Community Resources for Interest-Driven STEM Learning

Libraries serve vital roles in communities not only for access to print media but also to educational programs and to digital technologies. Because of their wide-spread local presence in communities, libraries are "at the forefront of tackling social inequalities by providing access to online information and supporting digital literacy" (Aspen Institute, 2014). In the Seattle Public Libraries specifically, a 2010 survey indicated that "providing materials and technology to those who otherwise might not have access" was the second most important service provided (Seattle Public Libraries, 2010, p. 11). These results indicate the Seattle Public Libraries are a key resource for technology and programming for both children and adults across diverse communities in the region.

Importantly, the role of libraries and librarians is also changing, with less emphasis on curating and storing physical collections and more emphasis on creating spaces for people to collaborate and generate new ideas (Aspen Institute, 2014). Librarians, then, need to become facilitators of learning, partnering with community resources to gain domain expertise and deliver contemporary content and physical materials. This is exemplified by the proliferation of makerspaces in libraries (Aspen Institute, 2014) and an increasing emphasis on providing technology-related education programming in addition to being vital access points for free resources. As informal learning spaces available to most communities, libraries offer opportunities to engage youth and families in dynamic learning experiences around new technologies, to explore new STEM-related interests, and to prepare for participation in community life and the workforce. This issue comes to the fore with both the emphasis in the NRC *Framework for K–12 Science Education* vision (and the resulting *Next Generation Science Standards*) on engineering design practices (NRC, 2012) and recent research findings on the importance of out-of-school learning on identity building and STEM learning in the ecology of learners' lives (Barron, 2006; Barron & Bell, 2015; Bell et al., 2009; Ito et al., 2013). The question remains, however: how can librarians gain the expertise and institutional capacity they need to provide effective STEAM programming that engages families in learning that leverages their cultural and linguistic resources and supports multiple interest-driven learning pathways?

Library Context

The Seattle Public Library's mission is "to bring people, information, and ideas together to enrich lives and build community." The system consists of twenty-seven locations plus mobile services, more than 650 employees, and works in a service area of approximately 670,000 people. There are three important pieces of context for our work with the library and for the library's involvement in Tech-Tales: (1) the City of Seattle's Race and Social Justice Initiative (RSJI), (2) the library's *Community Listening* process, and (3) emerging priorities regarding youth and family learning and community engagement in order to reimagine how the library could better serve the diverse youth population in Seattle given community feedback on library services as well as new research findings on learning, including expanded digital media tools and programs.

RSJI is an "effort to end institutionalized racism and race-based disparities in City government" (RSJI, 2015). In 2004 when the initiative began, Seattle was one of the first cities in the United States to develop a comprehensive plan to "explicitly focus on institutional racism." Seattle's mayor signed an executive order that "requires City staff to establish new goals, track outcomes over time, and report on the City's progress. The Executive Order calls on the City to apply a racial equity lens to all Citywide initiatives." As a city department, Seattle Public Library is accountable to this initiative and must report back to the city how it is addressing institutional racism and actively working to end it. In this way, an equity-focused learning project like TechTales falls squarely within both the library's mission and the city's initiative.

The library is working toward a community-centered model for all of its programs and services. As part of this effort, librarians systemwide have engaged in a Community Listening process. Using an equity lens, they examined demographic and economic information about their neighborhoods and then reached out to community members to do intentional listening about their interests, needs, issues, and concerns. Library staff then began work developing or adjusting library programs and services in response to those priorities, working in partnership with communities. This process is part of the library's efforts to support more equitable outcomes in its work. Their model of community listening involves listening and learning from communities, building relationships with community partners, and codesigning community programs that "reach people where they are," "bring people together," "prioritize equity," and "showcase community voices."

This results in library programs that are out in community settings, sometimes with community partners cofacilitating.

TechTales: Make. Share. Learn.

Over the course of five 3-hour sessions, TechTales centers nondominant families' stories and story-making processes as a means of repositioning and desettling (Bang et al., 2012) families' relationships to technology. Rather than positioning families as consumers or users of technology—in other words, simply showing them *how to*, TechTales invites families to imagine new relationships with technology that are deeply interwoven with cultural, familial, and place-based historicity. At the center of the design is the recognition that all learning is cultural and that all families and family members come to the workshop space with deep expertise around their own histories but also possible fraught relationships with technologies, especially if those technologies have served to erase, make invisible, or assimilate their communities (Bang et al., 2012). Importantly, our workshops frame technologies as also cultural; emergent and reflective of the cultural communities from which they have emerged. We were intentional about positioning families to take a critical view of technologies by asking them to reflect on the technological histories, uses, and expertises embedded in their own families and communities and to consider how these have evolved.

The intervention was designed to leverage the resources family members bring to the environment (i.e., interests, knowledge, practices, identities) and position them as developing experts in authentic project spaces in order to support progress along cultural learning pathways (Bell et al., 2012; Van Horne & Bell, 2017). As families animate their stories through robotics and programming through Scratch, they engage in playful and creative interactions, connecting relations and stories (stargazing, eagle relatives visiting, returning to Africa to reunite with family) with contemporary technologies (LEDs, motors, sensors) and identify and explore new (or prior) interests while developing new competencies in multidisciplinary forms of work (art, computer science, electrical engineering, and robotics).

TechTales is a three-year project funded by the National Science Foundation that has three phases: (1) designing family workshops to engage families with robotics, e-textiles, coding, and scientific phenomena, (2) designing family "robotics backpacks" to be checked out from libraries and community settings that contain all materials (laptop, robotics components, challenges, and wireless hotspots) for families to engage in engineering learning at home, and (3) disseminating the program to more library branches. We also have designed "booster days," or drop-in half-day events for families who have already attended TechTales to build on and extend their learning from the original workshops. These booster days take up the storytelling aspect of the original family workshops by being centered around storybooks such as *Those Darn Squirrels* (Rubin, 2011) and challenge families to take up part of the books and apply their robotics knowledge.

PDR With Libraries and Community Partners

Participatory design research (PDR) is a form of design research (Bell, 2004) that takes the work of equity as central to design and research aiming to both contribute to sustainable social change and to expand foundational knowledge of human learning. PDR makes specific theoretical and methodological commitments to equity through attending to (a) critical historicity, (b) power, and (c) relational dynamics that shape processes of partnering and their impacts on the resultant designs and enactments of interventions (Bang & Vossoughi, 2016). PDR works to link structural and historical critiques of power in the unfolding of activity in order to more deliberately disrupt unintentional or intentional forms of normativity. Thus an important part of PDR work is understanding the affordances, tensions, and challenges in the various roles, relations, and processes that unfold during design and implementation, especially when engaged in cross-sector partnerships.

In PDR, points of tension are often indicators of key areas in need of transformation and, when engaged in productive ways, are often moments of learning that allow for new forms of expertise, identities, and senses of agency that enable new forms of practice and participation to emerge—or what we might call role remediations. More specifically in PDR, the roles that people come to the partnerships with (practitioner, family member, researcher, and so forth, or similarly computer scientists, artist, engineer) are porous and fluid positionings that enable new ways of being both in design and in enactment. These role remediations often become central processes by which historicity, power, and relations are transformed and evolve to create important innovations.

Cross-sector partnerships of the kind associated with TechTales bring multiple stakeholder perspectives and institutional histories, routines, and value systems into sustained interaction. The participatory stance to the work opens up spaces for sharing, negotiation, and agentic participation in the collaborative design and capacity building work (Bell, 2016). We are interested in understanding how the project is perceived to fit within the different institutional frames by different stakeholders and how to describe tensions, remediations, and shifts that occur within the work of the partnership.

We conducted interviews with the key library staff on our project, most of whom are also coauthors on this chapter. These include the manager of the Youth and Family Services group (Rekha Kuver), the manager of informal learning within Youth and Family Services (Amy Twito), the digital media and learning program manager for Youth and Family Services who was a part of our project for the first year (referred to here as Roberto), and the main librarian who piloted TechTales in the first year of implementation (Ashley Braun). The purpose of these interviews was to understand more deeply the impact that our partnership has had on the library—but also to use these interviews as a way for our team to reflect on the extent to which we were really "walking the talk" of a more equitable form of partnership. In this section, we describe the evolution of our PDR process itself, highlighting some key lessons learned on organizing ourselves as a complex, multi-institutional design team.

Our design team experienced a deep evolution of the role of the library within the design team over the course of the first year. When we first conceptualized each institution's role within the project, SPL simply wanted to be the setting for the program. As Rekha put it, at the beginning of the project,

> I think that I knew that you all on your team were coming in with a really high level of expertise in designing programs and youth development . . . And so, when I first came in, I was like . . . bring it. Let's sponge this up.
>
> *(RK interview, 2017–05–31)*

This kind of university-as-designer perception mirrors dominant power relations that have historically existed as universities do research *on* communities rather than *with* them. However, we were seeking a collaborative participatory approach from the onset and worked to desettle this expectation by systematically structuring openings into the various phases of the design work. Our process eventually experienced deep role remediation (Bang & Vossoughi, 2016), or profound shifts in role within the team, as individuals from different sectors shifted their understanding of the codesign approach and found ways of contributing. What might have started out as a top-down university designer-to-library implementer relationship shifted to university, library, community, and science center staff collectively giving extensive feedback, designing and running professional development, conceptualizing and designing the curriculum, and collaborating on the research.

We argue that this type of active resistance to dominant power paradigms that often exist between university–community design projects or between program developer–client models provided not only different subject–subject relations to emerge (Bang & Vossoughi, 2016), but in the process, new forms of design and praxis-through-design (Zavala, 2016) that might not otherwise have been possible. The major lessons we learned were the importance of (1) making visible the tensions between institutional frames in order to work towards more equitable partnership structures, (2) developing trust and shared understanding while maintaining porous and open-ended roles within the design team to allow for transformative agency to emerge, and (3) systematically working to disrupt normative power relations that might otherwise exist between institutional actors on the design team.

Making Visible the Tensions Between Institutional Frames in Order to Work Toward More Equitable Partnership Structures

Bang and Vossoughi (2016) warn us that to ignore historicities of design context is to make invisible or, worse yet, reify existing oppressive and colonizing structures that we are actively designing to resist. TechTales is a collaboration between several institutions, each with its own history of relations with communities and with each other.

While we were careful to articulate our design conjectures (Sandoval, 2014), theoretical commitments, and design principles—we were not as explicit around what the cyclical, iterative process of design-based work itself looks like and how this process may be in tension with institutional frames related to program design and implementation. One challenge that the library faced at the beginning of our process, therefore, was not always knowing where and when to contribute. The team was collectively ideating on possible approaches to take with the program (e.g., defining the focus of family projects, learning goals, pedagogical practices, timelines) relative to design commitments that were not fully understood by the whole team. Amy, the informal learning program manager for the library, points out how different this process was from other program development efforts she has been involved with:

> I've done other grants that were much more structured. We're going to cre-
> ate this and we're going to do 50 of these . . . this was very different from
> that. To me, because I didn't know any better, it felt really unstructured. And
> some of the people from my team were very uncomfortable with it and
> were like maybe we don't need to be at all these meetings.
>
> *(AT interview, 2017–06–08)*

Amy's quote indicates to us that, at the beginning of our design process, we had not cultivated a sense of "mutual responsibility" (Bang & Vossoughi, 2016) or agency towards either the process or the products of design—and this participatory mode of collaborative design was at odds with historical patterns of program development within the library. This points to the importance of making the process itself a shared object of inquiry and negotiation at the beginning of our work together. For the learning scientists on our team, this participatory, learner-centered process was business as usual, but for our library partners, this was a fundamentally different way of developing programs, one that at times was in tension with their usual way of developing programs or developing relationships. Amy's quote also reminds us of how close we came as a group to an *in*equitable partnership: by leaning on decontextualized conversations about the design-based research process and not engaging in the embodied enactment of collaborative design from the onset of the project (e.g., through pilot work as we launched the effort), we risked continued reification of normative power relations by making the library feel peripheral to design decisions.

As we developed a fully drafted program, enacted it in a library-supported context, and reflected on the enactment, we identified problems with the current design, identified trade-offs and tensions, and made likely improvements to the program. When asked about her perspective on our team's design process at this stage, the lead librarian on our team, Ashley, admits being "bewildered" by the process and the ways in which the team interacted to share ideas and feedback.

> I think, in the beginning, I was a little bit bewildered about how things are
> working, 'cause this . . . It's not that it's not normal. I think we all work with
> feedback and constructive criticism too, but just like sort of easing into the

way that this works was really important for me, and kind of observing how everyone talks with each other and communicates to each other.

(AB interview, 2017–06–09)

Ashley's quote reminds us that, in addition to forming a shared sense of responsibility to the design process, it was important for all design partners to develop new professional frames (Goodwin, 1994) from which to view the work. As Zavala (2016) reminds us, "design is itself a learning process," one that we all approach through our own social positions and histories. We now know that the team needed to spend time developing a shared understanding of constructs from learning sciences (e.g., multiple ways of knowing) while seeing how they relate to the institutional goals of the library (e.g., multiple literacies). Concrete instances of learning-in-action (e.g., debriefing shared observations, shared watching of videos) were used to develop this shared understanding around these constructs. In addition, the team needed to be disciplined to systematically invite contributions from all stakeholders, including community collaborators and families, which deeply centers on issues of trust.

Developing Trust and Shared Understanding While Maintaining Porous and Open-Ended Roles to Allow for Transformative Agency to Emerge

Multisector partnerships need to operate from a position of mutual trust between the participants (Bell, 2016). Trust allows for continuity in the work beyond any inevitable complications that come up. It also allows for the participatory design work to unfold in ways that leverage the distributed expertise brought by specific partners—which is needed to successfully engage in such multifaceted work. For example, Rekha talks about her evolving understanding of SPL's expertise in the communities they serve and the need to assert that expertise in the design process:

> But the thing I think that I have really appreciated and learned more about is what our expertise is on our side, and what we can bring to the conversation in terms of practitioners and what we know about . . . What we know about our communities. Not that I didn't think that we had that expertise. *But I wasn't thinking in terms of that.* I was sort of thinking in terms of like, you guys [from the university] are gonna come in and do just a bunch of stuff. And we're gonna be receiving the info, and then we're gonna run with it. But now that other folks are kind of coming onboard, one of the things that I'm really hammering for them is you guys [from SPL] know stuff. And *you should assert what you know and really be active parts of that creation process.*
>
> *(RK interview, 2017–05–31)*

Rekha's quote initially reflects a classic normative power expectation that can exist when universities engage in community-based design work. However, she then goes on to describe deep transformational agency as she articulates her shift in expectation and framing. While the community-based knowledge and expertise were always there, normative power relations can make that expertise invisible unless we actively work toward more equitable partnership models. Speaking as a supervisor within the library, the other aspect of transformative agency in Rekha's quote is her encouragement of new librarians coming on board to "assert what you know" and to be "active parts of that creation process." This represents not only Rekha's own shift but a subsequent collective shift within the design team itself, as evidenced by Amy's quote that follows as she also expresses her understanding of the importance of having a librarian at the design table from the beginning of the process:

> I think because we have a better understanding of the importance of having a librarian involved or one of the people who is going to be teaching it . . . So if we went back right now with what we know and we were rewriting it at the beginning, I would have structured our whole team internally and on SPL a little bit different for it . . . I think I would have wanted to hire a librarian to be dedicated the development team maybe for like the first two years or something.
>
> *(AT interview, 2017–06–08)*

By coming to understand the importance of the Library's expertise in the partnership, the makeup of the design team itself was transformed, deeply shifting the types of "subject–object relations" (Bang & Vossoughi, 2016) that are possible to imagine and design for. From the perspective of DBIR, the deep involvement of practitioners from the very beginning of the project allows for the work to be centered on problems and opportunities of educational practices—as opposed to working from researcher-identified areas of emphasis (Bell, 2016; Penuel et al., 2011).

Working to Disrupt Normative Power Relations Between Institutional Actors on the Design Team by Cultivating a Culture of Contribution to a Shared Enterprise

Finally, our process highlights the importance of putting structures in place in the design process that allow for more equitable relations between institutions. This requires that processes of inclusivity and even epistemic heterogeneity are intentionally built, modeled, and explicitly attended to. Ashley describes how she eventually became comfortable contributing to the process:

> how receptive you all are of feedback that we give is just . . . I mean, I feel completely comfortable now in the whole dynamic of things, and my hesitation was only for maybe a couple weeks, when I was like, "Oh, I don't know." And I think that's just part of multiple organizations coming together. And

I guess more so this feeling of like, "Let's just give feedback and not get hurt about it." You know? And this idea that ideas aren't someone's own possession, and it's not someone's idea, *it's our idea* [emphasis added]. Stuff like that. And that might be just individual to me, 'cause this is kind of new to me, to treat things like that and to treat it without personalities getting pushed to the forefront. So I really like that. And then also . . . Yeah, just love the open sharing of feedback, and the respect that it seems everyone gives to everyone's opinion, this is really good. So it's really just a healthy culture in general.

(AB interview 2017–06–09)

Ashley's process of moving from an "I don't know" stance to an "it's our idea" stance represents, for us, deep role remediation but also a collective shift in accountability and reciprocity among the design team. Rather than predefining design roles on the team (for example, putting Ashley in a "facilitator only" box), Ashley's quote indicates that she came to *own* the collective design ideas of the group—strong evidence that the team came to be engaged in a shared endeavor. By actively and regularly attending to processes such as constant and collective feedback, debriefing, and reflection, roles were necessarily fluid and shifting in the group, allowing for multiple forms of expertise to emerge at different times in the process. While Ashley was frequently in the role of facilitator of the workshops and showed her expertise at storytime and while managing family dynamics in large groups, she was at other times codesigner and practitioner-researcher who could shape other parts of the program being designed.

Intentionally cultivating a culture of contribution to a shared enterprise helped facilitate this remediation of roles. Design sessions need to be architected to support collaborative ideation and contribution as well as safe dissent and creative problem solving. Such strategies can help disrupt hierarchical power relations and develop a more equitable platform for sustained collaboration.

Opportunities and Tensions of Equity-Focused Making With Libraries

We have also come to understand how our PDR/DBIR work pushes against some institutional factors of the library system, presenting both opportunities and constraints for supporting equity-focused, intergenerational making within libraries. We identified three factors that were both constraints and opportunities for us as we engaged in this project together: (1) designing for learning contexts beyond the library branch, (2) designing programming for intergenerational learning, and (3) designing for deep equity-focused STEM learning.

Designing for Learning Contexts Beyond the Branch

When we first conceptualized our project, we imagined that working within a large library system meant working in *branch libraries*—that because these branches were geographically located within most communities within Seattle, we would have a reach far beyond one science center, school, or community setting. What we quickly realized, however, was that the library was itself in the process of making its walls more porous. While librarians have historically worked both in and outside of branches (by visiting schools, for examples), the Library was undergoing a deep transformation itself by centering community needs in the codevelopment of programs with and within community organizations.

All Seattle Public Library staff on our project identified community listening as crucial to the work they are now doing, and that it addresses the reality that they were all noticing: that there were large pockets of their demographic that they were not getting "in the building." As Amy puts it:

> We serve some people really, really well. Parents who are very engaged with their children's learning, that have two-parent families, maybe one parent doesn't work or there's a nanny, and they are comfortable navigating our website and finding out all the great stuff we have . . . I think to be better situated to serve our community with an equity lens, we really need to do a lot more community listening and community conversations and be engaged with the community where the need is greatest.
>
> *(AT interview, 2017–06–08)*

Having a library branch in a community does not mean that all people in that community have equal access to those resources. Through the community listening process, the library is learning how to engage audiences who are otherwise not being currently served. While this could mean making in-building programming more relevant and convenient to their needs, it could also mean bringing that relevant programming out to community members. By bringing specific library programs to communities in order to match specific needs, a single library branch's reach can be greatly magnified.

What this meant for us as a design team was designing not only within a library system (and understanding the systemic structures within that system) but also designing with the community sites partnered with the library. In our first year of running TechTales, the community partner was a low-income housing alliance that offered permanent housing to families. TechTales was delivered three times on site in the housing complex in the first year of enactment; case workers within the site were liaisons to the families and helped us recruit and maintain communication with them. They also attended professional development, all family workshops, and worked as trusted contacts in the workshop space as we worked to gain trust with families. They provided some support to families in between the weekly sessions and ultimately assumed roles as design consultants, giving us feedback on the design based on their extensive knowledge of the families they work with.

This also meant that we had great stability and continuity in our TechTales participants: because families lived on site, they simply walked downstairs to the workshops from home and transportation was not an issue (something that is always a challenge in other informal education settings). Because this was a close-knit community, word of the workshops spread within the site, and this facilitated recruiting families into subsequent runs of the workshops. Because the case workers had close contact with families, they could knock on families' doors to remind them of upcoming workshop sessions. It also allowed us to easily hold "drop-in" help sessions for families in between workshops to offer help with projects without any implications for travel for families. When we held our follow-up booster days, we had an 85% return rate of families. Ashley says,

> It's just been amazing to see the interest that families have had for this . . . I think part of that is we've gotten to a place where the relationships are more stable now, and so they know us. But, you know, you never know with library programs if people are going to want to come back. And so this is the thing that just like continues to impress me and boggle my mind, frankly. When these kids . . . they're like, "We love TechTales. We want more!" I mean the ingredients are all there, and clearly there's a deep interest in what we're doing, for . . . so many reasons. Not just the fancy robotic tech, the shiny stuff, but also the family time and the community building and stuff.
>
> *(AB interview, 2017–06–09)*

Finally, Ashley touched on another key component in designing for this site: because the housing complex was such a tight-knit community, she attributed the success of the program not only to the "fancy robotic tech" but to the community building that TechTales affords. The stability of the context importantly allowed for personal relationships to develop between family members and the librarians. The relationships and the physical convenience supported ongoing participation in ways that promoted more extended cultural learning pathways for participants—across sessions, help and booster days, and soon across other programs in development.

Since TechTales began at the housing complex in the summer of 2016, the library's partnership with the housing alliance has deepened and grown. While TechTales was just one component in that partnership, it was one of the catalysts for building trust and demand for more technology-based programming. We therefore see the community listening and engagement process as both a way for us as a TechTales design group to add another stakeholder voice to the design table but also as a way for SPL to deeply partner with a community organization and meet its needs. Designing beyond the branch has pushed us to reconceptualize what it means to conduct equity-focused design *with libraries* to meet the needs of the communities they serve.

Designing Programs for Intergenerational Learning

At SPL, librarians are organized into age-specific service groups: children's, teen, and adult librarians. This presents an obvious challenge to an effort like TechTales aimed at family learning, where the focus is not just to design in service of youth learning, as many library and informal science learning programs do, but to focus on intergenerational learning. We heard from our library partners that this represents a shift that has both pedagogical and structural implications within the system. In our project, we work with the children's, teen, and supervising librarians. One hallmark of the children's librarian role is running storytime, or reading storybooks aloud to children and their parents or caregivers. While this represents one form of family learning, Rekha reflects on how our intentional focus on family learning is a shift in practice, especially for youth who are upper-school age and older:

> We tend to design from just what age is this and let's design for them, and if their parents come, awesome. So, I think that to have the intention . . . With the exception of early learning. Early learning, of course, you know that parents and caregivers will be there. So, to do intentional kinds of family programming is a new thing and should really think about adults learning and not just helping their kids learn. That level is definitely something that is new.
>
> *(RK interview, 2017–05–31)*

The intentionality of designing with families as the central focus—rather than youth—is a shift in programming that does not often happen in the library except in Story Time, where librarians are intentional about educating parents around engaging their young children in reading strategies. In that case, however, the primary focus is still in service of the children's learning. TechTales provides an opportunity for children and teen librarians to build human capacity to work with intergenerational groups, something that Rekha reports as being organizationally useful to bring to adult librarians in the future.

Designing for family learning requires a librarian (or any facilitator) to pay attention not only to running learning activities but also to family dynamics (asking questions like "How do we learn together?" "How do we make sure all ideas are heard?") and norms and roles for all-family participation (to avoid parents taking over or letting youth do all of the creative work). It also means learning to recognize learning in many configurations across families and various negotiation styles. We see, however, that children's librarians like Ashley can apply their practices from Story Time into family learning situations:

> In our story times, we always say, "[just because] the kids are moving around doesn't mean that they're not absorbing or doesn't mean that they're not

learning at that moment." So reminding myself of all of those things and then . . . the way that people come to it can be different, and everyone has something to contribute. So that's one thing that, as a facilitator, I need to keep in mind and, you know, improve upon is definitely making sure to notice those things, then to encourage them. Respecting the family negotiations that go on. Kind of trying to stay out of that, and let it happen the way they need it to happen.

(AB interview, 2017–06–09)

Fishman et al. (2013) emphasize the need, within DBIR, to design supports to build capacity "through efforts to develop organizational routines and processes that help innovations travel through a system" (p. 144). Part of our strategy for this was to hold debrief sessions after each workshop meeting in which we called out "moments of learning" that we each recognized (Vossoughi, Hooper, & Escudé, 2016). In this way, facilitators learn to recognize the various ways that family learning can emerge through interactions—and learn their role in facilitating that learning.

Designing for Deep Equity-Focused STEM Learning

Libraries have not historically been sites for deep engagement with STEM learning. TechTales therefore represents not only a shift in expertise needed to facilitate programming, but part of a deeper, evolving identity of libraries and the identities of all levels of library staff. All of our library staff recognized the importance of STEM learning to serving their communities and preparing people for the future, but they also recognized that this meant a (re)positioning of librarians from their traditional roles as knowledge holders to learners. Amy says,

> . . . it [TechTales] challenges the past assumptions of what a librarian is and does. And I feel like it places us where I think libraries in general, and our library specifically, should be moving with what a librarian does and how they do their work and where they do it. So I feel like it fits in with the future . . . So librarians have always been the keeper of all knowledge. It's putting people in a position where they don't know the answer. Because it attracts people who like to know all the answers and how to find everything and that's why they became a librarian, and suddenly now they're asked to do something very unfamiliar that makes them uncomfortable . . . is really, really a big stretch.
>
> *(AT interview, 2017–06–08)*

As Amy alludes to, repositioning how librarians themselves are situated with respect to knowledge both is part of the evolution of the librarian's role and also can be unsettling for library practitioners. The library staff all agreed that facilitating STEM programming was a growing expectation among librarians, one that was aligned with larger goals of meeting the present and future needs of their patrons and their communities. It is important to note that this new professional learning was happening while significant areas of existing library staff expertise were also being marshaled, specifically storytelling, reading, connecting patrons with resources and information, and staying centered on patrons' current and future needs. The narrative design focus for families benefited from the storytelling expertise of library staff. This promoted staff confidence and participation in the design work—which helped them manage the anxieties associated with the new professional learning they were doing while simultaneously contributing to the effort in meaningful ways. This is how cross-sector partnerships provide productive spaces for safe learning and capacity building and the leveraging of needed expertise for the shared endeavor (Bell, 2016).

Another way TechTales represents a shift in programming is the focus on deep engagement in learning rather than the "drop-in" programming that is more typical for libraries. Ashley says,

> This is unlike anything I've ever been able to do at the library because . . . our programming tends to be a little more superficial learning so people will come in one time and learn something. And outside of storytime, storytime probably the closest example that I say to this, because storytime is continuously offered . . . this would be the closest thing that I can think of that we do. Just at a different age, I guess, and with technology in such an exciting way. So yeah, that deeper learning is new.
>
> *(AB interview, 2017–06–09)*

This deeper learning also allows TechTales to design for focusing on families as "cultural, historical, and political actors" (Vossoughi et al., 2016) in their own stories and learning around STEM—and for supporting participants along more extended cultural learning pathways related to STEM competencies (Bell et al., 2012). Because these take time to cultivate, they are a challenge with drop-in programming and were reasons why we designed a five-part workshop series. However, orienting some librarians to facilitate this kind of equity-focused, intergenerational, multisession STEAM learning can be a challenge. Roberto, who was a digital media and learning manager when he participated in our program in its first year, develops technology-based programs within SPL for youth and adults and trains librarians on how to facilitate those programs. While he is no longer with TechTales (but is still at SPL), he describes his work with a librarian in facilitating a program to center youths' community experiences:

> It's easy, right, to do a drop in. You just come in and you do your thing, and that's it. You're done. A series, I think, is more planning and effort . . . So she [a librarian] wanted to do that e-textiles thing. So I wanted her to

start by prompting the kids about community, like what's a community? And then going into like, what's your community? What communities do you belong to? And then going into representations of community. What kind of things do you use to represent your community? So going in that path . . . I think that that was completely informed by your approach on how to build stories.

(Roberto interview, 2017–06–08)

TechTales pushes librarians/facilitators to think deeply about learning as cultural and about setting up learning environments so that all voices are heard. This also means actively working against deficit narratives of learners and their communities.

Implications for Professional Development and Sustainability

For the lead librarian on our project, TechTales also offered another dimension to her professional growth: she became so interested in the theoretical foundations underlying our project that she is now enrolled in the Youth Experience Certificate program (https://yx.umd.edu) to "train librarians to facilitate 21st century skill development among youth." Through this program and facilitating TechTales, Ashley is actively repositioning herself in relation to knowledge, learning, and patrons. Rather than, as Amy puts it, "knowing all the answers," she finds herself learning "side by side" with people and recognizing that this is a new position relative to "outdated" ideas of what it means to be a librarian. She also recognizes that "power sharing" with families in the workshop is a part of this:

> *You can learn side by side with people. This whole concept of power sharing that you all talk about is really important for just, how do I say this, basically just sharing skills more widely, providing wider access.* And access is always an issue for libraries, no matter what we're providing access to, if it's information or skills. Definitely thinking more concretely about the adult's role, and a sort of inter-generational programming in this way. Seeing that the technology, even if I don't feel like I have this expertise about it, it's fine. I just do it anyway, and we can learn through it together. That's been a big breakthrough for me, and I think that's gonna be a big breakthrough for a lot of librarians once they try it, because it is. . . *This is kind of getting back to the radical change theory thing that I was mentioning. This idea that librarians as experts is sort of an outdated model. And also the keepers of knowledge, that's not what we're going for anymore.* And this program has definitely helped me to implement those ideas a lot, and I'm just more open to trying new technology, even if I don't feel perfectly competent in it.

(AB interview, 2017–06–09)

We see Ashley's shift here—around how she views learning and around the role of technology in her life—as indicative both of building the kind of capacity for this work that will be necessary for programs like TechTales to take hold within the library system and also of the kind of repositioning in relation to families and knowledge that broader scale implementation will require. She describes her own role remediation in relation to families ("learning side by side") and also a fundamental (re)positioning of power relations between the library and its audience. We also see her reflecting on deep shifts in the institutional identities of librarians themselves: "This idea that librarians as experts is . . . an outdated model." Ashley represents, in this case, an "individual who experience(s) transformative agency and change" and then goes on to "intervene and impact new spaces and sets of relations at particular scales of time" (Bang & Vossoughi, 2016).

The question becomes, for us, how we set up the conditions within a PDR/ DBIR effort that make space for this deep transformational agency in institutionally sustainable ways. We argue that our practice of *cofacilitation* was integral to this, as it engaged all of us in a process of role remediation. In this model, Ashley cofacilitated the workshop with another codesigner, choosing how and when to take the lead. She was able to do so when she was comfortable, observe an enacted version of the design when she was less sure, but still engage in one-on-one support of families throughout. Over time, she gradually took on more of the workshop facilitation until she independently facilitated it by the third iteration of the program. However, by holding to the fluidity of roles between designer, facilitator, and researcher, we collectively fostered trust and transformative relationships that fed back into the codesign process itself. When we all put ourselves in the cofacilitator roles, we were all willing to be vulnerable (and model that vulnerability) by stepping in to facilitate a newly designed experience. We were all engaged in the giving and receiving of feedback and, in this way, gained a collective pedagogical expertise but also a shared sense of accountability and responsibility toward each other and our joint design effort. Ultimately, by engaging in new subject–subject relations—as cofacilitators, as facilitator-coach, and so forth—we shared our emerging pedagogical insights and promoted the idea that we were all engaged in a shared endeavor that fed into the newly imagined design possibilities.

Implications for PDR/DBIR Work With Libraries

All substantial learning happens across social settings over extended periods of time through concerted effort and often with guidance and support from others with more or differing expertise. Libraries represent democratizing contexts for meaningful learning and more just outcomes for individuals from nondominant groups. Library staff—with their expertise and connections to community organizations—represent a scalable strategy for promoting the development of multiple literacies, including those related to STEM fields. This will require capacity building and the development of new work routines that build upon the institutional history and value systems of libraries in sensible ways.

As we have shown, mutually beneficial partnerships—between librarians, social workers, science center staff, and educational researchers—engaged in participatory design can create, refine, and enact expansive learning experiences for families. This necessarily involves working against the historical power dynamics associated with university–community collaborations, the development of a shared understanding of participatory design processes, a desettling of specific norms and ways of working (e.g., age-banded vs. intergenerational programming), and the sustained effort associated with working in partnership. Innovative designs can result from the work of cross-sector partnerships: developing trusting relationships, negotiating the shared focus of the work, managing the complex endeavor, and engaging in the collaborative and cooperative work involved programmatically (Bell, 2016).

The promise of engaging in PDR through a DBIR approach is to develop resources and human capacity that support innovation and improvement over time—in ways that are more sustainable because they come to be embedded in the routines and structures of the institutions. We have some encouraging evidence that both researchers and library staff recognize the importance of these strategies and are engaged in shifting their routines and structures accordingly. The TechTales approach is supporting a growing number of equity-centered STEAM learning environments for families. Researchers are developing their capacity to assist the partners in these expanded offerings. Library staff are enacting these expanding offerings while also delivering other technology programs built on the competencies developed through TechTales. We are encouraged that we will be able to cultivate a growing number of powerful STEAM learning environments for families from nondominant communities that are equity centered over time—while developing fundamental knowledge about how best to arrange for equity-focused broad-scale implementation.

References

Aspen Institute. (2014). *Rising to the Challenge: Re-envisioning Public Libraries*. Washington, DC: Amy K. Garmer.

Bang, M., & Vossoughi, S. (2016). Participatory design research and educational justice: Studying learning and relations within social change making. *Cognition and Instruction, 34*(3), 173–193.

Bang, M., Warren, B., Rosebery, A. S., & Medin, D. (2012). Desettling expectations in science education. *Human Development, 55*(5–6), 302–318.

Barron, B. (2006). Interests and self-sustained learning as catalysts of development: A learning ecology perspective. *Human Development, 49*, 193–224.

Barron, B., & Bell, P. (2015). Learning environments in and out of school. In L. Corno & E. Anderman (Eds.), *Handbook of Educational Psychology* (Third Edition) (pp. 323–336). New York, NY: Routledge, Taylor & Francis.

Bell, P. (2004). On the theoretical breadth of design-based research in education. *Educational Psychologist, 39*(4), 243–253.

Bell, P. (2016, April 17). *The Work of Design-focused Research-Practice Partnerships*. Presentation at the National Association for Research in Science Teaching (NARST) Annual International Conference, Baltimore, MD.

Bell, P., Lewenstein, B., Shouse, A. W., & Feder, M. A. (eds.) (2009). *National Research Council: Learning Science in Informal Environments: People, Places, and Pursuits*. Washington, DC: National Academies Press.

Bell, P., Tzou, C., Bricker, L., & Baines, A. D. (2012). Learning in diversities of structures of social practice: Accounting for how, why and where people learn science. *Human Development, 55*(5–6), 269–284.

Bell, P., Van Horne, K., & Cheng, B. H. (2017). Designing learning environments for equitable disciplinary identification. *Journal of the Learning Sciences, 26*(3), 367–375.

Center for the Future of Museums. (2008). *Museums & Society 2034: Trends and Potential Futures*. Washington, DC: AAM Press.

Farrell, B., & Medvedeva, M. (2010). *Demographic Transformation and the Future of Museums*. Washington, DC: AAM Press.

Fishman, B. J., Penuel, W. R., Allen, A. R., Cheng, B. H., & Sabelli, N. (2013). Design-based implementation research: An emerging model for transforming the relationship of research and practice. *National Society for the Study of Education, 112*(2), 136–156.

Goodwin, C. (1994). Professional vision. *American Anthropologist, 96*(3), 606–633.

Ito, M., Gutiérrez, K., Livingstone, S., Penuel, B., Rhodes, J., Salen, K., Schor, J., Sefton-Green, J., & Watkins, S. C. (2013). *Connected Learning: An Agenda for Research and Design*. Irvine, CA: Digital Media and Learning Research Hub.

Moorefield-Lang, H. (2015). Change in the making: Makerspaces and the ever-changing landscape of libraries. *TechTrends, 59*(3), 107.

National Research Council. (2012). *A Framework for K–12 Science Education: Practices, Crosscutting Concepts, and Core Ideas*. Board on Science Education, National Academy of Sciences. Washington, DC: The National Academies Press.

Penuel, W. R., Fishman, B. J., Cheng, B. H., & Sabelli, N. (2011). Organizing research and development at the intersection of learning, implementation, and design. *Educational Researcher, 40*(7), 331–337.

Race and Social Justice Initiative. (2015). *Where We've Been: The Story of the Race and Social Justice Initiative*. Retrieved from http://rsji.org/where-weve-been/

Rubin, A. (2011). *Those Darn Squirrels*. New York, NY: Houghton Mifflin Harcourt.

Sandoval, W. (2014). Conjecture mapping: An approach to systematic educational design research. *Journal of the Learning Sciences, 23*(1), 18–36.

Seattle Public Libraries. (2010). *The Seattle Public Library Community Survey Summary*. Seattle, WA: Seattle Public Library.

Van Horne, K., & Bell, P. (2017). Youth disciplinary identification during participation in contemporary project-based science investigations in school. *Journal of the Learning Sciences*.

Vossoughi, S., Hooper, P. K., & Escudé, M. (2016). Making through the lens of culture and power: Toward transformative visions for educational equity. *Harvard Educational Review, 86*(2), 206–232.

Zavala, M. (2016). Design, participation, and social change: What design in grassroots spaces can teach learning scientists. *Cognition and Instruction, 34*(3), 236–249.

5

DESIGNING ALTERNATE-REALITY GAMES FOR THE PUBLIC LIBRARY'S SUMMER READING PROGRAMS

Elizabeth Bonsignore, Derek Hansen, and Kari Kraus

Introduction

This chapter summarizes the design process used by a youth services librarian and her small group of teen volunteers as they developed and implemented three small-scale alternate-reality games (ARG) (over the course of three summers) to promote the summer reading programs for their rural community's public library system. Their story offers a design-based view (Sandoval & Bell, 2004) into the evolution of approaches that a small public library team employed to make the traditional ARG format more accessible to youth (11–17 years old) and to encourage greater participation by their local community members in library and literacy-related events. (For more on small community libraries developing programming, see Chapter 9 by Phillips, Lee, and Recker, in this volume.) The chapter offers two sets of take-aways for librarians considering the potential of designing and implementing ARGs with their teen patrons: (1) lessons learned and recommended practices for tailoring ARGs for youth audiences and (2) the new media literacies and design-thinking practices that are triggered when cocreating ARGs with teens.

Alternate-Reality Games as Participatory Platforms for Practicing Transmedia Literacies

An ARG is a form of transmedia storytelling (Jenkins et al., 2006) whose narrative context is not bound within any single communications platform or media type. Its story fragments can be scattered and hidden on billboards or in websites, phone calls, text messages, or books (Kim et al., 2009; Martin, Thompson, & Chatfield, 2006). An ARG is also a participatory experience. Because of the ways in which its narrative elements are hidden, players must collaboratively hunt for clues, solve puzzles, and synthesize disparate information to assemble and advance the ARG's ever-evolving storyline (Kim, Allen, & Lee, 2008; McGonigal, 2003). In a *Sherlock Holmes* adaptation of an ARG, for example, players might receive a text message from Watson that contains GPS coordinates to an encrypted clue, which, once found, decoded, and shared with other players on a discussion forum, could be emailed back to Holmes in order to advance the story. Rather than being confined to the pages of a book or the reels of a film, the story spills out into the everyday world. Rather than taking on imaginary roles or using avatars, players participate as themselves.

Just as the ARG's narrative and character arcs are distributed across multiple communications media, players use everyday technologies such as blogs, chat, and online community forums to collaborate as they make sense of the unfolding story. During *The Beast*, an early ARG based on the Steven Spielberg film *A.I.*, in-game characters encoded and distributed narrative clues across various websites and online videos worldwide; likewise, more than one million players across the globe shared and puzzled over information that they uncovered via discussion forums and individual blog posts (McGonigal, 2003). A well-designed ARG can thus engage learners in twenty-first-century literacy practices, such as evaluating and sharing information across multiple media, analyzing complex problems, and using new media tools to reinterpret existing content or create new expressions (Jenkins et al., 2006; American Association of School Librarians [AASL], 2008; (P21) Partnership for 21st Century Skills, 2009).

In addition, ARGs possess unique characteristics in terms of player participation. First, players engage with ARG content and each other as themselves, not a fictional character or avatar. "ARGs do not require there be an avatar to build up . . . the only demand is that you interact with these as yourself" (Martin et al., 2006, p. 7). The direct, personal connection with ARG content may hold potential for players to internalize what they have learned into sense-making and problem-solving strategies that they can apply in their own lives. Players assume a central role in assembling the story world as they collect, connect, and share the distributed story bits that comprise the game's narrative. These skills encapsulate transmedia literacy and navigation skills necessary to be productive, effective citizens in a digital society (Jenkins et al., 2006). Because ARGs "present the evidence of [the] story, and let the players tell it" (McGonigal, 2008a, p. 202), players often begin to view *themselves* as detectives, storytellers, and problem solvers. Furthermore, most ARG designers demand that players *collaborate* to gather and assemble the story pieces by creating "puzzles and challenges that no single person could solve on their own" (McGonigal, 2008a, p. 203). Here again, well-designed ARGs are uniquely situated to support twenty-first-century literacy practices such as collaborative problem solving and transmedia navigation (Bonsignore et al., 2012, 2013; Johnson et al., 2011; Whitton, 2008).

When embedding gameplay and story seamlessly into everyday communication technologies, ARG designers often strive to "deny and disguise the fact that it is even a game" (Szulborski, 2005, p. 1). This is known as the "This Is Not a Game" (TINAG) ethos by ARG designers and players, because their goal is to blur the lines between "what's real" and "what's not." From an authentic learning perspective, blurring the lines between "real" and fictional worlds creates a design tension that presents both opportunities and challenges. TINAG can serve as a means for prompting critical thinking and information-evaluation practices, because *players are responsible for distinguishing "truth" from fiction*. Players must imagine and inhabit alternate visions of their world, looking critically at the information they find, constantly asking "what if" questions. Considering such "what-if" scenarios is called *counterfactual thinking* (Byrne, 2007). It can be a tool that fosters investigative reasoning across multiple disciplines, including science, history, and business (Gaglio, 2004; Hawkins & Pea, 1987; Owens, 2010). However, striking a meaningful balance between fact and fiction using the TINAG mantra poses an ethical dilemma for designers, particularly those who work within educational contexts that place high value in the accuracy and authenticity of information (e.g., schools, libraries, museums). For instance, consider the rise of "fake news" and our responsibility as information and learning scientists to ensure that educators must offer young learners clear signals for credibility, accuracy, and authenticity.

As highly social, interactive media experiences, ARGs have received widespread interest across commercial and academic enterprises (McGonigal, 2011; Martin et al., 2006). Examples of popular commercial ARGs include *I Love Bees*, which promoted the *Halo* videogame series, and *The Lost Experience*, used to retain and attract viewers to the popular television series *Lost*. Although ARGs were initially developed for entertainment, they have also garnered attention as a potentially transformative vehicle for education, specifically in terms of the ways in which they promote (1) information literacy skills across various media formats (i.e., transmedia literacies), and (2) collaborative problem solving (Johnson et al., 2011; Bonsignore et al., 2012, 2013; Battles, Glenn, & Shedd, 2011; Eklund, 2008). A small number of ARGs have already been developed with educational goals in mind, such as *World Without Oil*, which asked players to imagine their world in the midst of a global oil crisis, and *Black Cloud*, which engaged at-risk high school students in scientific investigations of environmental issues in their local neighborhoods (Niemeyer, Garcia, & Naima, 2009). These education-oriented ARGs can be enacted on a global scale, such as *Urgent Evoke*, an award-winning ARG that attracted more than 20,000 players from 150 countries to brainstorm solutions to the world's "most urgent social problems" (Alchemy, 2010). Alternatively, they can be targeted at a local level, such as *ARGOSI*, which engaged a small number of new students at a university in the UK to practice information literacy skills with classmates while exploring their school's neighboring community (Whitton, 2008).

Overall, ARGs hold promise to engage players in several new media literacies; however, they also present challenges to designers. How might libraries take on both the promise and challenges of implementing ARGs in community contexts? In 2008, Heather Owings, a youth services librarian and teen volunteer coordinator for her rural county's branch library in western Maryland, decided to find out.

Can ARGs Be Designed by Teens for Teens?

The opportunities that ARGs present for engaging teen patrons in transmedia literacy practices piqued Heather Owings' interest and imagination. During her work on an Institute of Museum & Library Services (IMLS) -funded Library Services & Technology Act (LSTA) grant project, *TeensConnect*,[1] Heather saw a presentation on ARGs by game design expert Jane McGonigal (McGonigal, 2011, 2008a). Heather was inspired to see how she could transform the online information literacy work she had been doing with teens in a way that would enable them to codesign interactive transmedia stories together. She invited McGonigal to a videoconference with a group of teen volunteers to demonstrate how the social media tools they had been using during the school year might be integrated into mixed-reality games' experiences like ARGs (McGonigal, 2008b). During that videoconference, Heather recruited three teen girls who would become her core ARG designers for the next three years.

Heather led her team from the Finksburg Branch of the Carroll County Public Library system, a rural area in western Maryland. They dubbed themselves the "Finksbrary" team, after the YouTube channel that they used to publicize the ARGs they created as part of the county library's summer reading program over the course of three summers. The Finksbrary team included Heather and one of her colleagues, along with three teenage girls. All of their design efforts were focused on an informal, out-of-school context. The team implemented three ARGs over the course of three summers (June 2008–August 2011), with a one-year design cycle taken for each ARG (the specific ARGs are described in the next section). Immediately after the videoconference with McGonigal, Heather recruited seven teens; however, once three of the initial volunteers realized that ARGs were *not* like videogames, they lost interest and decided not to participate. This presents one of the perpetual challenges of designing and describing ARGs: when encountering ARGs for the first time, many people mistakenly assume that they are akin to videogames. However, ARGs are not bound by a single platform, like a videogame console or mobile interface. The transmedia nature of ARGs makes them attractive as a potential platform for learning, since players have opportunities to interact with a variety of multimedia, but those who have never experienced the live scavenger-hunt-like nature of ARG gameplay often mistakenly equate it to more conventional digital games. Interestingly, the four girls who remained later noted in interviews that the teens who left "were boys who didn't get the story part of ARGs and only wanted to play videogames anyway" (Rose,

2012). Of the four who remained after the "videogamers" left, three teen girls became Heather's core design team. The fourth girl's family moved just before the first ARG launched, and though she remained close to the design team via email, she was no longer able to participate actively.

The three teens who Heather recruited included Rosie, a 14-year-old home-schooler who had not been part of Heather's TeensConnect program but had heard about the McGonigal videoconference from the community outreach that Heather had done with teen volunteers at the county library. Rosie had become enamored of McGonigal's design work on the *Lost Ring* ARG that had been part of the 2008 Summer Olympic Games in Beijing. A second teen was Caroline, who also signed up after the videoconference with McGonigal. She was a 13-year-old who had participated in TeensConnect at a local public school. Finally, Kitty joined the Finksbrary design team when she was 12 years old and was its youngest member; however, she had also participated in the TeensConnect program and was familiar with Heather's work. (Note: all teen names are pseudonyms to protect their privacy.)

When the girls first began the ARG design group, they ranged in age from 12 to 14 years old, and all of them required transportation by adults to their volunteer design sessions. Toward the end of their ARG design experience, the oldest girl was almost 18 and driving herself to all of the design sessions, while the youngest was in the process of earning her learner's permit. In effect, over the three-year program, the girls were not only growing as ARG designers, they were growing into adulthood. As one of the teen designers noted during her interview,

> Yeah, I mean I just voted [in government elections] this year . . . I **just voted**. I mean it's so crazy to think how much has changed. And it's so awesome. This is totally a little bit off-topic—but **because of this game** I'm actually going into Library Science. Like, I'm going to go get my master's degree and become a librarian. 'Cuz I wanna do stuff **like this**. I wanna be invested in kids' programs because . . . I grew up in the library for pete's sake.

Three ARGs for Three Summer Reading Programs

The three ARGs that Heather and her teen team designed evolved from a complex, multisited mystery that followed the typical design tropes found in popular adult-oriented ARGs in their first summer to a single-sited extension of a well-known fairy tale that maintained core elements of ARGs while also echoing the library's more traditional information "scavenger hunt" style by their final summer. For each of the ARGs, the team tried to fashion a story that aligned with the themes of their summer reading program, to capture and sustain the audience of readers who typically participated in summer programs, while also attracting youth who might be interested in the more novel interactive format characteristic of ARGs.

The first summer reading program theme was related to water, so the Finksbrary team decided to craft a mystery that involved a lost city in the Chesapeake Bay (similar to the legend of Atlantis). Planning started not long after the McGonigal videoconference in the summer of 2008, with the team holding design meetings once or twice a month on Saturdays throughout the school year (2008–2009). They dubbed their first ARG *Find Chesia* and envisioned a mystery in which a 14-year-old girl, Chelsie, would engage teens in the community to help her find her parents, who had disappeared while working at an archeological dig. Chelsie believed that a bracelet her parents gave her was tied to their mysterious disappearance, and she asked players for help in an introductory online video. Eventually, through her online interactions with two other archeologists, she learned that her parents may have been on the verge of discovering a Native American city that had disappeared under the Chesapeake Bay hundreds of years before. However, Chelsie was not sure whom to trust: the two other archeologists were also competing for whatever secrets were buried with the remains of the ancient city of Chesia. The *Find Chesia* narrative was distributed across multiple blogging sites (e.g., one for the teen protagonist, Chelsie, and one for an archeologist who was suspected as a competitor and possible enemy of the main character's parents), Twitter accounts, and video channels. As detailed in the lessons learned section, the Finksbrary team found that this approach, while exciting, was not only far too complex and resource intensive for a small library team to carry out, but it was also far too sprawling for most of the teen and child library patrons who they were trying to target.

Postgame feedback that Heather received from her library's Teen Advisory Board was that those who participated were unsure how and where to start. Others never went beyond perusing the materials in their summer reading packages

FIGURE 5.1 A snapshot of the promotional video for *Find Chesia.* Note the official "from Carroll County Public Library" caption. Here is an excerpt of Chelsie's related blog post: *"Hi my name's Chelsie. I got this bracelet for my 14th birthday. My aunt says it's from my parents, but the thing is that I haven't seen them in a year. They disappeared after my last birthday. They were working on an archaeological dig and one morning they were just gone. The bracelet is the only link I have to my parents. I'm hoping it can help me figure out what happened to them. Do you think you can help me?"*

because they were uncertain what alternate-reality games were. Unfamiliarity with the term—"ARG jargon" as the team later referred to it—prevented many teens from going to the *Find Chesia* sites in the first place. If they did visit Chelsie's blog, they weren't sure how to respond—or if they should respond—to her questions and requests for help. As teen designer Kitty noted,

> If an adult saw a rabbithole . . . they would have already been on that website. Once they're there, they click on the secret links. [She is referring to a URL shown in promotions for the movie, A.I., that was a link to the ARG *The Beast*.] For us, having the website on a paper invite object in the summer reading stuff . . . Well, you have to get them to **go** to that site . . . People looked at the paper and they were like—Oh—that's cool. But then, they didn't **go** there . . . I mean, you can't force people to take that first step . . . and even then, they had to stick with it . . . over the summer.

Consequently, during the following year, the Finksbrary team developed an ARG whose multimedia content was delivered primarily through one community website (Doh, 2010). This structural change helped the designers maintain the second year's ARG storyline within *one* access point for players, and they also hoped that it would reduce the players' confusion about "where to start" and "what to do next." In addition to modifying the way that they would present the structure of the narrative to players, the team decided that using an existing, well-known story or character would simplify the amount of original narrative that they would have to create. This strategy had the added benefits of (1) aligning more closely to the library's summer program goals to promote reading and (2) providing players with a familiar narrative context with which to access the game activities.

To start, one of the teen designers suggested that they present players with a library dilemma: a mysterious character has fallen out of an unknown book. The players' goal would be to identify the character and get him/her back into his/her story. They decided that the Mad Hatter from *Alice in Wonderland* would be their mysterious, mischievous character. In addition to the fact that the Hatter character was a plausible troublemaker, Lewis Carroll's story is in the public domain, so the team did not have to be concerned about copyright issues. The teen designers were excited to be able to extend a story that was familiar to both themselves and their peers. During the ARG, the teen designers blogged as players themselves, finding and sharing their clues, thoughts, and questions for the rest of the teen player community in their own voices rather than trying to play adult characters, as they had for *Find Chesia*. Not only did the teen designers feel more comfortable, the target teen players also felt more connected to these in-game characters, given their closeness in age and vernacular (Owings, 2010).

For their third and final ARG, the Finksbrary team wanted to repeat and build upon their success with the Mystery Guest. In much the same way that second-language learners have engaged in literacy practices by creating fan fiction that extends well-known texts popular with youth (Black, 2009), the Finksbrary team wanted to build their final ARG on a familiar foundation. Their goal was to balance a storyline that would be familiar to teens and children in their community with something new. The summer reading theme was focused on global narratives (i.e., themes that transcend time, geography, and cultures), and the team felt that well-known fairy tales and folk tales that have been retold across cultures held potential to be familiar yet remixable (e.g., Snow White and Little Red Riding Hood). They had learned from their experience with *Find Chesia* that creating an entirely new plot and story world required too many resources—in writing, in role-playing, in managing story-related websites—for their small volunteer group. They wanted to continue to use existing, well-known narratives with the success that they had experienced with *Mystery Guest*. At the same time, they also wanted to ensure that they presented something that felt new. They settled on the mystery of a modern Red Riding Hood who is lost in the forest with no cell phone coverage. Players would be tasked with helping "Red" find a way home to her grandmother by finding and decoding clues from characters who visit from other fairy tales. It would be called *Run Red Run*.

The opportunity to build something new from existing, familiar stories also enabled the Finksbrary teens to take advantage of their own "funds of knowledge" as they developed their budding design skills and design thinking. *Funds of knowledge* refers to experiences, skills, values, and dispositions that an individual possesses that are rooted in the families and communities s/he comes from (Barton & Tan, 2009; Basu & Barton, 2007; Moje et al., 2004). The concept of funds of knowledge is often used to refer to the life experiences and knowledge that youth possess that should be tapped to help make learning situations personally meaningful (Basu & Barton, 2007; Moje et al., 2004). The Finksbrary teen designers were excited to apply their funds of knowledge as avid readers in order to craft new tales from existing literature, as Rosie explained: "We had the entire realm of literature to work with . . . Like that's just—that's every teenage kid's dream—to be able to muddle with literature." Finding ways to balance between the familiar and the novel remained a consistent ARG design mantra throughout the Finksbrary design case, from the team's experiences with *Mystery Guest* through the end with *Run Red Run*.

Lessons Learned: Tailoring ARGs for Teens

The summer ARGs that the Finksbrary team designed and implemented over the course of 2008–2011 never quite took hold of their library community's attention in the ambitious ways that Heather had hoped. At most, Heather estimated that teen patron participation peaked in the tens and twenties during their second summer with *Mystery Guest*. Despite the modest community turnout overall, the Finksbrary team felt that they had learned several useful lessons that could serve future designers who might want to appropriate and tailor the core elements of ARGs (such as TINAG) for teens in a public library community.

Teens and Central, Single-Sited ARG Interface Versus Multisited Interfaces

From the time that the Finksbrary ARG team launched *Find Chesia* through the end of *Red*, one of their most salient lessons learned was that the pervasive, fragmented, distributed narrative characteristic of most adult-oriented ARGs did not work well with their target audience of teen library patrons. Overall, they found that *distributed transmedia narratives were overwhelming and confusing for teen players to follow and overly complex for teen designers to manage.* Although many teens visited Chelsie's blog after seeing the initial video, they did not seem to know how to respond to her request for help, or they did not follow links to sites of other characters that were embedded in Chelsie's blog or the physical paper clues that the Finksbrary team put in summer reading program packages. Moreover, although Heather and her team followed McGonigal's model of employing social media technologies like the popular microblogging tool Twitter to share character updates, the parents of many teens did not allow them to use any social media tools, and some teens did not know that they could read Twitter feeds without an account. The team's use of Twitter did garner interest from existing ARG communities like ARGnet, along with modest publicity, because Jane McGonigal followed some of *Find Chesia*'s character Twitter streams; however, there was little to no interaction from their target audience of teens. For the most part, teens did not seem to know how to venture forth into the game of their own accord.

The primary interface design strategy that the team employed to overcome this issue was to *use a single community website* to present the game's narrative and player challenges. This strategy seemed to be less confusing for a teen audience based on feedback that Heather received from teens in her branch's Teen Advisory Board. The Finksbrary team's experience suggests that *establishing a single community site from the outset* can promote initial and more sustained interaction from youth audiences, especially if the site enables players to interact with characters from the ARG storyline.

Guided Transmedia Narratives and Guiding Characters for Teens

In addition to presenting a single entry point and interface to an ARG for teens, Heather and her team also uncovered several design strategies related to the ARG's characteristic participatory narrative. First, they learned that teen players needed a "librarian-mentor" character that could act as a guide or mentor to help point out connections in clues that might be scattered throughout the ARG site over time. (For more on the role of librarians as mentors, see Chapter 8 by Clegg

☆ Steps for Creating an ARG

⊙ Page history

Jane McGonIgal shared with us 10 steps for creating an ARG in June 2008. I don't think we followed through on all the steps in our first attempt aka Find Chesia. So this is a reminder page, that we need to think about ALL of these steps, especially those highlighted in **bold**:

10 Steps to Inventing an Arg:

1. Start a puppet master team! (Check! We did this REALLY well imho)
2. Brainstorm your theme or story. What's the game about?
   (Again we did this really well last time)
3. **Pick the game "verbs." What are you asking players to DO in the game?**
   (Hmmm ... not so well done the first time)
4. Make a "media plan." What sites and technologies will you use?
5. **Design your community. What collaboration sites and technologies will you use?** I don't think players of "Find Chesla" worked together. I think we really need to Incorporate teams In the 2010 game.
6. Decide on a launch date - when does the game start? How long will It last?
7. Identify your team's strengths and pick design roles: story writer, researcher, game director, etc.
8. Make a game timeline.
9. Create the content!
10. Decide who to invite. (No bralner! Teens in the Summer Reading program of course!)

4 Secrets to an Awesome ARG:

1. **Make sure your players know EXACTLY what to do. ("This Is your mission! ")**
2. Help your players show off their superpowers.
3. **Make It super-social!**
4. **Your players are the real stars of the game.**

FIGURE 5.2   In wiki pages for the ARGs they created, Heather summarized McGoni-gal's pointers: "10 Steps to Inventing an ARG" and "4 Secrets" to an awesome ARG (McGonigal, 2008b). The team's mantra for most of their ARG design sessions were "*What are the verbs?*" For all their game content, they strived to clearly point players toward the tasks that they needed to complete to successfully solve the clues and advance the story.

and Subramaniam, in this volume.) Second, the Finksbrary teen designers found that their peers—and they themselves—felt the most comfortable if the characters they created were teens themselves rather than adults.

Find Chesia helped the team realize that they would need to add a character who could act as a sort of guide or mentor for players—someone who would answer any questions they had about how to play as they were interacting with the in-game website. Even after receiving background information on ARGs in their summer reading information packages and learning about ARGs in librarian recruiting talks, teen players showed that they *needed clear mechanisms and models for how to interact with the ARG narrative.* While adult players in popular ARGs like *The Beast* and *I Love Bees* might take the initiative to create and share their own directions with other players, teens seem enculturated to wait for an adult to give them license to act. Heather observed that her teen patrons needed structure and models for action to help them get started, especially in an informal, unguided context: "[T]eens really, well, they're in a culture of education and they are looking for directions on how to do this. Once they know the **structure**, then they are more than happy to interact." In *Mystery Guest*, the librarian character offered authoritative, in-game guidance to navigate through the main story beats and to receive clues about the puzzles. Heather's goal was for the librarian character to model the process of gathering disparate clues and synthesizing them into puzzle solutions for players.

In addition to establishing a mentor character to help guide players and to model problem-solving behaviors that are a core characteristic and game mechanic in ARGs, the Finksbrary teens felt that they were most successful when they created protagonists who paralleled their own personalities and ages. After investing a great deal of time and effort to develop backstories for their adult characters in *Find Chesia*, the teen designers revealed to Heather that, even as puppetmasters, they were uncomfortable portraying these adults during the live game. Throughout their design sessions, the teen designers were consistently concerned that they would be accused of misrepresentation if they tried to play adult characters, even characters whom they themselves had created. In *Find Chesia*, while the teens enjoyed developing the archeologist characters, they realized that they did not feel comfortable playing adult characters; rather, they wanted *adults* to portray them. In *Mystery Guest*, the teen puppetmasters were more comfortable "using their own voices," as Heather explained, by presenting narrative clues and puzzles as themselves (under pseudonyms), through video log (vlog) and blog posts. Teen players also noted that having more than one teen character portrayed on the ARG site was more engaging. As Heather observed, with "four different voices, four different girls," players could choose a favorite character to follow.

Extending New Stories From Existing Fictions

In terms of narrative design, the Finksbrary team's world-building strategy evolved from one that was original and required the creation and maintenance of many new narrative artifacts—both digital and physical, in-library objects—to an approach that took advantage of existing story worlds familiar to their target teen audience, such as novels like *Alice in Wonderland* and fairy tales like *Red*

Riding Hood. For example, in *Find Chesia*, the team's initial strategy was to build a completely new story world for players to explore (the lost city of Chesia, competing archeologists, and a teen in search of her parents). Like the evolution of most ARG storylines, *Find Chesia* grew as a counterfactual extension to existing knowledge (Bonsignore et al., 2012, 2013; Compeau & MacDougall, 2014). For instance, the significance of the gems in Chelsie's bracelet were drawn from the team's research on the use of various crystals by Native Americans, and the lost city of Chesia was inspired by various Native American tribes that existed before and during European colonization in the sixteenth and seventeenth centuries. When Heather and her teens realized that the complexity of this strategy was not only challenging for the players but also a taxing design process for their small team, they reconsidered how they could benefit from *existing* story worlds in the books and media that they were trying to promote for the library's summer reading program.

Their new narrative design strategy involved extending new interactive stories from well-known, existing narratives that children and teens would likely be familiar with (e.g., *Alice in Wonderland*, fairy tales). As Kitty noted in her post-game reflection:

> We wanted to use an **actual** person . . . a character. We didn't want to make a completely new story. Like the first year . . . it was so complicated, like inventing your own person. . . . For *Chesia* we had to invent an entire new life—lives! We thought—well, we would make it a lot less complicated if we could like use someone that other people knew.

Rosie agreed, elaborating on the excitement that the team felt about extending familiar stories:

> It was fantastic because . . . it was **our** take on *Alice in Wonderland*. We got to be like: What would happen if the Mad Hatter came out of the book? We had a foundation. We could write about it and we could change it . . . because it's public domain now. And the Rabbit . . . rabbit-holes? Yeah—it's like the perfect laboratory setting for an ARG form.

This strategy worked well for several reasons:

- It reduced narrative design complexity and media creation requirements for a small team.
- It allowed the team to take advantage of existing story world resources and not concern themselves with copyright issues, since the base narratives they selected were in the public domain.
- It was aligned with their library's goals of engaging teens with existing works of literature and building from there.

Both the teen designers and players were excited about this approach, given their growing interest in online fan fiction, or the practice of crafting new story extensions from existing texts, such as novels, television shows, or movies (Black, 2009; Jenkins, 2006). In addition, it was also used successfully by Angela Colvert (2009), whose puppetmaster team of 10- to 11-year-olds designed an ARG for younger classmates (9- to 10-year-olds) that was based on a novel that they had read for one of their classes. Indeed, building from existing story worlds has proven effective for the most successful ARGs from the entertainment industry, such as *ILB*, which extended the virtual world of the *Halo* videogame series; *The Beast*, in which "sentient machines" from the movie, *A.I.*, need therapists as much as humans do; or *MetaCortechs*, which grew directly from the *Matrix* film series and videogame franchise.

TINAG Is Tricky With Teens

The topic of internet safety was a recurring theme throughout the design process for all three Finksbrary ARGs. Online safety remained a concern throughout gameplay as well. As a librarian charged with educating youth about issues ranging from authoritative sources, self-presentation, and privacy, copyright, and fair-use regulations, "netiquette," and cyberbullying, Heather often wondered how she could balance the openness of adult-oriented ARGs with the concerns of parents and some of her own colleagues, as well as her teen designers (ALA, 2016; "Children and the Internet: Policies That Work," 2004). Initially, after being inspired by McGonigal's presentation to librarians about the potential of an ARG as a platform with which teens could practice digital literacies, Heather found that the distributed, frameless nature of ARGs was not only confusing to players, it also raised the concerns of some of her colleagues and parents. Prior to launching *Find Chesia*, she and her design team had wanted to create a story whose design followed McGonigal's pointers by being distributed across multiple types of sites and multiple characters. After hearing feedback from *Find Chesia*'s players and from Heather's Teen Advisory Board at the library, the Finksbrary team realized that multiple sites were difficult for their small group to maintain, hard for players to follow, and alarming for parents who were not sure that their children should be exploring sites that did not explicitly acknowledge a connection with the county libraries or their summer reading program.

Heather was not the only one who confirmed that internet safety and privacy issues were a concern for teen players and their parents/adult guardians. Many of the issues were raised by the teens themselves during their design sessions. It might be the case that the Finksbrary teens were more conservative than other teens across the U.S. or that they were more heavily influenced by adults/parents or even that they were trying to show Heather and me that they cared about internet safety more than they actually did. Questions remain on whether teen players outside the Finksbrary county system (e.g., in a more urban setting) would respond more favorably to a distributed ARG like *Find Chesia*, whose online feeds also did not identify themselves as "credible" library program sites. Existing and emerging research on adolescent use of social media and other digital content has shown that teens are not only aware of legal and societal concerns about the level of access that adults control in the name of "privacy" and "child protection" but that teens also actively seek social media that is *beyond* adult oversight and protection (boyd, 2014; boyd et al., 2009; Livingstone, 2008; Shapiro & Ossorio, 2013). Instead, many teens view privacy differently than adults: they seek privacy *from* adults, not protection by adults (boyd, 2014). However, the Finksbrary design team *did* encounter resistance to their efforts to follow design guidelines for adult ARGs rather than addressing concerns that they encountered so often in school and at home. Consequently, designers should be aware that these issues and concerns exist and that they must continue to be negotiated as they develop ARGs and similar transmedia experiences for teens.

The Finksbrary Teens: Practicing New Media Literacies

In most prior ARG studies, designers have focused on how ARGs can be crafted to engage *players*. However, the experiences of Heather and her teens suggest opportunities for future studies that explore the effects of involving youth in the ARG design process. The Finksbrary teens' active participation as the creators of their library's summer reading ARGs afforded them opportunities to engage in "design thinking," or ways of viewing and analyzing problems that lead to the identification, testing, and implementation of creative, systems-based solutions (Brown, 2008; Peppler & Kafai, 2009).

Research in game-based learning, game design, and e-textiles design has demonstrated the problem-solving expertise and increased agency that children can derive from their active participation in design thinking (Fields, Kafai, & Searle, 2012; Kafai, Fields, & Searle, 2012; Kafai, 1996; Squire, 2011). Several of these studies have found that when involved in game design or "Maker" processes, youth are not only learning skills that may help them earn jobs in the game industry or craft guilds (e.g., film production), but they are also building "technical, technological, artistic, cognitive, social, and linguistic skills suitable for our current and future world ... displaying media literacy in both old and new forms of reading and writing" (Salen, 2007, p. 304). Designing with youth can also enhance our understanding of the conceptual processes of the learners themselves (Ahn et al., 2012; Bonsignore et al., 2013) and has shown potential to benefit the learners who participate in their design (Guha, Druin, & Fails, 2010). In this section, we consider the literacy practices that the Finksbrary teens engaged in through their role as designers of participatory transmedia experiences like ARGs.

Creativity and Innovation

One of the core literacies in the Partnership for 21st Century Skills that is also promoted by the IMLS is "creativity and innovation," which includes the application of creative ideation techniques, demonstrating curiosity and imagination, and elaborating, analyzing, and refining ideas ((P21) Partnership for 21st Century Skills, 2009; IMLS Project Team and Task Force, n.d.). Throughout their three-year involvement in the Finksbrary ARG team, the teen designers created many different types of content: they wrote character posts for in-game characters such as Chelsie and the two archeologists; they developed fictional reasons why the crystals would be important to Chesia, building upon what they had learned about the resources that Native Americans used; they made new story extensions for existing works like *Alice in Wonderland* and *Little Red Riding Hood*; they helped write the scripts for and act out videos for their characters and also recorded audio. Their sample blog posts demonstrated the unique teen voices that they brought to the projects, as well as a growing understanding of "register": writing to a specific player audience (their fellow teens) with subtle clues and questions to guide them. Before posting them publicly, they shared and discussed revisions for the following draft blog entries on the Finksbrary design wikis for *Find Chesia* and *Mystery Guest*. The teens' involvement as ARG designers was, in some cases, the first experience they had with wikis and online collaborative writing.

In addition to the blog posts that the teens created for their ARGs, they began to experiment with writing and creating in other venues. Kitty and Caroline won teen writing contests during the summer that they worked on *Mystery Guest*. Rosie started her own personal blog about the same time as they were writing blogs for *Find Chesia*. During her postgame interview, Rosie noted that although her own blog and the posts that she wrote for the Finksbrary ARGs were "so little," she still felt as though she had made a statement for her library community:

> Imagine. 14 years old. Blogging. You're not gonna get many people to read **that**. Like, something so little—I mean, I just put words out onto the blogosphere . . . and heaven knows that that's a really big place for putting words . . . but it was an experience that definitely changed me for the better. I feel like I created something that . . . did something. It definitely brought awareness to the fact that libraries aren't just for books, dude.

Finally, the teens' responsibilities and identities as teen puppetmasters proved very important to them and spurred them to continue to create. In her interview, Kitty noted that "It was like writing a **BIG** story with lots of people . . . that was cool" (2011).

Respecting Others (Acting Ethically, Respectfully, and Legally)

Respecting others and collaborating on diverse teams is another core literacy from both the Partnership for 21st Century Skills and the ALSC's 21st Century Learner (AASL, 2008; (P21) Partnership for 21st Century Skills, 2009). The Finksbrary teens demonstrated their efforts to respect others most when they discussed internet safety issues with Heather and each other and when they told Heather about the concerns they had about misrepresenting themselves online. This theme recurred repeatedly during design sessions in which the teens discussed the pros and cons of adhering closely to the TINAG principle of ARG design. In addition to the awareness that the teen designers repeatedly displayed regarding internet safety, they were also sensitive to the fact that their ARGs were also played by children younger than teens, so they wanted to ensure content was accessible. For example, Rosie had the following to say about the team's design decision to keep all online game content on one site only:

> [W]e wanted to make sure that kids that were younger, that, 9 or 10 year olds . . . trying to get on the blog . . . It would be easier for them to follow . . . So that they didn't have to be hopping around all over the internet . . . which can kind of be **potentially** dangerous. We wanted to make sure that one: kids were safe, and two: it was easy to access.

The teen designers' concern for respecting others and acting ethically was not just limited to online safety or parental oversight, however. When they started to develop their ARG narratives by building from existing works of literature, Heather took the opportunity to discuss issues related to intellectual property and intellectual rights, such as the concept of fair use and how to determine if a work is in the public domain. On the design wikis for both *Run Red Run* and *Mystery Guest*, Heather compiled a brainstorming list of fairy tales and other works that were in the public domain so that the teens could brainstorm how they might build from the existing stories to create new extensions. In addition to their growing awareness of online policy-related issues like fair use and internet safety, Rosie and Kitty mentioned that they both felt as though creating the ARG was more than a collaborative exercise, but it was an opportunity to be part of a larger community, Kitty commented, "a conglomeration of people coming together to try to meet an end-goal."

The Importance of Play

A key activity that Heather tried to promote with her teen designers is part of the New Media Literacies and Participatory Cultures framework (Jenkins et al., 2006): "Play: the capacity to experiment with one's surroundings as a form of problem-solving" (Jenkins et al., 2006, XIV). Heather's willingness to give her teen designers room to experiment, brainstorm, and play with many ideas and many different storylines contrasts with more "teacher-centered" approaches to learning, in which "student responses provide springboards for teacher explanations" (Hmelo-Silver & Barrows, 2006, p. 22). Instead, Heather's actions during the team's design sessions resembled a technique known as the "reflective toss" (Hmelo-Silver & Barrows, 2006; Schoenfeld, 1998). In a reflective toss, an educator takes a student statement, paraphrases or summarizes it, and then "throws responsibility for elaboration back to the student" (Hmelo-Silver & Barrows, 2006, p. 22). For example, the educator/facilitator will ask for clarification on a problem or will ask the group what they think about proposed concepts or opinions. The metaphor of the reflective toss is grounded in the notion of interactive play—that an educator or facilitator gives learners the permission to play and to enable them to take risks rather than fearing failure in an assessment-driven culture.

In interviews, Heather continually emphasized that ARGs could give her teen designers and players more opportunities to play around without concerning themselves with making mistakes. She compared play to Tina Fey's "rules of improvisation" (2013) and emphasized that developing a confidence in and ability to "play" was a skill that should be developed through the ARG design process. Heather worked to promote both her designers' and players' efforts to participate in positive, humorous ways rather than emphasizing what they should *not* do online. Her approach underscores an important strategy for future designers and researchers who develop ARGs and similar interactive experiences with and for teens.

Conclusion

Game design and play have often been described by games-based learning scholars as models of interaction that are "rooted in reflection-in-action" (Salen, 2007, p. 302; Salen & Zimmerman, 2003). Effectively, game designers engage in a reflective design process as they iteratively develop rules of play and then playtest, evaluate, and modify those rules. The Finksbrary teens actively engaged in reflection-in-action over the course of the three years that they honed their ARG design craft.

In addition, Heather approached her design sessions using a Young Adult Library Services Association (YALSA) concept known as "radical trust," which involves the practice of involving teens in library planning and management decisions typically relegated to adult staff members only (Braun et al., 2014; Vieau, 2009). Radical trust is related to the concept of legitimate peripheral participation, which allows individuals who are newcomers to a community to engage in small but meaningful and productive tasks that, in turn, support that community (Lave & Wenger, 1991). For Heather, radical trust with her teens often meant allowing a high giggle count during design sessions. Regardless of how silly the girls were during design sessions, however, their "intuitive, spontaneous performance" (Schön, 1984) of being savvy and silly youth also shed light on their ability to think systematically and carefully about the experiences they were designing for their peers.

Heather and her teens never lost their exuberance for the potential of interactive, transmedia experiences like ARGs to be an exciting space for teens to play. Perhaps most importantly, as avid readers and library aficionados, they always viewed ARGs as a rewarding design space. During interviews about their experiences, all of the teens commented that they felt as though they had been part of larger creative community. As Rosie noted,

> [Y]ou can get so many people together and they come together and they **support** each other and they **help** each other out and you're getting a **great community** factor there. I mean an ARG doesn't just have to be a game. It can be a chance to get a community together to work for something.

Note

1 The *TeensConnect* project was a collaborative effort between the countywide public library system and the county's public schools to educate teens about so-called Web 2.0 tools (e.g., wikis and blogs) and to "encourage them to use online technology to cross geographical and cultural boundaries" (Owings, 2010).

References

Ahn, J., Subramaniam, M., Fleischmann, K. R., Waugh, A., Walsh, G., & Druin, A. (2012). Youth identities as remixers in an online community of storytellers: Attitudes, strategies, and values. *Proceedings of the American Society for Information Science and Technology, 49*(1), 1–10. doi:https://doi.org/10.1002/meet.14504901089

Alchemy. (2010, January 27). *'Urgent Evoke' About the EVOKE Game.* Retrieved from http://blog.urgentevoke.net/2010/01/27/about-the-evoke-game/

American Association of School Librarians. (2008). *Standards for the 21st-Century Learner in Action* (New Edition). Chicago, IL: American Association of School Librarians.

American Library Association. (2016). 'Internet use policies' policy. *Libraries and the Internet Toolkit* (blog). Retrieved from www.ala.org/advocacy/intfreedom/iftoolkits/litoolkit/internetusepolicies

Barton, A. C., & Tan, E. (2009). Funds of knowledge and discourses and hybrid space. *Journal of Research in Science Teaching, 46*(1), 50–73.

Basu, S. J., & Barton, A. C. (2007). Developing a sustained interest in science among urban minority youth. *Journal of Research in Science Teaching, 44*(3), 466–489.

Battles, J., Glenn, V., & Shedd, L. (2011). Rethinking the library game: Creating an alternate reality with social media. *Journal of Web Librarianship, 5*(2), 114–131. doi:https://doi.org/10.1080/19322909.2011.569922

Black, R. W. (2009). English-language learners, fan communities, and 21st-century skills. *Journal of Adolescent & Adult Literacy, 52*(8), 688–697. doi:https://doi.org/10.1598/JAAL.52.8.4

Bonsignore, E., Ahn, J., Clegg, T., Leigh Guha, M., Yip, J. C., & Druin, A. (2013). Embedding participatory design into designs for learning: An untapped interdisciplinary resource? In *To See the World and a Grain of Sand: Learning Across Levels of Space, Time, and Scale: CSCL 2013 Conference Proceedings Volume 1—Full Papers & Symposia* (1: pp. 549–556). Madison, WI: International Society of the Learning Sciences.

Bonsignore, E., Hansen, D., Kraus, K., & Ruppel, M. (2012). Alternate Reality games as platforms for practicing 21st-century literacies. *International Journal of Learning and Media*, 4(1), 25–54. doi:https://doi.org/10.1162/IJLM_a_00086

Bonsignore, E., Hansen, D., Kraus, K., Visconti, A., Ahn, J., & Druin, A. (2013). Playing for real: Designing alternate reality games for teenagers in learning Contexts. In *Proceedings of the 12th International Conference on Interaction Design and Children* (pp. 237–246). New York, NY: ACM.

Bonsignore, E., Kraus, K., Visconti, A., Hansen, D., Fraistat, A., & Druin, A. (2012). Game design for promoting counterfactual thinking. In *Proceedings of the SIGCHI Conference on Human Factors in Computing Systems, Austin, TX* (pp. 2079–2082). New York, NY: ACM.

boyd, d. (2014). *It's Complicated: The Social Lives of Networked Teens*. London: Yale University Press.

boyd, d., Marwick, A., Aftab, P., & Koeltl, M. (2009). The conundrum of visibility: Youth safety and the internet. *Journal of Children and Media*, 3(4), 410–419. doi:https://doi.org/10.1080/17482790903233465

Braun, L. W., Hartman, M. L., Hughes-Hassell, S., Kumasis, K., & Yoke, B. (2014). *The Future of Library Services for and with Teens: A Call to Action*. Academic. Chicago, IL: American Library Association: Young Adult Library Services Association. Retrieved from www.ala.org/yaforum/sites/ala.org.yaforum/files/content/YALSA_nationalforum_final.pdf

Brown, T. (2008). Design thinking. *Harvard Business Review*, 86(6), 84.

Byrne, R. (2007). *The Rational Imagination: How People Create Alternatives to Reality* (First edition). Cambridge, MA: MIT Press.

Children and the Internet: Policies That Work. (2004). Association for Library Service to Children, Librarians & Educators Online, Public Library Association. Retrieved from www.ala.org.proxy-um.researchport.umd.edu/alsc/issuesadv/internettech/childrentheinternetpoliciesthatwork

Colvert, A. (2009). Peer puppeteers: Alternate reality gaming in primary school settings. *Breaking New Ground: Innovation in Games, Play, Practice and Theory: DiGRA, Brunel University, London*. Retrieved 14 May 2012, from www.digra.org/dl/db/09287.19018.pdf

Compeau, T., & MacDougall, R. (2014). Tecumseh lies here: Goals and challenges for a pervasive history game in progress. In K. Kee (Ed.), *Pastplay: Teaching and Learning History with Technology*. Ann Arbor, MI: University of Michigan Press.

Doh, J. (2010, September 8). *Interview with Mystery Guest 2010 Creator Heather Owings | ARGNet: Alternate Reality Gaming Network*. ARGNet: Alternate Reality Gaming Network. Retrieved from www.argn.com/2010/09/interview_with_mystery_guest_2010_creator_heather_owings/

Eklund, K. (2008, May 1). *'Meet the 8TSO': World Without Oil—Serious Game for the Public Good*. Retrieved from https://wwolives.wordpress.com/2008/05/01/meet-the-8tsoc/

Fey, T. (2013). *Bossypants* (Mass market edition). New York, NY: Little, Brown & Company.

Fields, D. A., Kafai, Y. B., & Searle, K. (2012). Functional aesthetics for learning: Creative tensions in youth e-textile designs. In J. van Aalst, K. Thompson, M. J. Jacobson, & P. Reimann (Eds.), *The Future of Learning: Proceedings of the 10th International Conference of the Learning Sciences (ICLS 2012)—Volume 1, Full Papers* (pp. 188–195). Sydney, NSW, Australia: International Society of the Learning Sciences.

Gaglio, C. M. (2004). The role of mental simulations and counterfactual thinking in the opportunity identification process★. *Entrepreneurship Theory and Practice, 28*(6), 533–552. doi:https://doi.org/10.1111/j.1540-6520.2004.00063.x

Guha, M. L., Druin, A., & Fails, J. A. (2010). Investigating the impact of design processes on children. In *Proceedings of the 9th International Conference on Interaction Design and Children* (pp. 198–201). Barcelona, Spain: ACM.

Hawkins, J., & Pea, R. D. (1987). Tools for bridging the cultures of everyday and scientific thinking. *Journal of Research in Science Teaching, 24*(4), 291–307.

Hmelo-Silver, C. E., & Barrows, H. S. (2006). Goals and strategies of a problem-based learning facilitator. *Interdisciplinary Journal of Problem-Based Learning, 1*(1). doi:https://doi.org/10.7771/1541-5015.1004

IMLS Project Team and Task Force. (n.d.). Museums, libraries, and 21st century skills: Education. *Institute of Museum and Library Services: Issues* (blog). Retrieved from www.imls.gov/issues/national-initiatives/museums-libraries-and-21st-century-skills/definitions

Jenkins, H. (2006). *Convergence Culture: Where Old and New Media Collide.* New York, NY: New York University Press.

Jenkins, H., Clinton, K., Purushotma, R., Robinson, A. J., & Weigel, M. (2006). *Confronting the Challenges of Participatory Culture: Media Education for the 21st Century.* Chicago, IL: MacArthur Foundation.

Johnson, M., Clapp, M. J., Ewing, S. R., & Buhler, A. G. (2011). Building a participatory culture: Collaborating with student organizations for twenty-first century library instruction. *Collaborative Librarianship, 3*(1), 2–15.

Kafai, Y. B. (1996). Learning design by making games. In Y. B. Kafai & M. Resnick (Eds.), *Constructionism in Practice: Designing, Thinking and Learning in a Digital World* (pp. 71–96). Mahwah, NJ: Erlbaum.

Kafai, Y. B., Fields, D. A., & Searle, K. (2012). Making technology visible: Connecting the learning of crafts, circuitry and coding in youth e-textile designs. In J. van Aalst, K. Thompson, M. J. Jacobson, & P. Reimann (Eds.), *The Future of Learning: Proceedings of the 10th International Conference of the Learning Sciences (ICLS 2012)—Volume 1, Full Papers* (pp. 188–195). Sydney, NSW, Australia: International Society of the Learning Sciences.

Kim, J., Lee, E., Thomas, T., & Dombrowski, C. (2009). Storytelling in new media: The case of alternate reality games, 2001–2009. *First Monday, 14*(6). Retrieved from http://firstmonday.org/ojs/index.php/fm/article/viewArticle/2484/2199

Kim, J. Y., Allen, J. P., & Lee, E. (2008). Alternate reality gaming. *Communications of the ACM, 51*(2), 36–42.

Kitty, P. (2011). Interview with Kitty.

Lave, J., & Wenger, E. (1991). *Situated Learning: Legitimate Peripheral Participation.* Cambridge, England; New York, NY: Cambridge University Press.

Livingstone, S. (2008). Taking risky opportunities in youthful content creation: Teenagers' use of social networking sites for intimacy, privacy and self-expression. *New Media & Society, 10*(3), 393–411. doi:https://doi.org/10.1177/1461444808089415

Martin, A., Thompson, B., & Chatfield, T. (2006). *Alternate Reality Games White Paper—IGDA ARG SIG.* Retrieved from www.christydena.com/wp-content/uploads/2007/11/igda-alternaterealitygames-whitepaper-2006.pdf

McGonigal, J. (2003). This is not a game: Immersive aesthetics and collective play. In *Melbourne DAC 2003 Streaming Worlds Conference Proceedings* (Vol. 1). Melbourne, Australia: RMIT University. Retrieved from http://citeseerx.ist.psu.edu/viewdoc/summary?doi:10.1.1.107.4842

McGonigal, J. (2008a). Why I love bees: A case study in collective intelligence gaming. In K. Salen (Ed.), *The Ecology of Games: Connecting Youth, Games, and Learning* (pp. 199–227). The John D. and Catherine T. MacArthur Foundation Series on Digital Media and Learning. Cambridge, MA: MIT Press.

McGonigal, J. (2008b). *Make an Alternate Reality Game!* Presented at the TeensConnect Project Meeting 2008, Slideshare, June. Retrieved from www.slideshare.net/avantgame/ make-an-alternate-reality-game

McGonigal, J. (2011). *Reality Is Broken: Why Games Make Us Better and How They Can Change the World.* New York, NY: Penguin Press.

Moje, E. B., Ciechanowski, K. M., Kramer, K., Ellis, L., Carrillo, R., & Collazo, T. (2004). Working toward third space in content area literacy: An examination of everyday funds of knowledge and discourse. *Reading Research Quarterly, 39*(1), 38–70.

Niemeyer, G., Garcia, A., & Naima, R. (2009). Black cloud: Patterns towards da future. In *Proceedings of the 17th ACM International Conference on Multimedia* (pp. 1073–1082). Beijing, China: ACM.

Owens, T. (2010). Modding the history of science: Values at play in modder discussions of Sid Meier's Civilization. *Simulation & Gaming, 42*(May), 481–495. doi:https://doi.org/10.1177/1046878110366277

Owings, H. (2010). *Initial Interview 2010 Transcription.*

(P21) Partnership for 21st Century Skills. (2009). *Framework for 21st Century Learning.* Washington, DC: (P21) Partnership for 21st Century Skills. Retrieved from www.p21.org/index.php?option=com_content&task=view&id=254&Itemid=120

Peppler, K. A., & Kafai, Y. B. (2009). Gaming fluencies: Pathways into participatory culture in a community design studio. *International Journal of Learning and Media, 1*(4), 45–58. doi:https://doi.org/10.1162/ijlm_a_00032

Rose, A. (2012). *Interview with Rosie (pseudonym).*

Salen, K., & Zimmerman, E. (2003). *This Is Not a Game: Play in Cultural Environments.* In DiGRA Conference.

Salen, K. (2007). Gaming literacies: A game design study in action. *Journal of Educational Multimedia & Hypermedia, 16*(3), 301–322.

Sandoval, W. A., & Bell, P. (2004). Design-based research methods for studying learning in context: Introduction. *Educational Psychologist, 39*(4), 199–201.

Schoenfeld, A. H. (1998). Toward a theory of teaching-in-context. *Issues in Education, 4*(1), 1–94.

Schön, D. A. (1984). The architectural studio as an exemplar of education for reflection-in-action. *Journal of Architectural Education, 38*(1), 2–9.

Shapiro, R. B., & Ossorio, P. N. (2013). Regulation of online social network studies. *Science, 339*(6116), 144–145. doi:https://doi.org/10.1126/science.1219025

Squire, K. (2011). *Video Games and Learning: Teaching and Participatory Culture in the Digital Age.* New York, NY: Teachers College Press.

Szulborski, D. (2005). *This Is Not a Game: A Guide to Alternate Reality Gaming.* Macungie, PA: New-Fiction Publications.

Vieau, J. (2009, February 24). 28 days of advocacy #24—Radical trust: Academic. *YALSABLOG: Official Home of the Young Adult Library Services Association Blog and Journal* (blog). Retrieved from http://yalsa.ala.org/blog/2009/02/24/28-days-of-advocacy-24-radical-trust/

Whitton, N. (2008). Alternate reality games for developing student autonomy and peer learning. In *Proceedings of Learners in the Co-Creation of Knowledge (LICK) 2008* (pp. 32–40). Edinburgh, Scotland: Edinburgh Napier University. Retrieved from http://lick2008.wikispaces.com/file/view/Strand+1+-+Nicola+Whitton+-+V1+Paper.pdf

6

IMPROVING DIGITAL EXPERIENCE THROUGH MODELING THE HUMAN EXPERIENCE

The Resurgence of Virtual (and Augmented and Mixed) Reality[1]

Diana Hellyar,[2] Renee Walsh, and Micah Altman

Virtual Reality—a Broad View

We interact with digital information constantly. The aim of virtual reality (VR) is to improve the digital experience and enable people to interact with information in ways that they perceive as real. More precisely, "virtual reality," in its broad sense, denotes a set of computer–human interface methods, related technologies, and environments created by these methods that render information in the form of simulated objects, presenting these objects to the user through sensory stimuli, and offer physical modes of interaction (Blade, Padgett, Billinghurst, & Lindeman, 2014; Bailenson et al., 2008). This definition is intentionally broad and encompasses not only binocular three-dimensional visualization methods (such as those provided by VR headsets) but also "augmented reality" such as the Microsoft Hololens, "mixed reality," "virtual environments," and even realistic video games.

In the last year, building on decades of research and experimentation, effective tools that support VR have become widely available and affordable. For example, low-cost hardware offers surprisingly rich stereoscopic information visualization, head and body tracking, and environmental sensing and imaging. Further, the current generation of the now ubiquitous smartphone offers some form of all of these. Whether they recognize it or not, people all over the world are increasingly encountering the methods of VR in games, at work, and in "third places" such as libraries and museums.

This new generation of tools shows substantial promise. With thoughtful design and implementation, VR tools and methods can be used to enhance how people interact with computers, with information, and with each other. VR methods can be used to make interactions easier, richer, more immersive, and more realistic—and ultimately increase the engagement, efficiency, and satisfaction of these interactions.

This chapter is designed generally to introduce information professionals and researchers to the topic of VR, to characterize its potential to enhance human experiences, and to identify the concepts that are critical to its application. The chapter is also intended specifically for professional librarians and applied library information science researchers who aim to integrate new interface technologies and design concepts into library systems.

As authors, we are embedded in the research and practice of libraries. We have sought out both the literatures of interactions in virtual reality and the emerging technology of its implementation. This is new territory for libraries. So while we conjecture that the new affordances that VR and related technologies supply have substantial potential for libraries, the pathways are necessarily speculative.

Pokémon Are (Literally) Everywhere! The Spread of Augmented Reality

Pokémon GO was released by Niantic Labs in July 2016. Users downloaded this game to their mobile devices and attempted to find, catch, and train Pokémon. The first Pokémon game was originally released in 1996 for the Game Boy. Since then, the Pokémon franchise released more electronic games, card games, and even an anime series. *Pokémon GO* revolved around the same concept as the rest of the franchise, to find, catch, and train Pokémon to become the best Pokémon trainer. The difference in *Pokémon GO* is that the game utilizes a player's GPS systems on their phone to find Pokémon in the real world. These Pokémon could be found in parks, stores, libraries, and other public places around the world. Instead of staying in one place, the game forced players to walk around their neighborhoods to find new Pokémon to capture. When a player comes across a Pokémon, they can see an image of the monster in front of them through their phones (Thier, 2016).

Libraries embraced the *Pokémon GO* phenomenon. Many libraries created Pokémon-related programs and displays. Some libraries even became pokéstops. Pokéstops are landmarks that users must visit to collect objects in order to continue with the game. They allow users to interact with each other and the pokéstop itself. The New York Public Library wrote a blog explaining the game and showing where to find Pokémon around the library. The Skokie Public Library in Skokie, Illinois, created *Pokémon GO* Safaris for K–5 patrons (Spina, 2016).

Pokémon GO utilizes a form of VR called augmented reality. Augmented reality combines the real world with virtual objects (van Krevelen & Poelman, 2010). There are many ways to experience augmented reality. With recent technology advancements, mobile devices are one of the easiest ways to utilize augmented reality technology. In *Pokémon GO*, for example, the Pokémon will only appear in the player's environment if they are looking at it through their phones or other devices. Augmented reality allows users to interact with their real-world environment in new ways.

Design Principles for Applying VR

Enhance Emotional Experiences

Libraries act as places that inspire the people who visit them in addition to providing information. Often inspiration can be provided by innovative architecture that encourages exploration, thinking, and collaboration. In a similar way, carefully designed use of VR can support richer and more positive emotional experiences. These positive emotional experiences can in turn enhance learning (Tyng et al., 2017).

For an example of how VR can heighten emotion, consider the work *Man on Spire* from the *New York Times* VR (Chin, Solomon, Pirog, & Walsh, 2016). Even experienced on a smartphone, using an inexpensive viewer, such as Google Cardboard, this work can induce awe. The four minute and thirty four second video depicts Jimmy Chin, a professional mountaineer and filmmaker, as he climbs to the top of the spire atop the newly built One World Trade Center in New York City. The title of the video makes reference to the 2008 documentary *Man on Wire*, about Philippe Petit's 1974 high-wire walk between the twin towers of the former World Trade Center. We see Chin climb the needle-like spire of the new World Trade Center along with Jameson Walsh, the person certified to conduct the annual inspection of the site. Chin refers to the skyscrapers of New York as the mountains of the city, with the World Trade Center as the tallest mountain. Upon reaching a platform at the top of the building, we see Chin slowly ascend the ladder-like tower that reaches another 408 feet into the sky. Entering the last portion of the spire, Chin clips the carabiner from his harness to the ladder and leans out to take pictures of the skyline. We look out, up, and down with him.

Looking down at the buildings and the water below induces awe—and perhaps a little anxiety. Chin comments,

> It's a very intense feeling to be up there. There you are on the top of this needle above eight million, ten million people. You get that very visceral experience of feeling insignificant. It was really just beautiful and almost lonely. I think that is what makes it special.
>
> *(Chin et al., 2016)*

Although these emotions are cognitive phenomena, they are often triggered, in part, by specific sensory experiences and visual designs. These technologies offer new opportunities to incorporate richer sensory experiences into how patrons and visitors interact with digital material and data and use these to generate positive emotional experiences.

VR affordances are often employed with the goal of inducing a sense of presence. Informally, presence is the feeling that one is really within a virtual environment and interacting with it. Presence is often promoted by increasing immersion, or sensory fidelity, of the experience. Immersion is most often enhanced through visual elements, such as field of view, display resolution, stereoscopy, graphics rendering (image synthesis) features (e.g., shading, lighting, texture, reflection, depth of field), and head-based rendering (Bowman & McMahan, 2007; Cummings & Bailenson, 2016). Immersion can also be increased through elements of the virtual auditory interface including spatial auditory displays, cross-mode interactions, and selective auditory attention (Vorlander & Shinn-Cunningham, 2014).

More formally, presence might be broadly conceived as part of a holistic experience that integrates sensory, cognitive, affective, active (personal), and relational (social) interaction together in order to increase the sense that a person is really in a particular place, the accuracy of the experience, and its memorability (Chertoff & Schatz, 2014).

Nor is presence the only emotion that VR promotes. For example, VR is commonly employed in games with the aim of enhancing enjoyment. Although pleasure and enjoyment are often underrated in information system design, there is evidence to suggest that pleasure can be supported as an integral part of information seeking (see Dork et al., 2011 for a review, and for examples, Cauchard et al., 2006). This may, in turn, promote higher engagement, flow, and more effective learning.

Thoughtful use of VR affordances can enhance not only interactions with systems but with other people. Recent research suggests that VR may be useful to promote empathy and support prosocial behavior. Some approaches to enhancing empathy and prosocial behavior include enhancing social signals through capturing facial expressions and other behaviors (see Bailenson et al., 2008), simulating the perspective of others (Oh et al., 2016), providing interaction methods that prime behaviors (see Rosenbuerg et al., 2013), in which participants were given "superpowers."

There are even suggestions that VR may, through the induction of perceptions such as "vastness," be able to promote profound emotional experiences such as awe (Rauhoeft et al., 2015). Although for thousands of years, many civilizations have recognized awe as an unexpected and overwhelming emotion that is tied to epiphanic experience, it is only recently that researchers have begun to study the emotion systematically. According to Dachner Keltner and J. Haidt, awe is defined "as the emotion that arises when one encounters something so strikingly vast that it provokes a need to update one's mental schemas" (2003). Various studies on awe show that the emotion corresponds with feelings of well-being, engagement, and benevolence (Rudd et al., 2012) as well as increasing subjects willingness to "modify mental structures" (Shiota, Keltner, & Mossman, 2007; Silvia et al., 2015) and change attitudes.

Awe is induced by two cognitive properties: vastness and accommodation. Vastness, or so-called perceived vastness, can literally mean the impression of a vast or large space such as a galaxy of stars or a city skyline. Vastness can also be interpreted on a metaphorical level where it "describes any stimulus that challenges one's accustomed frame of reference in some dimension" (Shiota et al., 2007).

This is to say that a speech by an exceptional orator could be perceived as vast, as could a mind-altering or innovative novel.

In response to a vast event that is beyond one's usual frame of reference, the brain must accommodate or shift in order to assimilate this new experience into their worldview. Accommodation is the name of this reaction that occurs in the reaction to an awe-inducing event. Accommodation is both "an inability to assimilate an experience into current mental structures" as well as the "willingness to modify mental structures" in order to integrate the new experience into an evolved worldview (Keltner & Haidt, 2003; Shiota et al., 2007).

Psychological research on creativity shows that experiencing events or imagery that is "outside of habitual thought patterns can lead to enhanced cognitive flexibility and creativity" (Kaufman & Gregoire, 2015, p. 93). In their 2012 article, scientists from UC Davis and Radboud University Nijmegen hypothesized that students who experienced an "unusual or unexpected experience" would demonstrate greater "flexible and creative thinking." To test this process, students watched events in VR that violated the laws of physics. For example, a bottle knocked over from a table started to float or levitate in the air instead of falling to the ground. After viewing this imagery, students were asked to answer the question "What is sound?" by generating as many answers as possible. The scientists found that "actively (but not vicariously) experiencing unusual and unexpected events enhances people's cognitive flexibility" (Ritter et al., 2012). Simone M. Ritter defines cognitive flexibility as, "the ability to break old cognitive patterns . . . and thus, make novel (creative) associations between concepts" (2012). Therefore, it is possible that brainstorming techniques or exploration in VR, which alters patrons' self-schema, can promote greater creativity as well as innovation in the research and learning process.

In 2016, David B. Yaden and Jonathan Iwry and several other scientists completed a study on the so-called overview effect, which is the term created by Frank White for the epiphanic, euphoric, and self-transcendent feeling astronauts experience when seeing the earth from space. In writing about the overview effect, Yaden et al. note that the experience corresponds with "changes to the observer's 'self-schema'—the particular framework through which they imagine themselves in relation to the world" (Yaden et al., 2016). As a next step, Yaden would like to try to replicate the overview effect through VR technology as a way to "foster that feeling of connectedness" that is generated by an awe-inspiring overview effect (Rosenfeld, 2016).

Imagine being able to pick up rare illuminated manuscripts or to wander the ancient libraries and cities in which they were stored. Imagine being able to command a library of hundreds of millions of books to reorganize itself, enticing you to wander serendipitously. VR has the potential to enable this and more. Further, as physical places, libraries have long functioned as treasured "third spaces"— places with both intellectual and emotional resonance. VR provides an opportunity to extend this resonance into the digital domain.

In sum, VR enables one to create experiences that are emotional as well as informative. By thoughtfully designing the sensory affordance in VR to enhance the intellectual and psychological interactions, one can create a substantial impact.

Designing Interfaces to Enhance Engagement

One of the most prevalent functions of VR technology is the ability to feel "present" in a different environment through sensory immersion. These immersive experiences increase user engagement in these environments. There are three different types of engagement: behavioral, emotional, and cognitive. Behavioral engagement focuses on participation. Emotional engagement includes positive and negative reactions to those around oneself and willingness to do the work. Cognitive engagement incorporates thoughtfulness and willingness to put forth the necessary effort to understand complex ideas. While there are distinctions between the three types of engagement, they come together to form a single multidimensional process (Fredricks, Blumenfeld, & Paris, 2004).

One example of a virtual environment that enhanced engagement was *Second Life*. *Second Life* was a three-dimensional, desktop based virtual world created in 2003 by Linden Labs. It allowed users to create avatars and interact with other users in a virtual environment. Avatars could imitate the real world by purchasing clothes, constructing buildings, and meeting new people. *Second Life* offered people with a space in which they could collaborate together in the virtual world (Inman, Wright, & Hartman, 2010).

Universities explored *Second Life*'s potential to create virtual immersive learning environments for students. The School of Library and Information Science at San José State University created a 16-acre virtual campus modeled after their physical campus. The faculty at San José State University were encouraged to move their classes to their new virtual campus on *Second Life*. Some professors embraced the idea of hosting classes on *Second Life*. Faculty found that there was less geographic or physical constraint by hosting classes through *Second Life* which allowed for freedom to create experiences that were difficult to achieve in real life. For example, one professor created simulations so students could practice skills such as interviewing (Luo & Kemp, 2008). Creating these virtual immersive learning environments on *Second Life* helped achieve an enhanced learning environment and increase the engagement of online students who may be missing the experience of in-person classes.

Designing Systems to Support Collaboration

Virtual worlds like *Second Life* allowed for people all over the world to collaborate and create a shared task space in a virtual environment. For example, virtual conferences created a new way for avatars to come together in the virtual world. Creating a shared task space in VR gives people the ability to meet and collaborate in a virtual environment without the limitations of a physical space.

Virtually collaborative environments could emulate face-to-face collaboration. Allowing for a shared task space and shared manipulation gives users the opportunity to collaborate together in the same environment and to create with each other. Web-based word processors such as Google Docs allow for this type of collaboration. In Google Docs, users can add content to a shared document and see each other's edits in real time without needing to download it to a computer (Karpova, Correia, & Baran, 2009). Collaboration in VR could take this a step further and incorporate more elements of face-to-face interactions. Other ways that collaboration can be enhanced are by allowing users to see where someone else is looking or by being able to view, manipulate, and annotate a physical object in a virtual space.

Mixed reality, a subclass of VR, provides a different way for people to collaborate virtually. Mixed reality is a form of VR that mixes real and virtual worlds within the same experience (Milgram & Kishino, 1994). Carnegie Mellon University and Microsoft teamed together to work on a method to utilize mixed reality without requiring every participant to have a mixed-reality device such as Microsoft's Hololens. They envisioned a method utilizing Skype in which a single user would have a head-mounted display to allow others to see and annotate the primary user's space (Lee, Swift, Tang, & Chen, 2015).

The article gave the example of a student participating in an exploration of a cave. In this example, the professor could not accompany the student. The student could use a Hololens device while the professor uses Skype from their office to see exactly what the student is seeing. The professor could annotate the student's environment, and the student would be able to see the professor's annotations in real time (Lee et al., 2015). While the consumer version of the Hololens has yet to be released, this method could have a great impact on virtual collaboration in education and other fields alike. For instance, libraries often provide meeting spaces for their patrons. Both public and academic communities could greatly benefit from exploring the idea of virtual meeting spaces. It would be a natural fit for libraries to try out these options and provide a space for virtual collaboration.

Support Physically Richer Modes of Interacting With Systems/Content

Creating a realistic environment goes beyond the visual aspects of a virtual world. It is also important to consider how the user interacts with the environment. Realistic modes of interacting with the virtual world can help users feel immersed in the environment. VR can support richer modes of interacting with an environment by creating methods that are similar to how users interact with the real world. Gaze tracking follows where a user focuses their attention. Body motions can be tracked, allowing for a user to walk around in the virtual world while physically walking in the real world. Hand tracking would allow users to interact with the world in a realistic way instead of using a game controller. These movement tracking methods enhance the VR experience by creating a deeper level of immersion for the user (Lee et al., 2015). These methods allow users to interact with a virtual environment in previously unknown ways.

Hand tracking systems in VR help to create a life-like environment for those using VR technologies. These systems allow users to use hand gestures to interact with objects or manipulate the virtual environment. There are various proposed methods for tracking hand gestures. Many hand tracking systems require some device on the hand itself to track motions due to the difficulty of tracking the bare hand. The bare hand is hard to track by itself since it is a highly articulated flexible object (Pan et al., 2010). One proposed method that tracked the bare hand used a multicue hand tracking algorithm based on velocity weighted features and color cues in the hand (Pan et al., 2010).

Other methods track the hand by using devices on the hand. Wang and Popović (2009) utilizes a multicolored glove and a single camera to track the motions. They demonstrated the applications of this method in three ways. They demonstrated the ability to control a character's walking motions, interact with building blocks to create a virtual 3D structure, and recognize the American Sign Language alphabet to create a fingerspelling application (Wang & Popović, 2009). Frati and Prattichizzo (2011) proposed a method using Microsoft Kinect and sensors on the fingers to track a user's hand motions. They presented an algorithm to allow for the animation of the hand in the virtual environment (Frati & Prattichizzo, 2011). While there are various methods for hand tracking systems, these examples show the variation in achieving accurate hand tracking.

There are many possible benefits to creating realistic forms of interaction. Instead of the users holding a game system controller, these realistic interactions with the virtual world allow for further immersion in their environment. However, there are benefits beyond creating these immersive experiences. These forms of interacting are also helpful for medical purposes by allowing patients to use realistic hand movements while playing a game.

In one study, a leap motion controller was utilized to aid elderly patients affected with subacute stroke (Iosa et al., 2015). A leap motion controller captures the motions of the hands to control a virtual environment while playing video games designed to help improve the patient's hand functions. Four elderly patients participated in the study and their hand ability and grasp force were measured. At the end of the study, patients showed significantly improved hand ability and grasp force.

The sample size for this study is small due to the fact it served to provide a proof of concept that a leap motion controller can be suitable for elderly patients with subacute stroke. Despite the sample size, this study does show how hand tracking, such as with the leap motion controller, can be utilized to simulate real-life hand motions and allow users to interact with these systems in realistic ways.

Incorporate Elements of User Environment/Content

Augmented reality, a form of mixed reality, allows for digital elements to be incorporated into the real world. Augmented reality was first prototyped in the 1960s by a computer graphics professor, Ivan Sutherland, and his students at Harvard University and the University of Utah. In the 1970s and 1980s, research continued with a small group of people from the U.S. Air Force's Armstrong Laboratory, the NASA Ames Research Center, the Massachusetts Institute of Technology, and the University of North Carolina at Chapel Hill. Augmented reality was a distinct field of research by the late 1990s after several conferences began presenting on the topic (van Krevelen & Poelman, 2010).

Augmented reality aids users in incorporating elements into the user's environment. *Pokémon GO*, as mentioned earlier, helped the general public understand how augmented reality could be used to create this concept. However, *Pokémon GO* is not the only way augmented reality can be used to enhance the user's environment.

Libraries could help patrons receive book reviews by creating a book display of augmented reality–enabled covers accessible through an app on their phones (Goerner, 2016). Posters hung around a classroom or library can trigger videos and come to life when viewed through a tablet or mobile device (Baird, 2016).

There are many key components needed to create an augmented-reality system. Essential components including displays, sensors, and tracking user position and orientation are necessary to combine the virtual world with the real world. Also, graphic computers and software technologies are key components to allow for real-time, 3D interactions (van Krevelen & Poelman, 2010).

Augmented reality creates dynamic modes of learning. One study examined how augmented reality affects students' understanding of a difficult concept in a science museum (Yoon, Anderson, Lin, & Elinich, 2017). They found that the use of augmented reality improved the students' understanding of the concept because they were able to learn it in a new way. A study by Estapa and Nadolny (2015) found that students using augmented reality to learn math concepts demonstrated higher motivation than the other students. Augmented reality can create new ways for students to understand concepts and be motivated to learn.

Developing a Strategy to Enhance Digital Interactions With (and Within) Libraries

Targeting Library Interactions and Audiences

For librarians, this discussion may raise questions about how the affordances of these new technologies may be applied in libraries—for example to increase inclusion and access: Could VR be used to increase engagement and attention by using immersion to convey a sense of place of being in an historic archive? Could we reduce the barriers to those seeking library instruction and reference by using avatars to enhance social communication? Could we enhance discovery and interaction with library collections by using physical interaction to make navigation of information spaces seamless?

The conceptual diagram below (Figure 6.1) illustrates the conceptual connections between areas of library services; the enhancements to interaction that VR can possibly provide; the interaction features that promote those enhancements; and the current technologies that support these features.

Vertically, the diagram is organized from high-level features to lower-level features. The arrows between illustrate how features at one level promote features at a higher level. The top of the diagram shows the four overarching contexts within the libraries that which patrons interact with information. These interactions may be potentially enhanced through designing the interaction experience to promote high-level cognitive or emotional experience. In turn, these experiences are promoted through specific high-level interaction characteristics, which are provided by input and display technologies.

VR may potentially be used to enhance any of the major areas in which patrons interact with libraries and collections: discovery, access, reference, and

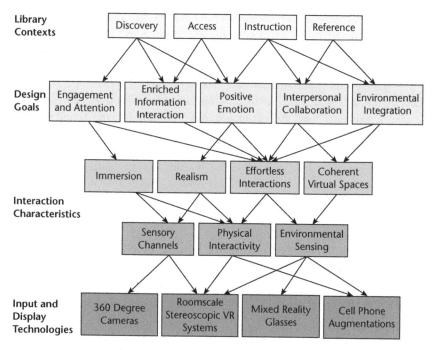

FIGURE 6.1 Links between library contexts, design goals, interaction characteristics, and input/display technologies

instruction. VR technologies can enhance interactions with information and with other people in a variety of ways through enhancing emotional experiences such as presence, curiosity, pleasure, empathy, and awe; enhancing engagement through forms of immersion; supporting collaboration by reducing barriers to communication and by providing shared task spaces; providing richer modes of interacting with information; and by incorporating elements of the user's environment in the experience.

However, VR experiences must be carefully designed—as the various VR affordances (and supporting technologies) target different parts of the interaction experience. Each area of library services may use VR in different ways—in pursuit of different interaction goals. When libraries move to pilot a VR experience, they should carefully consider how the target audience and interaction might benefit from selected enhancements, which areas of enhancement to target, and thus which VR features to support.

For example, library discovery may benefit from the use of VR to improve engagement, offer richer information interaction, and induce emotional experiences such as "flow"—whereas library instruction may benefit more from VR's potential to facilitate more seamless interpersonal interaction and to incorporate elements of the user's environment into the interaction. As a library prepares to engage with VR, it should carefully consider which area of interactions it is targeting, what current or additional audiences it intends to reach, and how these audiences can be better served.

Once a target audience, area of interaction, and enhancement goal has been selected, one should target the features of VR that are most closely associated with that enhancement goal. For example, sense of presence is strongly enhanced by the ability to direct the direction of gaze (e.g., through 360-degree video), by binocular video, and by head tracking, while collaboration is more strongly promoted by shared task spaces and facial tracking. Select specific technologies only once the most important interface features have been identified.

Exploring Strategies: Four Ways of Looking at Medieval Manuscripts

When a library has a particular need for its collection, one that is difficult to solve with staffing, current collections technology, or funding, one place to turn may be VR. VR can allow access to certain library materials and spaces without the constraints of time, space, staffing, and perhaps most importantly, physical availability of the collections or item in question. VR may also help libraries raise the profile of certain collections and make them available to the entire internet-enabled world.

While VR technology at the level of an HTC Vive or similar device is not yet entirely common, YouTube is available on every internet-connected device. 360-degree videos are supported by YouTube and can be used on desktops or mobile devices. The 360-degree videos can also be watched via VR devices and are relatively inexpensive to create and produce. For example, if one wanted to give patrons a more immersive experience, they could create a 360-degree video tour of a special collection. This will allow patrons to feel immersed in the environment. The University of Adelaide Libraries in Australia created a VR project to explore two key forms of VR. They used the GoPro 360 Heros rig to shoot three short videos around and outside of the library (Weatherall, Miller, & Thomas, n.d.).

VR experiences such as these may allow for remote browsing, cut down on wear and tear on specific items, and make the collections available to a wider audience. The library may want to allow for anyone to view, for instance, their manuscripts as well as allow patrons to interact with the manuscripts by being able to add comments or tags to the images or take screenshots. Items may be available for online browsing, and patrons may be able to get a better feel of a rare or fragile item by allowing the entire item to be scanned and manipulated in VR.

These immersive experiences may also allow patrons the magic of serendipity. It may make finding different or unknown items easier and assist with better searching and suggestions based on previous searches. This type of experience should also, ideally, allow patrons to take screenshots or download the entire text and provide an easy way for patrons to access and ask questions about the material. They can create digitized books of manuscripts like an ebook. A VR tour can achieve these goals by having all the texts live on a virtual bookshelf. It can be hosted on the library's own website via a virtual reference desk interface.

If patrons want to use a manuscript in the special collections room for heavy research, a program could be created for use on a desktop computer with high resolution. The library could put aside one or two computers that contain the program. This would allow patrons to write notes in their own notebooks, and people could potentially work together if they wanted to look at the same thing. However, this experience is not immersive. If patrons want to use this option for educational purposes or just to explore, the institution could create a program that is supported on a high-end VR device such as Oculus Rift to create an immersive experience. If both seem like good options, then both could be created so patrons can use whichever method is best for them. One example of this is a social platform called AltspaceVR. This platform allows users to interact with each other in an immersive environment. While AltspaceVR is intended for use with VR devices, users can also access it on mobile devices or computers ("AltspaceVR," 2017).

The library may want to enhance the experience of browsing the physical collection. Patrons could see comments, annotations, and tags on physical items created by other patrons as well as add in their own. Patrons can use their own mobile devices for this purpose. The library can utilize an app that will allow patrons to do this by hovering over a book cover or a certain page, and the other comments or annotations will appear. This app will also assist patrons in their search for items or topics within a collection. They could search for a topic on their phone or tablet and then find an item and select it. They could hold their mobile device up to the shelves or the room and it will show on the screen where their item is located and, possibly, where other similar items are. Such an app could help orient patrons around special collections as well. Such a patron-oriented app could also function as a map. Patrons could hold their mobile device up at eye level and look at the screen, and subject areas will be highlighted. This could help patrons discover the materials around them and enhance the magic of serendipity.

The library could create an app that uses augmented reality to achieve these goals. For example, media experience designer Pradeep Siddappa created an app called LibrARi that allows patrons to locate books on the shelf by utilizing augmented reality. The app is designed to enhance information discovery and make it easier for patrons to find books (Siddappa, 2014).

These are just a few examples of how a library could enhance various interactions utilizing VR. There are many more ways that VR could help solve a need in the library. Critically evaluating the needs of the library can help one to decide how VR can be used to enhance patron experiences.

Negative Design Considerations

VR technology imposes costs for equipment, development, and maintenance and can impose burdens on ease of use. For example, the need to use expensive, bulky VR equipment might well be justified in the experience of exploring a volcano—but it would be counterproductive if used to reproduce the experience of sitting in an ordinary classroom. To avoid being seduced by novel features or becoming lost in technical choices, it is useful to consider past design misuses (also known as "antipatterns").

Avoid Technology Demos

VR is a new technology, and many applications of VR function more as demonstrations of the technology than as well-designed solutions to particular interface problems. While some of these demos may be initially attractive, they will not sustain user engagement unless they serve a purpose and provide a benefit. To avoid being entranced by technology experience identify the specific audience you intend to target, the specific ways in which you expect VR technologies to enhance the user-interface experience, and estimate the extent to which costs and barriers to use are justified by potential gains.

Avoid Creating New Barriers to Interaction

The aim of VR is to make interactions richer and easier. However, naïve application of new technologies can often have the reverse effects. Cutting-edge VR technologies are often expensive—thus requiring the use of these technologies for interaction with a system may create economic barriers to use. Further, even when equipment is supplied or widely available, bulky VR equipment may limit some interactions while enabling others: cords restrict movement, goggles obscure vision (and may prevent interaction with people in the same space), and specialized controls may interfere with use of keyboards.

Moreover, use of VR may create new cognitive barriers to interaction—resulting in a "steep learning curve" (see, for example, Luo & Kemp, 2008). While it may be natural for a user to perform direct physical manipulation of a physical model of information within a virtual environment, interacting with VR equipment and within virtual environments is not yet standardized. Thus VR environments may not support affordances (such as zooming in on an image) that users have come to expect or may find the mechanism for nonphysical UI interactions, such as displaying a menu, puzzling or nonintuitive. Further, even experiences based on physical manipulation may be more tiring or induce motion sickness in a virtual environment (Fox et al., 2009). Finally, although the new affordances offered by VR offer the potential to create new interfaces that are more accessible to neurodivergent and disabled users, many current VR systems are not developed with accessibility in mind.

Avoid Indiscriminate Realism

Reality is sometimes boring, unpleasant, or even dangerous. Thus when creating a virtual environment, it is important to consider both which aspects of reality one should and should not reproduce. For example, some early approaches by universities (and even libraries) to developing a presence in *Second Life* were to essentially duplicate the institutions physical environment—a campus, building, or lecture hall (for a partial review, see Jennings & Collins, 2007) Although this approach may be useful for an architectural walkthrough—for most students a better approach (such as that taken by San Jose State University, discussed earlier) would be to have the virtual environment not duplicate the classroom experience but take an opportunity to provide a more authentic experience of the object of study.

Launching VR in Libraries

Planning for VR Implementation

There are many components to consider when thinking about implementing VR in libraries or other settings. A fully developed plan will be helpful to make decisions for the entire process. First, deciding what type of experience the users of the VR pilot will participate in will inform the rest of the process. It is first important to decide on a set goal or outcome for the VR experience. There are other questions to ask at this point to help guide this decision. These questions may include: What interaction elements are most influential in achieving the goal? What experience will be improved, for whom, and in what way? There are many other aspects to consider at this point as well. Deciding on a set budget is critical before getting too far in the process. It will help inform many other aspects of implementing a VR experience. Other considerations at this point should include timeline, space available in the library, and staffing.

Another important component of this process is to decide how the pilot will be developed. There may be programs already produced that can be used for a VR pilot. This would be one of the simplest methods of implementation. It would not require much development, and the production cost could be lower. However, it may be harder to have a personalized experience. If the pilot needs to be produced from scratch, then there will be more questions to answer. Some questions to be considered could include: Who will develop the program? Will someone need to be hired to develop it? What would be the added cost? Does that fit in with the budget allotted for the pilot? Answering all of these questions is critical before making decisions on VR devices.

The final stage of planning would be to consider what technologies are affordable and feasible for the pilot being planned. There are many different VR devices that vary in cost and functionality. Carefully considering which device would be appropriate for the pilot will be critical for success. Designing an assessment plan would also be a consideration at this stage. Having some quantifying information that can be reported could be critical for the further implementation of a VR pilot.

Even at the pilot stage, one should consider how the new technology will integrate with existing library systems. Although some technologies, such as 360-degree videos, are relatively standardized and interoperate with a range of hardware and software, standards in other areas, such as body tracking, are still evolving. Thus, VR hardware and software may be tied to particular hardware and software platforms.

Finally, consider if there are any safety considerations before implementation. VR hardware is often accompanied by a long list of cautions—however, most risks are minor. For example, some lower- to medium-end devices are not ideal for long sessions, as they induce motion sickness: users can start to feel a bit sick after long stretches with the device (Grush, 2016). Other common potential safety considerations include obscured vision from wearing goggles and collisions and falls when a person is physically moving their body in space—especially if cords and goggles are involved. Finally, a potentially serious risk for those who have photosensitive epilepsy (which may be undiagnosed) is that full field-of-view visualizations could trigger seizures. Considering these concerns before implementation would not only inform decisions but allow you to plan ahead for when patrons begin use the devices.

Options for a VR Pilot

There are many different options to pilot a VR experience at a library or other institution. These options could range from being relatively inexpensive and easy to put together all the way to options that are costly and would be more complicated to produce. However, starting off with a smaller, less costly pilot could be helpful to introduce VR into a library to assess interest and future success.

An augmented-reality pilot could be achieved with very low cost, but it could take some time to produce. There are many programs and apps, including free programs, on the internet that allow users to create their own augmented reality experience. For example, one app called Aurasma allowed teacher Maria Baird to create an easy way for documents to be read aloud to students through their tablets. She even found a way to allow students to create their own experiences using the program (Baird, 2016). This option could be free to pilot if there are already smartphones or tablets available to use once the product is completed.

Another option for a VR pilot is to create 360-degree videos. Creating these videos could potentially have a low production cost. One of the benefits to creating 360-degree videos is that while users should use a VR headset to get the full experience, they can also view the video on a mobile device or computer. The 360-degree videos are used for a wide range of purposes. For example, colleges and universities use these videos to provide tours of the campus. It provides students with the opportunity to get a chance to look around campus and to get a feel of what it would be like to be there (Joly, 2016). Creating a 360-degree video would require the purchase of a special camera that supports 360-degree video recording. These cameras can cost around $200. These videos can be viewed with low-end VR devices such as Google Cardboard.

These two pilots are examples of smaller-scale projects that could help introduce VR into a library setting. After a pilot is implemented, it is important to assess the program to see if a larger-scale project could be successful. Some questions to ask could include: What could be learned from the pilot? How might it be improved for the future? What would a successful, larger-scale project for the library look like? What new experiences would the users want to explore in a new project? Asking these questions could help improve the smaller pilot and inform the design of the larger project.

Scaling Out a VR Pilot

Once a successful pilot has been implemented, libraries may be interested in scaling out the VR experience to a larger project. This project would most likely have a specific goal in mind based on a specific need of the library. The same questions that were asked before implementing a pilot should be asked when looking to scale out. However, there may be some new aspects to consider. It would be important to decide how a VR project would help this need. Once a specific goal is in mind, the next step would be to decide on specific design elements that will be highlighted in the program. For example, is creating an immersive environment important to the goal of the project?

It is also important to understand what types of VR devices are on the market and which ones would be best to achieve the goal of the project. There are varying levels of VR devices. These devices cover a wide range in cost. Devices such as Google Cardboard are among the least expensive. People can even build their own headset by using plans and designs available for free on the Google Cardboard website (Moorefield-Lang, 2015). These devices are compatible with most mobile devices (Powell et al., 2016). In the middle, there are devices such as the Gear VR and Google Daydream. Similar to Google Cardboard, these devices require the use of mobile devices to create the VR experience. However, unlike Google Cardboard, there are only a few mobile devices that are compatible with the Gear VR or Google Daydream. The highest level of VR includes devices such as the Oculus Rift and HTC Vive. Both of these devices require the equipment to be connected to a high-powered computer. Connecting the device to a computer instead of a smartphone allows for higher quality images (Swider, 2017).

Each of these devices can be useful for various tasks that can be accomplished with VR. Every device allows for head tracking, which gives the users the ability to look around the virtual environment in 360-degree views. For Google Cardboard, one of the main functions of these devices is viewing 360-degree videos and photos. These videos allow for semi-immersive experiences since most of these videos either do not allow users to move around or put them on a fixed path (Powell et al., 2016). Higher-end devices such as Oculus Rift or HTC Vive would be better for creating physically richer modes of interacting with the environment. These devices can support various technologies to allow for this functionality. For example, hand tracking systems would be able to be incorporated in higher-end devices and provide users with a more immersive VR experience (Lee et al., 2015). Lower-end devices may not be able to support these added systems.

After looking into various devices, limitations, and challenges, safety issues should be considered. Each device may have its own sets of limitations that would be important to know before purchasing and implementing the technology. For example, it is difficult to provide interactivity with the Google Cardboard. Some of these devices have a button built in, allowing the user to click, but the interactivity is limited (Powell et al., 2016). Also, heavy use of the phone inside a device such as Google Cardboard, Gear VR, or Google Daydream can cause the phone to potentially overheat (Grush, 2016).

Devices and programs may also have system integration considerations. For example, with high-end devices such as Oculus Rift and HTC Vive, the user must have a high-powered computer in order to run VR programs. The devices require a high amount of processing power to run without any issues (Eadiciccio, 2016). Some computer companies sell computers that are ready to run these devices;

however, they are relatively expensive. Standard desktop computers will not be able to support these devices.

Considering all of these elements when wanting to scale out will help the success of the VR project, and careful consideration before any equipment is purchased will allow for easy implementation and may help you to have fewer issues later. Thinking about how this project will fit into the library and how it will fulfill a need in the library will not only allow users to have an interesting VR experience but also to create a meaningful experience for the community.

Summary

VR is a collection of different tools and methods for enhancing interactions with digital systems and content. Although VR technologies have existed for decades, they are now improved and readily available to libraries. VR could improve browsing, access, reference, and instruction. To do this requires careful design to incorporate the key mechanisms and principles of VR such as creating immersive experiences to enhance engagement in virtual environments, enhancing the ability to collaborate virtually, to emulate face-to-face collaboration, enhance emotional communication, supporting physically richer modes of interacting with the environment, and incorporating virtual objects in the user's environment. Each of these design principles, whether taken separately or combined, can create a VR experience for a wide range of users.

VR may potentially be used to enhance any of the major areas in which patrons interact with libraries and collections: discovery, access, reference, and instruction. As a library prepares to engage with VR, it should carefully consider which area of interactions it is targeting, what current or additional audiences it intends to reach, and how these audiences can be better served. VR technologies can enhance interactions with information and with other people in a variety of ways. Thus, when libraries move to pilot a VR experience, they should carefully consider how the target audience and interaction might benefit from selected enhancements, which areas of enhancement to target, and thus which VR features to support. Select specific technologies only once the most important interface features have been identified.

There are many key questions to ask when thinking about implementing VR in a library. These considerations include deciding on specific goals or a set outcome for the VR experience. Other considerations include target audience, budget, timeline, space available, and staffing. Another important aspect is to look into who would be developing the program and what added production costs might be. All of these components should be planned out and carefully considered before deciding on devices or equipment. These questions will help inform what would be appropriate for the desired outcome.

Starting off with a smaller pilot project is helpful for learning about the technology and how it will be received by users before implementing a larger-scale project. Once you have decided to scale out to a larger VR project, there are more aspects to consider. It is important to have a specific goal in mind and think about the design elements that should be focused on in the project. Once these decisions are made, then it is important to look at the types of devices that are currently on the market and which ones would be appropriate for the project. Each of these devices can accomplish different goals. Some design elements that may be featured in the project may not be available in every device. Limitations, challenges, safety issues, and system integration considerations should be evaluated before any final decision is made to ensure easy implementation. Implementing VR into a library can bring meaningful experience for patrons. VR is not only for gaming; it can enhance people's lives in new, previously unachievable ways, and libraries can bring that experience to them.

Notes

1 This research is supported in part by National Science Foundation award 1418122.
2 We describe contributions to the paper using a standard taxonomy (see Allen, L., Scott, J., Brand, A., Hlava, M., and Altman, M. (2014). Publishing: Credit Where Credit Is Due. *Nature, 508*(7496), 312–313). D.H. served as lead author. D.H. and M.A. authored early versions of the manuscript; D.H. was primarily responsible for redrafting the manuscript in its current form; R.W. contributed to writing section on enhancing emotional experience; all authors contributed to review and revision. M.A. and D.H. led in the conception of the article (including core ideas, analytical framework, and statement of research questions). All authors contributed to research and analysis and to the writing process through direct writing, critical review, and commentary.

   VR, broadly conceived, has existed in concept and occasional practice for more than sixty years—with concepts dating back to science fiction and implementations including the mechanical, multisensory, 3-D "Sensorama" system introduced as an entertainment novelty in 1956. Over the last decade, many applications of VR have been created, including some, such as *Second Life*, that reached mass popularity. However, VR has only recently achieved a stage of democratization—in the last several years, mass-market, low-cost, high-performance hardware and complementary VR development software have become widely available. (See Blade et al., 2014, for a discussion of the history of VR in detail.)

References

Allen, L., Brand, A., Scott, J., Altman, M., & Hlava, M. (2014). Credit where credit is due. *Nature, 508*(7496), 312–313.

AltspaceVR. (2017). Retrieved from http://altvr.com/

Bailenson, J. N., Yee, N., Blascovich, J., Beall, A. C., Lundblad, N., & Jin, M. (2008). The use of immersive virtual reality in the learning sciences: Digital transformations of teachers, students, and social context. *The Journal of the Learning Sciences, 17*(1), 102–141.

Baird, M. (2016). Bringing lessons to life: Harnessing the power of Pokémon GO to make stories and classroom materials come alive. *Digital Literacies, 34*(3), 24–25.

Blade, R. A., Padgett, M. L., Billinghurst, M., & Lindeman, R. W. (2014). Virtual environments: History and profession. In K. S. Hale & K. M. Stanney (Eds.), *Handbook of Virtual Environments: Design, Implementation, and Applications.* Boca Raton, FL: CRC Press.

Bowman, D. A., & McMahan, R. P. (2007). Virtual reality: How much immersion is enough? *Computer, 40*(7), 36–43.

Cauchard, J. R., Ainsworth, P. F., Romano, D. M., & Banks, B. (2006, October). Virtual manuscripts for an enhanced museum and web experience 'living manuscripts'. In International Conference on Virtual Systems and Multimedia (pp. 418-427). Springer, Berlin, Heidelberg.

Chertoff, D. B., & Schatz, S. L. (2014). Beyond presence: How holistic experience drives training and education. In K. S. Hale & K. M. Stanney (Eds.), *Handbook of Virtual Environments: Design, Implementation, and Applications*. Boca Raton, FL: CRC Press.

Chin, J. (Director), Solomon, B. (Director), Pirog, J. (Producer), & Walsh, C. (Producer). (2016). *Man on Spire* [Video file]. NYT VR.

Cummings, J. J., & Bailenson, J. N. (2016). How immersive is enough? A meta-analysis of the effect of immersive technology on user presence. *Media Psychology, 19*(2), 272–309.

Dörk, M., Carpendale, S., & Williamson, C. (2011, May). The information flaneur: A fresh look at information seeking. In Proceedings of the SIGCHI conference on human factors in computing systems (pp. 1215-1224). ACM.

Eadiciccio, L. (2016, March 28). Review: Oculus rift is expensive, complicated, and totally wonderful. *Time*. Retrieved from http://time.com/4272506/oculus-rift-review/

Estapa, A., & Nadolny, L. (2015). The effect of an augmented reality enhanced mathematics lesson on student achievement and motivation. *Journal of STEM Education, 16*(3), 40–48.

Fox, J., Arena, D., & Bailenson, J. N. (2009). Virtual reality: A survival guide for the social scientist. *Journal of Media Psychology: Theories, Methods, and Applications, 21*(3), 95–113.

Frati, V., & Prattichizzo, D. (2011, June). Using Kinect for hand tracking and rendering in wearable haptics. In *World Haptics Conference (WHC), 2011 IEEE* (pp. 317–321). Piscataway, NJ: IEEE.

Fredricks, J. A., Blumenfeld, P. C., & Paris, A. H. (2004). School engagement: Potential of the concept, state of the evidence. *Review of Educational Research, 74*(1), 59–109.

Goerner, P. (2016). Augmented reality: What's next? *School Library Journal, 62*(9), 19–20.

Grush, A. (2016, August 18). Samsung Gear VR: Everything you need to know. *VR Source*. Retrieved from http://vrsource.com/samsung-gear-vr-release-date-price-games-features-479/

Inman, C., Wright, V. H., & Hartman, J. A. (2010). Use of second life in K–12 and higher education: A review of research. *Journal of Interactive Online Learning, 9*(1), 44–63.

Iosa, M., Morone, G., Fusco, A., Castagnoli, M., Fusco, F. R., Pratesi, L., & Paolucci, S. (2015). Leap motion controlled videogame-based therapy for rehabilitation of elderly patients with subacute stroke: A feasibility pilot study. *Topics in Stroke Rehabilitation, 22*(4), 306–316.

Jennings, N., & Collins, C. (2007). Virtual or virtually U: Educational institutions in second life. *International Journal of Social, Behavioral, Educational, Economic, Business and Industrial Engineering, 2*(3), 180–186.

Joly, K. (2016). Videos show 360-degree campus views. *University Business, 19*(3), 26.

Karpova, E., Correia, A. P., & Baran, E. (2009). Learn to use and use to learn: Technology in virtual collaboration experience. *The Internet and Higher Education, 12*(1), 45–52.

Kaufman, S. B., & Gregoire, C. (2015). *Wired to Create: Unravel the Mysteries of the Creative Mind*. New York, NY: Perigee.

Keltner, D., & Haidt, J. (2003). Approaching awe, a moral, spiritual, and aesthetic emotion. *Cognition & Emotion, 17*(2), 297–314.

Lee, A. S., Swift, M., Tang, J. C., & Chen, H. (2015, October). 3D collaboration method over HoloLens™ and Skype™ end points. In *Proceedings of the 3rd International Workshop on Immersive Media Experiences* (pp. 27–30). New York, NY: ACM.

Lee, P. W., Wang, H. Y., Tung, Y. C., Lin, J. W., & Valstar, A. (2015, April). TranSection: hand-based interaction for playing a game within a virtual reality game. In *Proceedings of the 33rd Annual ACM Conference Extended Abstracts on Human Factors in Computing Systems* (pp. 73–76). New York, NY: ACM.

Luo, L., & Kemp, J. (2008). Second Life: Exploring the immersive instructional venue for library and information science education. *Journal of Education for Library and Information Science*, *49*(3), 147–166.

Milgram, P., & Kishino, F. (1994). A taxonomy of mixed reality visual displays. *IEICE Transactions on Information Systems*, E77-D(12), 1321–1329.

Moorefield-Lang, H. (2015). Libraries and the rift. *Knowledge Quest*, *43*(5), 76–77.

Oh Song, H., Xiang, Y., Jegelka, S., & Savarese, S. (2016). Deep metric learning via lifted structured feature embedding. In *Proceedings of the IEEE Conference on Computer Vision and Pattern Recognition* (pp. 4004–4012).

Pan, Z., Li, Y., Zhang, M., Sun, C., Guo, K., Tang, X., & Zhou, S. Z. (2010, March). A real-time multi-cue hand tracking algorithm based on computer vision. In *Virtual Reality Conference (VR), 2010 IEEE* (pp. 219–222). Piscataway, NJ: IIEEE.

Powell, W., Powell, V., Brown, P., Cook, M., & Uddin, J. (2016, March). Getting around in google cardboard—exploring navigation preferences with low-cost mobile VR. In *Everyday Virtual Reality (WEVR), 2016 IEEE 2nd Workshop* (pp. 5–8). Piscataway, NJ: IIEEE.

Rauhoeft, G., Leyrer, M., Thompson, W. B., Stefanucci, J. K., Klatzky, R. L., & Mohler, B. J. (2015, September). Evoking and assessing vastness in virtual environments. In *Proceedings of the ACM SIGGRAPH Symposium on Applied Perception* (pp. 51–54). New York, NY: ACM.

Ritter, S. M., Damian, R. I., Simonton, D. K., van Baaren, R. B., Strick, M., Derks, J., & Dijksterhuis, A. (2012). Diversifying experiences enhance cognitive flexibility. *Journal of Experimental Social Psychology*, *48*(4), 961–964.

Rosenberg, R. S., Baughman, S. L., & Bailenson, J. N. (2013). Virtual superheroes: Using superpowers in virtual reality to encourage prosocial behavior. *PloS One*, *8*(1), e55003.

Rosenfeld, J. (2016, May 26). Scientists are trying to solve the mystery of awe. *New York Magazine*. Retrieved from www.thecut.com/2016/05/scientists-are-trying-to-solve-the-mystery-of-awe.html

Rudd, M., Vohs, K. D., & Aaker, J. (2012). Awe expands people's perception of time, alters decision making, and enhances well-being. *Psychological Science*, *23*(10), 1130–1136. doi:http://dx.doi.org/10.1177/

Shiota, M. N., Keltner, D., & Mossman, A. (2007). The nature of awe: Elicitors, appraisals, and effects on self-concept. *Cognition and Emotion*, *21*(5), 944–963.

Siddappa, P. (2014). *LibrARi*. Retrieved from www.pradeepsiddappa.com/design/librari/

Silvia, P. J., Fayn, K., Nusbaum, E. C., & Beaty, R. E. (2015). Openness to experience and awe in response to nature and music: Personality and profound aesthetic experiences. *Psychology of Aesthetics, Creativity, and the Arts*, *9*(4), 376–384.

Spina, C. (2016, July 12). Pokémon GO: What do librarians need to know? *School Library Journal*. Retrieved from www.slj.com/2016/07/technology/applications/Pokemon-go-what-do-librarians-need-to-know/

Swider, M. (2017, June 15). HTC Vive vs Oculus Rift: Which VR headset is better? *TechRadar*. Retrieved from www.techradar.com/news/wearables/htc-vive-vs-oculus-rift-1301375#

Thier, D. (2016, July 11). What is 'Pokémon GO,' and why is everybody talking about it? *Forbes*. Retrieved from www.forbes.com/sites/davidthier/2016/07/11/facebook-twitter-social-what-is-pokemon-go-and-why-is-everybody-talking-about-it/#158cc38d1758

Tyng, C. M., Amin, H. U., Saad, M. N., & Malik, A. S. (2017). The influences of emotion on learning and memory. *Frontiers in Psychology, 8*, 1–22. doi:https://doi.org/10.3389/fpsyg.2017.01454

van Krevelen, D. W. F., & Poelman, R. (2010). A survey of augmented reality technologies, applications and limitations. *The International Journal of Virtual Reality, 9*(2), 1–20.

Vorlander, M., & Shinn-Cunningham, B. (2014). Virtual auditory displays. In K. S. Hale & K. M. Stanney (Eds.), *Handbook of Virtual Environments: Design, Implementation, and Applications*. Boca Raton, FL: CRC Press.

Wang, R. Y., & Popović, J. (2009). Real-time hand-tracking with a color glove. *ACM Transactions on Graphics (TOG), 28*(3).

Weatherall, B., Miller, C., & Thomas, S. (n.d.). *Virtual Reality Pilot Project*. Retrieved from www.adelaide.edu.au/library/about/projects/vr/VRProjectFinalReport.pdf

Yaden, D. B., Iwry, J., Slack, K. J., Eichstaedt, J. C., Zhao, Y., Vaillant, G. E., & Newberg, A. B. (2016). The overview effect: Awe and self-transcendent experience in space flight. *Psychology of Consciousness: Theory, Research, and Practice, 3*(1), 1.

Yoon, S., Anderson, E., Lin, J., & Elinich, K. (2017). How augmented reality enables conceptual understanding of challenging science content. *Journal of Educational Technology & Society, 20*(1), 156–168.

PART III

Reconceptualizing Librarianship

7

DESIGNING FOR STEM IN LIBRARIES SERVING UNDERSERVED COMMUNITIES

Crystle Martin

Introduction

STEM programming creates opportunities for youth to develop interests and to envision potential avenues for those interests. Youth from backgrounds that are often underrepresented in STEM fields oftentimes have less exposure to STEM-related activities. This chapter focuses on design aspects of STEM workshops that can be implemented in libraries and facilitated by librarians who may be nonexperts in the subject matter. It presents empirical findings from interviews with youth and librarians who participated in or facilitate Scratch workshops in libraries. The interviews focus on the design aspects and effectiveness of the workshops and how the workshops influenced youth interested in coding and STEM careers. This chapter offers design consideration for impact when designing STEM programming in underserved libraries.

Understanding the Challenges

Creating STEM programming for underserved libraries is important for several reasons. There is a continuing equity gap in STEM fields, which is most prominent in the communities in which underserved libraries are located. Exposure to STEM-related content, even brief exposure, can have long-term effects like influencing a youth's career path. Libraries have an essential role to play in helping youth connect what they learn in STEM programming in informal settings to academic paths and future opportunities.

Equity

Equity gaps persist in employment diversity for many computing and science jobs. In computing, African-American women hold only 3% of available jobs, and

Latinas hold only 1% (NCWIT, 2015). Lack of representation in the workforce may be fostered by earlier interactions, in school and in informal learning environments. Current research highlights that despite attempts to address inequality in STEM through formal education, these inequalities persist.

Despite widespread access to physical technology (Lenhart & Page, 2015), barriers still exist to the benefits of digital technology. These benefits have been more recently explored using a sociocultural approach (Ito et al., 2009; Martin, 2014a), which identifies barriers to developing digital literacies. The dispersion of internet use skills varies based on gender, educational attainment of parents, and race/ethnicity (Hargittai, 2004, 2010; Zillien & Hargittai, 2009). Lack of access creates lack of opportunity to explore and develop skills and confidence.

Gender and racial/ethnic disparities represent a stratification, which is troubling from a sociocultural and social justice perspective (Riegle-Crumb & King, 2010). Women and girls from low-income families, research states (Domenico & Jones, 2007; Khallad, 2000; Toglia, 2013; Watson, Quatman, & Edler, 2002), face more obstacles, which in turn reduces their career aspirations and expectations. Research has demonstrated that mentors in various contexts are associated with positive academic, vocational, and behavioral outcomes (Dubois & Silverthorn, 2005; Schwartz, Rhodes, Spencer, & Grossman, 2013) and that mentoring relationships may strongly influence outcomes related to attitudes, interpersonal relationships, and engagement (Eby et al., 2008). Social connection allows for a dialogue to be established between peers, which fosters a conversation of trust with the intended purpose of learning, "improvement," and "goal attainment," (Hattie & Timperley, 2007). Based on previous work suggesting improvement in STEM opportunities could be obtained through interest-driven and informal learning spaces, this study focuses on coding in online communities. Interest-driven spaces offer youth the opportunity to explore identity and agency (Martin, 2012, 2014a), trying on different roles that they could transfer outside of that setting. Transfers can include connecting to related career paths. Ochsner (2012) found that people used their video game and fan fiction online communities as places to try out and visualize different career paths. These statistics bring to mind the question, what can we do to support engagement of underrepresented youth to develop equity?

Careers

There is a consensus forming that starting in early adolescence, youth begin to think concretely about their futures, and these early thoughts impact how the youth prepare for their chosen career (Auger, Blackhurst, & Wahl, 2005; Bandura, Barbaranelli, Caprara, & Pastorelli, 2001; Riegle-Crumb, Moore, & Ramos-Wada; 2011). Existing research already describes the importance of exposure to disciplines that could potentially lead to future opportunities and career pathways (National Research Council, 2011; Modi, Schoenberg, & Salmond, 2012).

Although there is no simple solution, digital media, which has a strong connection to STEM programming, has the potential to create opportunity for upward mobility, particularly for disadvantaged youth (DiMaggio, 1982).

Even brief exposure to a topic can spark a lasting interest (National Research Council, 2011; Modi et al., 2012). The path between brief exposure and lasting interest is not an automatic connection. It is necessary for learners to have access to continual opportunities for positive experiences (Ahn et al., 2014), as this helps to create stronger connection to the interest. When trying to observe and capture the phenomena of transfers and transitions from interest to opportunities, a framework like that of connected learning is useful for analysis.

In early adolescence, youth begin to consider their future in a concrete way. These early considerations often influence the development of interests in careers (Auger et al., 2005; Bandura et al., 2001; Riegle-Crumb et al., 2011). For most youth early exposure begins in school settings, but despite efforts to address inequality in career exposure through formal education, gender and racial/ethnic disparities have become more stratified (Riegle-Crumb & King, 2010). The National Women's Law Center released a report proposing steps to help eliminate educational disparity in STEM for diverse youth. These included "increasing access to educational opportunities that promote diversity and reduce racial isolation" and "ensuring access to curricula that will help students build strong academic foundations . . . such as STEM courses and courses . . . that develop critical-thinking, reading, and math skills" (NAACP, 2014, p. 38). The report goes on to encourage formal education settings to "improve extracurricular opportunities and participation among African American girls" and to "improve STEM opportunities and achievement for African American girls" (NAACP, 2014, p. 43). The report stops short of offering recommendations and action steps to implement the proposed changes.

In out-of-school settings, an analysis of extracurricular activities illustrates that an advantage in noncognitive and cognitive skills is developed by higher levels of participation in upper-income families (Covay & Carbonaro, 2010). This equity gap is not irreconcilable or irreversible. However, understanding that the gap is consistently widening between what upper-income and lower-income families spend on enrichment activities is important. Bottom-income quintile expenditure on extracurricular activities has been essentially stagnant since the early 1970s (Duncan & Murnane, 2011), whereas existing inequalities have widened as expenditure of the top income quintile has grown more than two and a half times during the same time period.

Research on impacting youth career paths through interest and exposure does offer potential avenues to combat existing inequalities. For example, research has shown that even brief exposure to a topic can spark a lasting interest or highlight a potential career that the youth may want to pursue (National Research Council, 2011; Modi et al., 2012). There is, however, a disconnect between initial interest in STEM and having that solidify into a career path. This is demonstrated in the fact that youth of color and white youth report almost equal rates of initial interest in STEM as a college major despite dramatic differences in the rates at which they pursue STEM majors (Anderson & Kim, 2006; Hanson, 2006). Many factors can impact the transition between interest and career path, including lack of support from caring adults and mentors, lack of understanding of career options, and structural and institutional barriers.

Not surprisingly, the equity gap exists along gender, race/ethnic, and socio/economic lines and has impact from K–12 education to career choices. Women make up only 25% of those in computing jobs, with women of color making up the smallest percentages of that 25%: 3% are African-American women and 1% are Latinas (NCWIT, 2015). This is compared to white women (16%) and Asian women (5%). Only 5% of scientists and engineers working in science and engineering occupations are African American and 6% are Hispanic, compared to 71% white and 17% Asian (NCSES, 2015). When trying to observe and capture the phenomena of transfers and transitions from interest to opportunities, a framework like that of connected learning is useful for analysis.

Connecting Informal Learning to Other Settings

The connection between informal, interest-driven learning and formal educational and career spaces can be seen as part of an ecology of learning. A learning ecology is "the set of contexts found in physical or virtual spaces that provide opportunities for learning" (Barron, 2004, 2006, p. 195). This framework elevated the idea that what youth do in their interest spaces is relevant for social and learning development, and that learning can connect to other settings beyond the setting it was initiated in. Out of the body of research on youths' learning in their interest spaces, a new framework has been developed, connected learning (Ito et al., 2013). Connected learning posits that there are many contexts of learning that can impact youth. Connecting these contexts in the larger learning ecology leads to the idea of pathways. Viewing youth learning through this lens encourages exploring the "learning lives" of youth not as isolated points in time but as connected across time (Erstad & Sefton-Green, 2012).

Building on the framework for learning ecologies, the framework of connected learning conceptually breaks the larger learning ecology into three spheres—peer, interest, and academic/future—and a design framework. The framework describes the interactions between the spheres as connected learning. However, connected learning is more than just enumerating the connections between parts of a youth's learning ecology. Connected learning "advocates for broadened access to learning that is socially embedded, interest-driven, and oriented toward educational, economic, and political opportunity" (Ito et al., 2013). It brings together the disparate parts of a youth's learning ecology, translating and linking that learning to academic success and future trajectories. This may be a new approach, but the ideas range as far back as Dewey (1938), who posited the idea of viewing education as seamless across all aspects of life. For some youth, mostly those from high socioeconomic households, this seamless education is already a reality. However, for a majority of youth it is not.

Another view of the connections that youth could potentially create between their informal and formal learning environments is Beach's (1999) idea of consequential transition. "Transitions are consequential when they are consciously reflected on, often struggled with, and the eventual outcome changes one's sense of self and social positioning" (Beach, 1999, p. 114). This idea of transition has limitation and is grounded in the idea of transfer, so a modified term, consequential connections, has been used by certain scholars (Ito et al., 2015). Consequential connections are mechanisms that support connections between young people's interest, peer culture, and academic, which create opportunities for youth to have their expertise and knowledge valued and can potentially lead to future opportunities or career paths. Just access to an interest is not enough; access to mentors and cultivated opportunities is needed as well. Learners must have continual opportunities for positive experiences that can offer up future trajectories (Ahn et al., 2014). Despite the challenges that this type of learning approach offers, it is achievable for youth who can connect learning the pathways between contexts, and libraries are a place that can bridge information learning with traditional academic pathways and future opportunities. Creating pathways to opportunities should be supported, and libraries are an excellent place to do this.

Libraries Bridging the Gap

Libraries offer great potential for bridging gaps in STEM access. With 9,082 administrative public library units and 98,460 school libraries in the United States (Number of Libraries in the United States, 2015), they could reach a very large portion of the population. The question is how libraries bridge this gap. Baek (2013, p. 5) offers six science-specific capabilities supported by informal learning environments like libraries, which I have modified for STEM more broadly:

1. Experience excitement, interest, and motivation to learn about phenomena in the digital and physical spaces.
2. Come to generate, understand, remember, and use concepts, explanations, arguments, models, and facts related to STEM.
3. Manipulate, test, explore, predict, question, observe, and make sense of the world through STEM.
4. Reflect on STEM concepts, like the scientific method and computational thinking, as a way of knowing; on processes, concepts, and institutions of science; and on their own process of learning about STEM-related topics.
5. Participate in STEM activities and learning practices with others, using scientific language and tools.

6.   Think about themselves as STEM learners and develop an identity as some-
     one who knows about, uses, and sometimes contributes to STEM concepts
     and fields.

Libraries support informal learning functioning as connected learning environments (Ito et al., 2013), connecting in-school learning and learning that happens
in interest spaces for youth, so that youth can receive value for it and find future
opportunities. STEM in libraries is not about the creation of a physical product
but about learning the underlying concepts, such as design thinking (Bowler,
2014) and computational thinking (Brennan & Resnick, 2012). These programs
can be a great opportunity for the participants to learn vital skills in the twenty-
first century and also opportunities for youth for development of career readiness
skills, like responsibility, agency, and leadership for youth who help facilitated the
programs (Salusky et al., 2014).

Research Context

The data presented in this chapter is part of a three-year study. The study was
multimodal and multisited and looked at ways to spread opportunities for STEM,
especially coding, in libraries through an ethnography of an online visual coding
community for youth called Scratch and a design-based research (Barab & Squire,
2004) project that focused on designing STEM workshops for libraries, especially
for libraries with limited resources. The data presented in this chapter will focus
on the design-based workshop development. The implementation of the workshops was developed using an iterative codesign process with the librarians who

TABLE 7.1 Description of Implementation Sites

Implementations	Location	Age of Youth	Number of Sessions	Number of Weeks
1	South Los Angeles	Middle/High School	16	8
2	South Los Angeles	Middle/High School	16	8
3	South Los Angeles	High School	2	1
4	South Los Angeles	Middle/High School	6	6
5	South Los Angeles	Middle School	6	6
6	South Los Angeles	Middle School	3	3
7	South Los Angeles	Elementary School	7	7
8	North Long Beach	Elementary/Middle School	6	6
9	North Long Beach	Elementary School	6	6
10	Orange County	Elementary–High School	6	3
11	Orange County	Middle School	5	1
12	Orange County	Middle/High School	3	3

were facilitating. Each librarian received facilitator guides and limited instruction prior to implementing the workshops. Librarians were specifically selected who had limited to no prior coding experience and worked in underserved libraries to help develop workshops and implementation strategies that were applicable to as many potential facilitators as possible.

Over the course of three years, I worked with librarians across eleven libraries in South Los Angeles, North Long Beach, and Select Areas of Orange County in California, for twelve implementations. Each librarian facilitated five to eight workshops in their libraries. The way the workshops were facilitated changed over time based on the needs of each setting and feedback from previous iterations. In total, 222 students have participated between May 2014 and the May 2017, 93 females and 129 males. Of the 222 participants, 33 were African-American/black, 111 were Latinx, 41 were Asian American, 12 were white, and 25 were unknown or declined to say.

FIGURE 7.1 Screenshot of the Scratch homepage

Scratch

Scratch is a free online visual coding language used for authoring multimedia projects. Scratch is designed primarily for ages 8 to 16 (Scratch, 2018) but the online community has participants younger than 8 through retirement age. The online community came into existence in 2007 when Scratch was updated to allow project sharing and remixing online, as opposed to creating and using projects on the local computer, which was Scratch's previous instantiation. Those who participate in the online Scratch community are called Scratchers. The online community is made up of two main areas. The first is the coding platform, where Scratchers create projects, which are individual creations, and studios, which are collections of projects that members of the community put together. Scratchers can comment on individual projects, studios, and the profiles of other Scratchers. The second area is the forums. Here members of the community ask and answer longer-form and more technical questions, as well as discuss and propose changes to Scratch as a coding program and as a community. Through Scratch, youth can have many entries into coding and connections to academic and career opportunities (Martin, 2018).

Designing for Impact and Accessibility

From this study, six design considerations have surfaced that provide a basis for designing STEM programming for underserved libraries, which fall into three larger themes of youth interest and voice, technological challenges, and challenges the librarians face. This section explores these design considerations in more detail.

Making Programming Youth Centered

Designing programming that is interest driven is an important starting point for youth-centered design in libraries. In order to do this successfully, the program designer should consider the interest of youth at sites individually and not rely on what is considered popular through "common knowledge" for a specific age group. Interests certainly vary by age but also by community. To determine what popular interests are for youth in a community, the youth librarian is the first and oftentimes best point of contact. They will know what is popular with the youth they serve and can potentially connect you directly to the youth to find out what interests they have. Talking to youth directly through Teen Advisory Boards at libraries is also an easy way to understand youth interest and youth needs at a particular library. This should be approached from a place of openness, with no judgment as to the perceived "quality" of the interest, in terms of educational value or "respectability." As research has shown, whether it is gaming, professional wrestling, or role-playing (Pfister, 2014; Martin, 2014b, 2017; Rafalow & Salen Tekinbaş, 2014), learning gains and skill development within many interest communities are evident. Talking to the librarians in this study, they reported youth interest in hip-hop, skateboarding, vampire and monster romance novels, Ninjago, *Minecraft, Adventure Time,* and graphic novels for middle school and high school-aged youth just as a sample.

Combining an interest with a program should be undertaken thoughtfully, not put on as a veneer. How the interest can be incorporated to meet program outcomes should be considered. For example, in this study, experts in hip-hop were consulted to help design the Scratch workshop. This led to a workshop that offered information to youth about the history of hip-hop, as well as underlying understanding of how coding is not dissimilar from hip-hop music and dance, or music and dance in general. The similarity lies in thinking of the component parts of music, dance, and coding. Describing these connections creates opportunities for youth who may have felt that coding was daunting and something they may not feel they have commonality or a connection with to have a starting point that feels familiar.

Supporting the Nonexpert

To support nonexpert librarians in facilitating STEM programs in libraries with limited resources and underserved communities, it is essential to consider their needs and their constraints. Librarians who participated in this study described the limited amount of time they have for learning new skills they might want to implement. Like teachers, they have extremely tightly scheduled days, but unlike teachers, many do not get an hour a day for preparation and professional development. This lack of time, as well as funding to buy new equipment, was expressed by those who facilitated the workshops for this study, as well as other librarians who participated in professional development workshops run at conferences on the topic of conducting hip-hop and Scratch workshops in libraries. Many participants stated that the only time they had to prepare for programming was in the time between questions while working at the reference desk. This meant for them video instruction was difficult, especially if the instructions were live and not recorded. Short snippets of video were easier, as they could occasionally fit one in, but they could not use headphones for long periods of time. The consensus was that guides, usually in the form of pdf documents, that walked them through the process were the easiest to fit into their schedule and limited preparation time. Most also could not commit to more than two hours of preparation time for a program. The librarians who participated, as mentioned, work in low-income, underserved areas where resources and staff time are limited.

Another way to support nonexperts is to offer multiple facilitation strategies for whatever the program is that is intended to be implemented. Each library is a unique context with its own strengths and limitations, so the more flexible a program can be the more likely it is to be adopted. Some of the most successful implementations from this study were those that utilized high school students as facilitators. The benefits from these implementations included youth being less hesitant to ask questions, librarians being able to leverage the expertise of some of their youth in program implementation, and the youth creating more flexible implementations than other facilitators. For example, in Implementation 4, the librarian, Alejandra, created a career-development opportunity for youth in conjunction with the program and hired two youth facilitators to run the coding programs. She advertised for the facilitators at a local high school, required the teens to apply and go through an interview process, gave feedback on the interview and application process to those who applied, and selected them based on interest and experience. The two youth selected were Laretha, a 16-year-old African-American girl, and Rodrigo, a 17-year-old Latinx boy. They decided to go with a hands-on approach to facilitating. They would show the basics of what the youth were going to do for the day: for example, they would describe how to make sprites change color, spin, and get bigger and smaller. Then they would demonstrate an example that they had made. On the computers the participants were using, Laretha and Rodrigo would already have open a tab to Scratch that offered a list of other people's shared projects to match the content of the day's workshop. Once they had pointed the participants to the potential examples, they supplied paper and writing utensils for those who wanted to design on paper before they started working in Scratch. Once the participants reached the design stage, they worked at their own pace with the help of the Laretha, Rodrigo, and Alejandra. Rodrigo describes his experience being a facilitator like this:

> I like how we have time beforehand in order to, like, make sure everything is going well. And we basically, like, debug it ourselves in a way the day before. And it's, like, enough time. We're not rushing or anything like that. And also the number of kids makes it easier for us to not be, like, you know, flooding with kids, but at the same time we have enough to have, like, time with each one individually and get to know them, like, the people that I've known from here. Like, I know some of them like games, and some of them like decorating and stuff like that. So that's actually been kind of nice to get to know them instead of just, like, talking to everyone at once and get a little bit of time with each one.

Rodrigo emphasized the importance of individual support of students in their exploration and use of Scratch.

Another facilitation approach that was consistently successful was fostering an atmosphere of the facilitator as colearner. This positioning helps the librarian feel more comfortable with their expertise level and at the same time sets up a culture within the program that allows the participants to get value for the expertise and makes asking questions and not knowing how to do things a normal part of participation. It is critical to help libraries feel comfortable in not being the expert and to make it clear that programs will have bumps and no program is perfect, but that is okay, and it is also okay to try and fail and try again.

Fostering a Productive Interest-Driven Learning Environment

To foster a productive interest-driven learning environment, several techniques can be used, including peer-to-peer learning, using creative examples, and balancing didactic teaching with free exploration. Peer-to-peer learning happens between participants when they work together to solve a problem or answer a question (Ito et al., 2013). Laretha describes the challenges of creating a peer-to-peer learning environment in a drop-in workshop situation with youth who do not know each other.

> Well, at first one of the most challenging aspects was to get them to talk. I noticed that at the very beginning everybody was quiet. And it was really awkward because it sounded like only the interns were the enthusiastic ones. And, you know, like, there's cliché situations where, like, there's a class teaching and then all the kids are just, like, staring at each other, like, "What?" [LAUGHTER] And so it took time. Like, we had to, like, slowly get them to speak up, and we had to find out their interests. Like, it takes time and patience. And you have to also give them, like, space, too. But it ended up being a blessing because now everyone's all happy.

Fostering peer-to-peer learning is useful for participant learning and their project development, as well as being helpful for the facilitators, because it spreads the sources of help across all participants in the workshop not just the facilitators.

Using creative examples helps to develop more diversity of content and variability. As mentioned in Laretha and Rodrigo's description of workshops, they used examples of other similar projects as a way to foster creativity and design. Rodrigo describes it:

> Yes, I think the beginning was the hardest part, because it was just a group of people you didn't really know. And they just sort of expected you to teach them stuff. But there was, like, no connection in the beginning, and they were just really awkward and stuff. And then even if they had a problem they'd rather just stay quiet and sit there than actually ask us for help. And when we went to them they'd just be, like, "No, I'm okay." And now they've opened up, so whenever they have a problem they ask us. Or when we walk around they'll be, like, "How do I do this?" or "How do I do that?" So that was the hardest part in the beginning.

There is also a balance to be reached with creative examples and didactic instruction. Some basic instruction is necessary to demonstrate how the project is supposed to work, whether for Scratch or another workshop. However, too much and like Implementation 1, the participants are likely to reproduce the example being described without adding their own creativity and voice to it. But if the workshop is too freeform, participants do not know where to start or what to do.

Understanding the Challenges of Libraries

One design challenge that comes up when designing multiday programs for libraries is that most library programs are drop-in, and even if there is a sign-up, there is often times an ever changing group of youth who participate from week to week. There will be a few who come consistently, but many others will come intermittently. When designing a curriculum to be implemented over multiple weeks, consider how a librarian or facilitator will be able to include and get up to speed a youth who has not participated in previous weeks.

Underresourced libraries face several challenges, as mentioned earlier. One of which is limited staff and staff time to put to new programs. The other challenge is technological. The libraries that participated in the study had limited Wi-fi capabilities. They also generally used tablet and laptops which had battery life issues. The librarians also did not necessarily have control over the computers they were using, so anything that needed to be installed required permission and the help of other departments. Many of the libraries did not have established computer labs that could be used for programming, so they used multipurpose rooms. These rooms were not designed to have large numbers of laptops that would need to be plugged in. This created a challenge for facilitators and participants as they participated in the workshop.

Keep Challenges of Youth in Underserved Communities in Mind

Many youth who participated in these workshops did not have reliable internet at home and were more likely to have access to mobile devices than to other types of computers. Mario describes his internet access: "No [I don't have internet access], it went down so we're just waiting for it to get back up." So when designing, if you want youth to do activities outside of the program, understand the community that you will be working with and make sure you design for the context at hand not an imagined context. In order to completely understand what that context is, you may need to do additional data collection before the design process.

Keeping Youth Voice in Your Design

Creating opportunities for flexible inclusion of youth interest allows youth the opportunity to create a connection to the project and to express their voice through their creative output. The youth who participated in the Scratch workshops felt this was an impactful part of participating in Scratch. Mario, a 12-year-old Latinx middle schooler, said,

> People are always helping you [in Scratch] and you're always in it trying to create everything you can, do the best you can do, just having fun. Just creating anything you want like in your own image. You could make your own image. It's really creative, like it could really inspire any kid that's at our school.

If you intend for youth to share online, do not assume that because they are youth they all share online. Results from this study demonstrated that most youth did not use social media and were reticent about sharing online. The causes of this seem to be apprehension about sharing unfinished work and fear of negative critique. A strategy to encourage and contextualize sharing online is important for this to be a successful part of a program. For example, in Implementation 2, Renata, the librarian, was trying to get participants to share their projects to a Scratch studio for the library program. Many were very cautious to share. Renata decided to try an approach in which she described all the projects on Scratch as works in progress, constantly being changed and improved, as a way to make the process seem less consequential. It worked. After she described the platform this way each time she asked them to post, more and more participants became comfortable with posting. Defining your intended outcomes and deciding what can facilitate those outcomes is necessary for success of the program.

Wrap-Up

Developing STEM workshops implementable in low-resourced libraries requires a confluence of several factors. Start by considering librarians, in the case of this research youth librarians, as design partners. No one knows more about their community and their facilities' strengths and barriers. As designers, work with the librarians, and youth, like those participating in a Teen Advisory Board, to create workshops that are relevant experiences targeted to a specific population. Youth engagement with the final product (i.e., the STEM workshop) depends on their interest in the broader topic. Work with practitioners to involve high school students as facilitators for the project. This offers exceptional opportunities for personal development and career skills acquisition for youth participants and creates opportunity to establish a culture of peer-to-peer learning. Librarians have extreme demands on their time and usually have no more than a few hours to prepare for a new program. Make training documentation easy to use and absorbable in short increments. Make your programs flexible so that they can be adapted for each new setting, as each library is a unique context. Libraries are an ideal place to reach youth who may feel disconnected with school, have access to less out-of-school enrichment, and are often less encouraged than other students to pursue STEM careers. Just like in schools, libraries offer their own set of challenges, but with thoughtful planning, they can offer impactful STEM programming.

Get Started!

This chapter lays out potential design considerations for creating STEM programs in underserved libraries based on data collected over a three-year period. These considerations are not the only ones and will change over time, as context changes. These design considerations offer a place to start and encourage you to do so. Look for a practitioner partner who is willing to work through the design process with you; they will be invaluable in creating your STEM programs. Remember that there will always be bumps in the road and revisions to make. Never consider the program finished; it can always be refined and improved. There can be a lot of fear on the part of those implementing STEM programming in areas where they are not experts. Always consider what you need to create to make them feel easily supported in implementing the program without you needing to be there for implementation or training. If you empower your practice partners in design and implementation, the programs created have the opportunity to reach more youth who visit underserved libraries.

References

Ahn, J., Subramaniam, M., Bonsignore, E., Pellicone, A., Waugh, A., & Yip, J. (2014). 'I want to be a game designer or scientist': Connected learning and developing identities with urban, African-American youth. In *Proceedings of the Eleventh International Conference of the Learning Sciences (ICLS 2014)*. Boulder, CO: International Society of the Learning Sciences.

Anderson, E. L., & Kim, D. (2006). *Increasing the Success of Minority Students in Science and Technology (No. 4)*. Washington, DC: American Council on Education.

Auger, R. W., Blackhurst, A. E., & Wahl, K. H. (2005). The development of elementary-aged children's career aspirations and expectations. *Professional School Counseling, 8*(4), 322–329.

Baek, J. (2013). Public libraries as places for STEM learning: An exploratory interview study with eight librarians. *StarNet Science-technology Activities and Resources for Libraries*. Retrieved from www.nc4il.org/images/papers/Baek_Public%20Libraries%20as%20 Places%20for%20STEM%20Learning.pdf

Bandura, A., Barbaranelli, C., Caprara, G. V., & Pastorelli, C. (2001). Self-efficacy beliefs as shapers of children's aspirations and career trajectories. *Child Development, 72*(1), 187–206.

Barab, S., & Squire, K. (2004). Design based research: Putting a stake in the ground. *The Journal of the Learning Sciences, 13*(1), 1–14.

Barron, B. (2004). Learning ecologies for technological fluency: Gender and experience differences. *Journal of Educational Computing Research, 31*(1), 1–36.

Barron, B. (2006). Interest and self-sustained learning as catalysts of development: A learning ecology perspective. *Human Development, 49*(4), 193–224.

Beach, K. (1999). Consequential transitions: A sociocultural expedition beyond transfer in education. *Review of Research in Education, 24*(1), 101–139.

Bowler, L. (2014) Creativity through 'maker' experiences and design thinking in the education of librarians. *Knowledge Quest, 42*(5), 58.

Brennan, K., & Resnick, M. (2012). New frameworks for studying and assessing the development of computational thinking. *Proceedings of the American Educational Research Association (AERA) Annual Conference.*

Covay, E., & Carbonaro, W. (2010). After the bell: Participation in extracurricular activities, classroom behavior, and academic achievement. *Sociology of Education, 83*(1), 20–45.

Dewey, J. (1938). *Education and Experience.* New York, NY: McMillan.

DiMaggio, P. (1982). Cultural capital and school success: The impact of status culture participation on the grades of U.S. high school students. *American Sociological Review, 47*(2), 189–201.

Domenico, D. M., & Jones, K. H. (2007). Career aspirations of women in the 20th century. *Journal of Career and Technical Education, 22*(2).

DuBois, D. L., & Silverthorn, N. (2005). Natural mentoring relationships and adolescent health: Evidence from a national study. *American Journal of Public Health, 95*(3), 518–524.

Duncan, G. J., & Murnane, R. J. (eds.) (2011). *Whither Opportunity? Rising Inequality, Schools, and Children's Life Chances.* New York, NY: Russell Sage Foundation.

Eby, L. T., Allen, T. D., Evans, S. C., Ng, T., & DuBois, D. L. (2008). Does mentoring matter? A multidisciplinary meta-analysis comparing mentored and non-mentored individuals. *Journal of Vocational Behavior, 72*(2), 254–267.

Erstad, O., & Sefton-Green, J. (2012). Digital disconnect? The 'digital learner and the school.' In O. Erstad & J. Sefton-Green (Eds.), *Identity, Community, and Learning Lives in the Digital Age* (pp. 87–104). Cambridge, UK: Cambridge University Press.

Scratch. (2017, July 1). For Parents. Retrieved from https://scratch.mit.edu/parents/

Hanson, S. L. (2006). African American women in science: Experiences from high school through the post-secondary years and beyond. In J. Bystydzienski & S. Bird (Eds.), *Removing Barriers: Women in Academic Science, Technology, Engineering, and Mathematics.* Bloomington, IN: Indiana University Press.

Hargittai, E. (2004). Internet access and use in context. *New Media & Society, 6*(1), 137–143.

Hargittai, E. (2010). Digital na(t)ives? Variation in Internet skills and uses among members of the 'Net Generation'. *Sociological Inquiry, 80*(1), 92–113.

Hattie, J., & Timperley, H. (2007). The power of feedback. *Review of Educational Research, 77*(1), 81–112.

Ito, M., Baumer, S., Bittanti, M., boyd, d., Cody, R., Herr-Stephenson, B., Horst, H. A., Lange, P. G., Mahendran, D., Martínez, K. Z., Pascoe, C. J., Perkel, D., Robinson, L., Sims, C., & Tripp, L. (2009). *Hanging out, Messing Around, and Geeking out: Kids Living and Learning with New Media.* Cambridge, MA: MIT Press.

Ito, M., Gutierrez, K., Livingstone, S., Penuel, W., Rhodes, J., Salen, K., Schor, J., Sefton-Green, J., & Watkins, S. C. (2013). *Connected Learning: An Agenda for Research and Design.* Irvine, CA: Digital Media and Learning Research Hub.

Ito, M., Soep, E., Kligler-Vilenchik, N., Shresthova, S., Gamber-Thompson, L., & Zimmerman, A. (2015). Learning connected civics: Narratives, practices, infrastructures. *Curriculum Inquiry, 45*(1), 10–29.

Khallad, Y. (2000). Education and career aspirations of Palestinian and US youth. *The Journal of Social Psychology, 140*(6), 789–791.

Lenhart, A., & Page, D. (2015). *Teens, Social Media & Technology Overview 2015: Smartphones Facilitate Shifts in Communication Landscape for Teens*. Pew Research Center. Washington, DC.

Martin, C. (2012). Video games, identity, and the constellation of information. *Bulletin of Science, Technology, and Society, special issue: Game on: The Challenges and Benefits of Video Games, Part I, 32*(5), 384–392.

Martin, C. (2014a). *Voyage Across a Constellation of Information: Information Literacy in Interest-Driven Learning Communities*. New York, NY: Peter Lang.

Martin, C. (2014b). *Learning the Ropes: Connected Learning in a WWE Fan Community*. Irvine, CA: Digital Media and Learning Research Hub.

Martin, C. (2017). Kayfabe: An in depth look at WWE and its fandom using digital ethnography. In L. Hjorth, H. Horst, A. Galloway, & G. Bell (Eds.), *The Routledge Companion to Digital Ethnography* (p. 244). London: Routledge.

Martin, C. (2018). Supporting youth to envision careers in computer science through an interest in computer coding. In W. Tierney, Z. Corwin, & A. Ochsner (Eds.), *Diversifying Digital Learning: Online Literacy and Educational Opportunity* (p. 126). Baltimore, MD: Johns Hopkins.

Modi, K., Schoenberg, J., & Salmond, K. (2012). *Generation STEM: What Girls Say About Science, Technology, Engineering, and Math*. New York, NY: Girl Scouts of the USA.

NAACP Legal Defense and Education Fund (LDF) and National Women's Law Center (NWLC). (2014). *Unlocking Opportunity African American Girls: A Call to Action for Educational Equity*. New York, NY: LDF Communications Department.

National Center for Science and Engineering Statistics (NCSES). (2015). *Women, Minorities, and People with Disabilities in Science and Engineering*. Bethesda, MD: National Science Foundation.

National Center for Women and Information Technology (NCWIT). (2015). *Women in IT: The Facts*.

National Research Council. (2011). *Successful K–12 STEM Education: Identifying Effective Approaches in Science, Technology, Engineering, and Mathematics*. Washington, DC: National Academies Press.

Number of Libraries in the United States. (2015, September). *American Library Association*. Retrieved from www.ala.org/tools/libfactsheets/alalibraryfactsheet01

Ochsner, A. (2012). *Typically Untypical Affinity Practices Making a Mass Effect*. Unpublished thesis. Department of Curriculum and Instruction. University of Wisconsin-Madison.

Pfister, R. C. (2014). *Hats for House Elves: Connected Learning and Civic Engagement in Hogwarts at Ravelry*. Irvine, CA: Digital Media and Learning Hub.

Rafalow, M., & Salen Tekinbaş, K. (2014). *Welcome to Sackboy Planet: Connected Learning Among LittleBigPlanet 2 Players*. Irvine, CA: Digital Media and Learning Hub.

Riegle-Crumb, C., & King, B. (2010). Question a white male advantage in STEM: Examining disparities in college major by gender and race/ethnicity. *Educational Researcher, 39*(9), 656–664.

Riegle-Crumb, C., Moore, C., & Ramos-Wada, A. (2011). Who wants to have a career in science or math? Exploring adolescents' future aspirations by gender and race/ethnicity. *Science Education, 95*(3), 458–476.

Salusky, I., Larson, R. W., Griffith, A., Wu, J., Raffaelli, M., Sugimura, N., & Guzman, M. (2014). How adolescents develop responsibility: What can be learned from youth programs. *Journal of Research on Adolescence, 24*(3), 417–430.

Schwartz, S. E., Rhodes, J. E., Spencer, R., & Grossman, J. B. (2013). Youth initiated mentoring: Investigating a new approach to working with vulnerable adolescents. *American Journal of Community Psychology, 52*(1–2), 155–169.

Toglia, T. V. (2013). Gender equity issues in CTE and STEM education. *Tech Directions, 72*(7), 14–17.

Watson, C. M., Quatman, T., & Edler, E. (2002). Career aspirations of adolescent girls: Effects of achievement level, grade, and single-sex school environment. *Sex Roles, 46*(9–10), 323–335.

Zillien, N., & Hargittai, E. (2009). Digital distinction: Status-specific types of Internet usage. *Social Science Quarterly, 90*(2), 274–291.

8

REDEFINING MENTORSHIP IN FACILITATING INTEREST-DRIVEN LEARNING IN LIBRARIES

Tamara Clegg and Mega Subramaniam

Redefining Learning in the Connected World

New technologies (e.g., ubiquitous computing, mobile computing, wearable technologies) have significantly lowered the bar of producing knowledge. For example, we can compare traditional video production to uploading videos to YouTube from a cell phone. Almost a decade ago, producing and distributing information in video format required numerous hours of setting up a video camera with perfect lighting, capturing and editing the footage needed, then figuring out how and where to host/upload the video to ensure that the targeted population would be able to view the video. Additionally, there were other considerations such as download speed of the user's access, server space to host the video, how to get more viewers to view the video, and so on. Due to these complexities in producing knowledge, only designated experts (and people who had privileged access to sophisticated technology) produced knowledge, while the public consumed this knowledge. The emergence of newer technologies such as mobile technologies and social media has revolutionized how information and knowledge can be created and distributed—leading to the birth of what scholars have described as "participatory culture" (Jenkins et al., 2009). The public, including young people, can now be problem solvers and experts themselves.

This participatory culture is transforming teaching and learning in all environments—from schools, workplaces, and informal settings such as homes and libraries. Across all of these settings, educators of young people are needing to reimagine their roles in supporting learning. Traditional literacies (such as reading, writing, and arithmetic) need to be expanded to be inclusive of literacies that are needed to be successful in productive participation, such as digital, information, and design literacies. Not only are young people learning from the "teacher," they are also learning from the technology that they are interacting with, the physical and virtual communities in which they are embedded, and seamlessly bridging learning that is happening across learning contexts such as home, school, libraries, and virtual communities. Ito and her colleagues (2013) describe such learning experiences as connected learning. Supporting connected learning for young people has thus become of critical importance for today's educators.

Connected Learning

Connected learning is driven by an equity agenda that strives to promote inclusivity in terms of providing physical, intellectual, and social access to personalized learning experiences for all young people (Subramaniam et al., 2017).

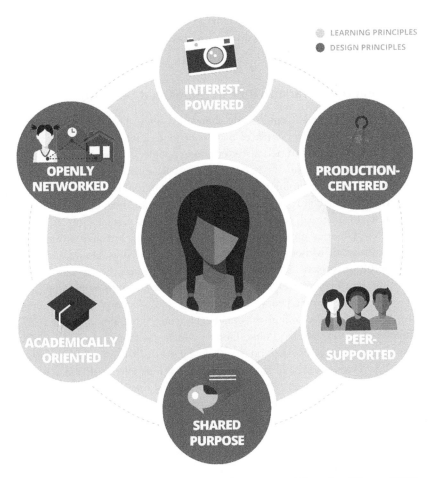

FIGURE 8.1   Connected Learning Framework (Connected Learning Alliance, 2018)

Youth from nondominant groups are often deprived of such opportunities due to insufficient resources and mentorship that is available to them. True connected learning environments promote connections across three learning principles: interest-powered, peer-supported, and academically oriented (Ito et al., 2013). Interest-powered learning environments "foster the drive to gain knowledge and expertise" (Connected Learning Alliance, 2018) by leveraging young people's existing interests and passions in the design of these environments. Peer-supported learning environments allow "young people [to] fluidly contribute, share and give feedback to each other," producing "learning that is engaging and powerful" (Connected Learning Alliance, 2018). Learning environments that connect informal learning experiences to formal education, civic, and career opportunities exemplify the academically oriented learning principle in connected learning (Ito et al., 2013). These three learning principles are complemented by three design principles in connected learning—shared purpose, openly networked, and production centered. Through a shared purpose, young people leverage openly networked infrastructures to participate in production-centered activities (Ito et al., 2013).

Redefining the Librarian's Role in Connected Learning

A recent Pew Research Center study shows that 49% of the American public generally think of libraries as places that "contribute a lot to sparking creativity in young people" and "a trusted place for young people to learn about new technologies" (47%) (Horrigan, 2016, p. 8). Trends such as participatory culture and connected learning are pushing librarians to transition from the traditional role of expert to that of facilitator (Braun et al., 2014) and shift the roles of libraries "from a repository for materials to a platform for learning and participation" (Garmer, 2014, p. XI). Libraries' growing emphasis on participatory learning, summarized by the Institute of Museum and Library Services (IMLS) as "doing, together" (Hill, Proffitt, & Streams, 2015), is "illustrated by the emergence in recent years of learning labs, makerspaces, and other library resources and programming that go beyond simply training people how to use library collections" (Hoffman et al., 2016). One of the most exemplary connected learning environments is the YOU-Media space in the Chicago Public Library, which was then replicated in thirty more learning labs across the country (Sebring et al., 2013). Young people are increasingly coming to the library to engage in various interest-driven activities that Ito and her colleagues (2009) have identified as *hanging out, messing around,* and *geeking out.* This insurgence of new library patrons necessitates peer support and results in libraries being used for production-centered goals. In essence, libraries become "places to do stuff, and not simply places to get stuff" (Williams as cited in Valenza, 2008). Libraries are thus a ripe out-of-school environment to engage young adults in connected learning experiences (Braun et al., 2014; Hill et al., 2015; Subramaniam et al., 2017).

The opportunities and challenges that librarians have to enhance peer-supported and interest-driven environments are definitely unique. In a recent study where researchers conducted interviews and focus groups with ninety-two youth-serving librarians nationwide to investigate the opportunities and challenges that librarians face with respect to implementing connected learning in their youth programming, researchers found that librarians are great in "giving young people what they want" but lack confidence in their ability to serve as mentors in technology-enabled environments (Subramaniam et al., in press). The following quote from a librarian in the study epitomizes the point on how librarians equate mentorship with needing to be the expert when working with young people in technology-infused learning environments:

> For the robotics and Raspberry Pis, I rely heavily on the instructor. I personally am not fluent with either one of those technologies . . . I think a lot of what would be holding us back is having staff that is well versed in how to use them and really have ideas on how to implement them.

For some librarians, letting go of the role of the expert to become a facilitator requires a change in mindset and a mastery of a new set of skills on how to facilitate programming and services that will allow young people to dictate the direction and outcomes of a connected learning program. Past and even current practices of youth librarianship position the librarian as the person who generates the idea for a program and service solely or within his or her team, plans the program, recruits young people to participate in the program through multiple channels, and then implements the program. When it comes to using technology in their programs, past practices have held to the mantra "Don't know it, don't use it," which exclusively relies on the expertise of the librarian in order to offer a technology-infused program or services to the youth in the community.

Realizing connected learning requires transformation in thinking about the roles librarians take on with youth—librarians do not need to be sole experts in helping young people master emerging literacies. Redefining their roles and the mentorship they can provide are the key to designing and implementing interest-driven environments that are truly youth led. In this chapter, drawing from research in the learning sciences, we will cover the types of help youth need and the types of mentoring relationships that mentors must foster to support connected learning experiences. We will then apply these mentorship models to library settings and conclude with the skills and training needed for librarians to nurture these types of mentorships.

Types of Help Young People Need

In order to serve as mentors to realize connected learning, it is vital that librarians understand what type of help young adults as learners need. We have identified three types of help that are critically important to enhance and realize connected learning experiences.

First, Barron, Gomez, Martin, and Pinkard (2014) point to the importance of *fostering skill development and common language around creativity, production, and critical approaches* to learning (i.e., design thinking and twenty-first-century skills) versus passive approaches to learning. While twenty-first-century skills are those espoused in Jenkins et al.'s (2009) discussion of participatory culture (e.g., information and digital literacy), design thinking is specifically a new movement that emphasizes applying the processes and philosophies of designers (i.e., empathizing with stakeholders, inventing innovative prototypes, and iterating to new solutions) to solve new challenges and realize new opportunities (Ogilvie & Liedtka, 2011). Supporting design thinking and twenty-first-century skills involves helping youth to retain and develop their artistic skills (Barron et al., 2014) and promoting their technology-development skills necessary for twenty-first-century information processing (e.g., judging information online, remixing and recreating digital products, etc.) (Jenkins et al., 2009). Establishing a common language for these practices involves helping learners develop collaborative dispositions whereby they cocreate ideas, designs, and products. It also involves elaborating ideas together and providing (and receiving) constructive criticism to one another (Barron et al., 2014; Jenkins, 2009; Druin, 2002). Learners must see constructive critiquing and ideation techniques modeled so that they can begin to use similar language and practices. Additionally, key to development of design-thinking skills is helping learners fully leverage the freedom to fail and iterative processes to creating new ideas and products (Brown, 2009; Ogilvie & Liedtka, 2011). Librarians must model, prompt, and scaffold these practices and language to effectively promote connected learning experiences.

Second, *supporting youth engagement in connected learning communities* is vital to promoting connected learning experiences, as peer and mentor support in communities often inspire and drive the learning that occurs (Nasir & Hand, 2008; Barron et al., 2014). Communities also provide safe spaces for learners to try out new roles and make mistakes that lead to learning and expertise (Clegg & Kolodner, 2014; Clegg et al., 2013). However, youth need help initiating engagement, or on-ramping, in new communities (Barron et al., 2014). Once they are integrated into these communities, they also need scaffolding to promote their deepened engagement, helping them participate in ways more integral to the community. To do this, mentors must identify learners' developing skills and interests and point to relevant contributions learners can make that leverage those skills and interests and help learners further develop them. As opposed to expert–novice models, apprenticeship models are often more helpful in this case, where even novices are engaging in activities that are contributing to the community endeavors. Joint endeavors common in apprenticeship models enable mentors to observe and identify youths' interests and skills as they develop. Following an apprenticeship model, mentors (including librarians) can also plan new projects that will require the skills learners are developing and showcase their emerging expertise (Barron et al., 2014; Barton & Tan, 2010; Clegg & Kolodner, 2014).

Last but not least, *helping youth begin to take on leadership roles in the community* becomes important. Barron et al. (2014) suggest making space for learners to take on new leadership roles—pushing learners to take on new information behaviors, start new groups and discussions, and share relevant media. Mentors must additionally enable and encourage learners to have the agency and ownership needed for these roles (Yip et al., 2012). Librarians can give learners autonomy in the direction of the learning activities themselves and helping them to navigate those leadership roles.

To illustrate the types of help that youth need and how such help is provided to them in a nonlibrary environment, we describe the Kidsteam intergenerational design team at the University of Maryland. Kidsteam is an excellent example of how this type of scaffolding and on-ramping can occur. As youth between the ages of 7 and 12 join the design team, in apprenticeship manner, they participate, along with the entire team—old-timers and newcomers—in a two-week summer "boot camp" at which they become familiar with the concepts and ideas around design, collaboration, and iterative prototyping of technology designs (Druin, 2002; Fails, Guha, & Druin, 2013). This boot camp consists of team-building activities in which they get to know members of the design team and develop an understanding of one another's strengths and dispositions. During this time, they also develop a common language around design through the techniques used on the design team to help children articulate and share their ideas alongside adults (Fails et al., 2013). These techniques are in the form of design activities that make the tasks of design concrete, simple, and easy to begin for children. Many of these techniques involve informal drawing and illustrating ideas with crafts in ways that spark children's creativity while maintaining a sense of fun and lightness needed for iteration (Walsh, Foss, Yip, & Druin, 2013). While these techniques are often used during the boot camp to on-ramp newcomers into the design team using fictitious design goals (e.g., designing the air conditioner of the future), once the actual design sessions start, youths' engagement is deepened in these design techniques through design prompts from industry and research teams who are creating products in partnership with the design team.

Through the design techniques and overall structure of the program, youth learn to ideate and share their ideas, valuing creativity and collaboration (Druin, 2002). Early on, they begin actual work on the team, engaging in the design process after one or two weeks of being on the team alongside other children and adults who have been there longer. They learn to ask one another questions and critically consider ideas together (Fails et al., 2013). Over time, learners begin to take on more leadership roles—initiating conversations in the whole group and even initiating and leading their own design sessions for new ideas that they have had (Yip et al., 2013). It then becomes important that facilitators scaffold such leadership, helping children to become comfortable sharing their ideas with the whole team of peers and adults. Additionally, in support of leadership, adult partners must offer learners opportunities to take on new leadership roles, such as making time and space for them to lead their own design sessions as the children express interest and initiative (Yip et al., 2013).

Types of Mentoring Roles

In order to support youth in these ways, mentors need a key set of skills. We have identified three types of skills especially critical for supporting youths' connected learning experiences.

First, because it is no longer sufficient to solely focus on the mentor as expert and the youth as learner, ***mentors must be comfortable taking on a variety of roles in the learning experience***, including but not limited to facilitator, learner, and the more traditional role of expert (Barron et al., 2014; Nacu et al., 2016). Specifically, mentors need to guide youth to new learning experiences, prompting them to ask new questions and pursue new types of learning (Clegg & Kolodner, 2014). This facilitator role then helps learners to fully explore their curiosities and to develop new and deepened interests. As learners explore these dynamic learning pursuits that change and develop as they go, mentors often find themselves also taking on the role of learner—asking questions that are new to the mentor(s) and the youth that they each must work together to address (Clegg & Kolodner, 2014). Additionally, with youths' growing familiarity with technology, they can often ease into the role of experts themselves, helping their mentors discover new knowledge (Yip, Gonzalez, & Katz, 2016). Finally, there will remain times when mentors must use their own expertise to guide and help learners as they explore their interests (e.g., Clegg, Gardner, & Kolodner, 2011). This type of expert guidance can help learners to find the information they need and/or explore more meaningful and rich topics.

For example, in the Science Everywhere program at the University of Maryland and the University of Washington, youth learn science through exploration of everyday topics like kitchen chemistry and everyday environmental sustainability practices. In these dynamic learning experiences, mentors must take on a variety of roles. For example, we held a set of sessions on the topic of filtration, led by a graduate student volunteer who specializes in the topic. Graduate students and faculty on our research team who had little expertise in this area helped learners to engage in explorations and ask new questions, taking on the role of facilitator and learner as we explored together with the youth. As guiding facilitators, we asked youth questions about the types of mixtures they use every day at home and in their day-to-day lives and ways it might be useful to filter such mixtures. However, as learners developed their own ideas for filters and for filtering investigations, they needed the expert graduate student to help them see what types of filtration would be possible given the constraints of the learning environment and the liquids they were working with. For example, learners wanted to turn regular household drinks (e.g., Kool-Aid or juices) into clear liquid, filtrating out the color in the liquids. While the expert mentor knew this was possible, she helped them to see that they would need to consider additional filtering constraints (e.g., speed of filtration and ways to slow the filtration down) when designing their filters. As such, it took a range of mentoring roles to support learners' choice-driven investigations.

While Kidsteam and Science Everywhere demonstrate great examples of how mentors transition among these facilitator, expert, and learner roles, these transitions are harder for librarians given the complexities of library program offerings and attendance. For librarians, coming to an understanding of when to step into which role is problematic given that (1) youth drop in to library programs whenever it is convenient and not on a regular basis; (2) library programs are one-off, weekly, or seasonal depending on the themes and resources that are available; and (3) it is unlikely that the same youth are participating in each session. Sustained interaction on a regular basis in Kidsteam and Science Everywhere helps the mentors to gauge the youth that they are working with and determine when to step into which roles. The Make Do Share resource developed by the Kitsap Regional Library (Braun, Ciotti, & Peterson, 2016) provides a library playbook (with an emphasis on STEM programming) that provides guidance on how these differing mentorship roles can be established in a library learning environment. The ConnectedLib project (http://connectedlib.ischool.uw.edu/) also has a Mentoring module in its upcoming toolkit for youth-serving librarians. We draw primarily from these two resources (unless otherwise indicated) to derive insights on when librarians should assume the roles of facilitator, expert, or learner.

Librarians can facilitate when:

- Youth already have an interest in something and need encouragement and feedback from the librarian. Through the interviews that were conducted in the ConnectedLib project, many youth librarians discussed ways to help young people build their self-esteem and increase their confidence by supporting their interests. For example, a librarian shares,

  > I have a young man who has attended maybe a few programs and he's a writer, and he's very insecure about his writing ability. But after me just offering my guidance, my assistance, and helping him develop who he is as a writer, he now frequently sends me some writing that he has done so that I can edit it and give him some suggestions on how to make it better.

- Librarians do not have the expertise that is needed for certain career and personal interests but can facilitate connection with outside mentors. At the Providence Public Library, youth interested in fashion and art connected with design educators and students from a local college through a connection that was made by the youth librarian. For instance, at one workshop, a male youth interested in fashion was able to meet a college student who shared a similar background (Connected Learning Alliance, n.d.).

- Youth can mentor other youth. Youth are best positioned to help each other prepare for completing school projects and experiment with new technologies at their library when they have shared interests (Larson et al., 2013). Youth librarians have encouraged young people to "geek out" by designing their own programming for other teens while a librarian facilitates by offering feedback (Hoffman et al., 2016)

Librarians can learn from youth or learn together with youth when:

- Exploring a new technology. Youth librarians interviewed in the ConnectedLib project discuss how their role as a digital media mentor is more about collaborating and working through problems together rather than being a technology expert. A librarian describes her approach to using technology with young people:

> If a teen comes to one of us and say[s] 'I want to do this thing' and if none of us know how to do it, we sit down and we figure out how to do it together whether it be trying to find information in the book, looking up a tutorial on YouTube, reaching out to maybe another mentor or someone else in our life, who might know what's going on.

- Youth are openly displaying their expertise (known as youth signaling) (Ching, Santo, Hoadley, & Peppler, 2017). Youth librarians can provide or mobilize resources that are needed when youth are openly displaying their expertise and learn together with other youth.

Librarians can serve as the expert when:

- Advising young adults on appropriate technology use. Youth librarians can serve as experts in finding high-quality, age-appropriate digital media for youth and answer parents' questions about media use (Haines & Campbell, 2016). Some librarians have created blogs with recommended educational and literacy apps for young people of all ages (Campbell, Haines, Koester, & Stoltz, 2015).
- They possess the domain knowledge that is needed for the programming. Youth librarians may already be expert game designers/players, photographers, makers, artists, and the like and may offer expert advice on the relevant knowledge and skills that are needed by youth to explore their interests and passion in these areas.

While it is important that mentors embrace the myriad roles needed for supporting connected learning, they must also **navigate the tensions they may face between** *taking on these diverse roles* (Barron et al., 2014). For example, as mentors take on facilitator, learner, and expert roles, balancing between life-relevant aspects of the experience and the academically oriented aspects of the experience becomes critical. Supporting life-relevant experiences often involves mentors taking on the role of "socio-cultural friend" (Barron et al., 2014), engaging in conversations with youth to learn more about their interests, motivations, and day-to-day life experiences. This also requires mentors' openness and willingness to share their own interests, backgrounds, motivations, and life experiences to build personal rapport with learners but also to set positive examples for them (Barron et al., 2014; Clegg & Kolodner, 2014; Nacu et al., 2016). However, facilitators must be aware, in taking these roles, how to navigate between engaging in social conversations with learners while also supporting youth learning and the academic aspects of their experiences (Clegg & Kolodner, 2014). Mentors must carefully engage socially with learners while helping them to slow down and reflect in the midst of busy, exciting activities (Gardner, Clegg, Williams, & Kolodner, 2006), all the while observing the youths' progress, developing interests, and learning.

In the Kitchen Chemistry program at the University of Maryland and Georgia Tech, youth learn science through cooking (Clegg & Kolodner, 2014; Clegg et al., 2012; Clegg et al., 2014; Gardner & Kolodner, 2007; Yip et al., 2012). This has been an ideal context for mentors to take on a variety of connected learning mentoring roles, as cooking lends itself quite naturally to social experiences (Nardi, 2005), and the learning environment was designed to foster scientific inquiry and engagement (Clegg & Kolodner, 2014). In this context, facilitators helped youth use science to perfect dishes of their choosing. Mentors engaged in cooking investigations with youth, pointing to new investigations learners could do to improve their dishes based on their goals and helping youth to take on investigator roles. Simultaneously, adult mentors conversed with learners about their food likes and dislikes, travels, and their day-to-day lives (Clegg & Kolodner, 2014; Clegg et al., 2014). One teacher in the environment reported that this increased exposure helped one of her students who was having challenges in science class begin to feel more comfortable reaching out to her for help when she did not understand (Clegg & Kolodner, 2014).

Kitchen Chemistry mentors often supported connected learning by helping youth to engage in scientific investigations on their own terms, using their own language, to achieve their own personally determined goals (Clegg et al., 2014). For example, one learner wanted to make fried chicken like his mother made at home. Facilitators helped him perfect the dish by investigating the effects of using different oils and types of breading for the chicken. The learner conducted experiments varying oils and types of breading with adult facilitators who guided the design of the experiment but were also colearners with him—not knowing which oils and breadings would produce their desired results. Once they compared the results of the experiment to the specified goals for their chicken (e.g., color, crispiness, texture), the learner concluded that his mom should switch from olive oil to canola oil when frying chicken. Key to this experience, however, were mentors' academically oriented guidance on designing experiments, analyzing results, and making claims as well as the socially oriented conversations needed to draw out the learner's personal goals with respect to his mom's fried chicken.

Allowing learners to have these informal learning experiences in which they can explore their interests in meaningful ways on their own terms then opens the door for more academically oriented connections later that help learners relate to the topic from the perspectives of their own interests and goals (Clegg & Kolodner, 2014; Barton & Tan, 2010). One Kitchen Chemistry participant reported that she realized she was engaging in sneaky learning later, when she was introduced to some of the techniques (e.g., measuring) we used for cooking in her math class (Clegg & Kolodner, 2014). She realized that she was learning math as she was cooking and did not realize it.

In the HackHealth program that was implemented at selected Title 1 middle school libraries in the Washington, DC, metro area, young people investigate their own health interests, whether it is information they personally need, information for a family member, or information they want simply out of curiosity. The primary goal of this program is to increase disadvantaged middle school students' interest in science and health, their health and digital literacy skills, and their health-related self-efficacy. During HackHealth, school librarians, in conjunction with researchers at the University of Maryland, all served as mentors to lead one- to two-hour weekly sessions for approximately eight to twelve weeks. During each session, we emphasized various information and health literacy skills, such as conducting effective internet searches, assessing the credibility of online information, and carrying out the steps of the research process. The central focus of this program has been to sharpen young people's skills in obtaining and assessing health information from the internet (St. Jean et al., 2015). As facilitators, the research team and librarians were often asked about methods that we use to assess credibility of the information, what sources to select when youth are looking for health information, and we were often bombarded with questions such as "Is this correct? Did I do it right? Can I trust this YouTuber? Is this website legit?" While the facilitators constantly engaged in conversations with youth and asked questions to learn more about their interests, motivations, and day-to-day life experiences, we consciously did not provide what we thought was the "correct" answer and often answered questions with questions that would allow young people to develop their own heuristics on why one website was better than the other and how to pick up cues on fake news and websites (Subramaniam et al., 2015). This is no easy task and requires librarians to walk a tightrope navigating the role of an expert, facilitator, and learner to be the best "sociocultural" friend.

As mentors take on these roles, they must also continuously *reflect on specific ways to promote equity and diversity in their learning context or community*, focusing on repeatedly positioning all youth in their contexts to take on engaged, leadership roles. This also involves continuously watching out for patterns that favor one group over another (Barron et al., 2014). For example, in the Digital Youth

Network, Barron et al. (2014) observed that more boys were taking up STEM opportunities than girls. They continuously monitored for this and introduced new ways to engage girls in STEM activities. They observe that this is not something that is just done once, but it must be continuously observed and addressed throughout the life of a program (Barron et al., 2014). Additionally, this requires welcoming nontraditional participation, specifically offering a variety of ways learners can contribute to the learning community (Gee, 2005). We have found in our work that allowing learners to share their thoughts, insights, questions, and ideas via social media with a range of media forms (e.g., photos, video, text, drawing) enables learners to draw on a variety of participation styles to contribute to the community (Ahn et al.; Clegg et al., 2014; Yip et al., 2014). This has allowed more reticent learners to showcase the science practices they were using that would have otherwise gone unobserved (Ahn et al.; Clegg et al., 2014; Yip et al., 2014).

Libraries have always been institutions that promote equality and oftentimes offer the only after-school opportunity that nondominant youth can attend. In the Washington, DC, metro area, between the years of 2011–2014, selected Title 1 middle school libraries ran a weekly after-school program called SciDentity that utilized science storytelling and new media to engage youth in STEM ideas. School librarians and researchers from the University of Maryland served as facilitators in the program. Throughout the three-year program (serving youth from grades 6 to 8), the researchers consistently noticed youth who would respond to our prompts and activities more positively than others. The connected learning literature emphasizes the importance of examining the larger ecosystem of resources and experiences that youth have access to—beyond our after-school setting. SciDentity facilitators attempted to do this through offering a variety of interest-driven participation opportunities and scaffolding throughout the program based on continuous observations and reflection and learning about their entire learning ecosystem (Ahn et al., 2014). This required mentors to constantly document practices and interest-driven moments and reflect on these moments to design the appropriate learning activity and scaffolding.

Building a Community of Mentors

As we realize the breadth of roles needed to promote connected learning for youth, the task of supporting such dynamic experiences might seem overwhelming. As mentioned earlier, one key for librarians to consider is the importance of developing learning partnerships with community organizations and institutions beyond the library to engage the entire community as mentors in connected learning (Barron et al., 2014). In this way, it is important for librarians to become community builders, helping parents, community volunteers, and even other youth to become mentors themselves for connected learning experiences. This involves *developing innovative ways to engage families and community members in youth learning experiences* (Barron et al., 2014).

Our Science Everywhere project engages both parents and learners as mentors for connected learning. We have leveraged participatory design techniques described earlier (e.g., drawing, crafting techniques) to engage families together in the design of new technologies (Yip et al., 2016). Having families interchange between working within their own families and working in groups with other families has been helpful in these contexts for engaging families as partners in the design process and helping all family members take on more engaged roles (Yip et al., 2016).

Second, as community builders, librarians must also provide the necessary scaffolding for mentorship to parent, community, and peer volunteers. Such scaffolding includes *helping community members/parents think of themselves as mentors*. Often, we have found that parents think of library programs as places in which they drop their children off and then leave. Helping them to see these experiences as places that they go and work together to engage in science learning required conversations and meetings with parents (Yip et al., 2016). Additionally, structuring sessions just for parents to learn more about the program's expectations and learning activities and to ask questions apart from their children (Yip et al., 2016) are excellent strategies to engage parents. Similarly, older learners in our Science Everywhere program can often become frustrated with younger learners who need more guidance or behavior management. Encouraging older learners to take on mentorship roles then involves communicating that expectation with them and positioning them as the older, more mature youth who can help guide younger learners.

It is also possible to develop new activities and experiences to help youth take on more leadership roles. In one session in Science Everywhere (several of our young adults described this session as their favorite), we positioned the youth as teachers and the adults as learners. We wanted to learn more about youth culture, particularly with regard to social media and other popular technologies, so we tasked the learners with the challenge of teaching the adults how to be cool with their technology. Youth worked in small groups with one adult per group. Using low-tech prototyping crafts called bags of stuff, they taught the adults how to use the most popular apps and technologies with style, creating craft props to help the adults demonstrate youth culture. At the end of the session, the adult learners had to act out what they learned about how to be cool with their technology. Such activities are key to helping youth begin to take on the mindset of leaders, mentors, and teachers.

In order for adults and youth to take on these mentorship roles, they also need strategies for interacting with youth mentees. Librarians thus need to communicate and demonstrate ways mentors can effectively interact with youth to provide the type of guidance they need (Barron et al., 2014). This guidance often involves encouragement to potential mentors to dig into the learning activity with youth and to become engaged learners alongside them. Helping others become effective mentors also involves debunking stereotypes about what it looks like or means to engage academically. Often mentors, especially adults, are hesitant to engage in learning activities with their children because they fear that expertise is needed that they don't have. However, when we communicate the role of colearner with mentors, it helps put adults at ease and develop a comfort in their role as mentors. We have found that activities that relate learning to everyday life contexts (e.g., cooking, gardening) that adults are familiar with can help increase their comfort with mentoring their kids as well as help broaden their own perspectives of what science is and how it can be done (Clegg & Kolodner, 2014; Yip et al., 2014).

Developing activities that adult mentors can do with youth to promote deeper learning is also helpful for positioning community members as mentors. Life-relevant activities are particularly useful for helping mentors to further their engagement together in connected learning activities in other contexts (e.g., at home, in the community). Parents in our Kitchen Chemistry and Science Everywhere programs, for example, often report going home and extending recipes and experiments on their own with their children (Ahn et al., 2018). Families have recreated and revised recipes from Kitchen Chemistry or tried out similar experiment procedures from Science Everywhere. Key to such activity extensions are activities that leverage everyday topics that are relevant in other contexts as well as tools families are likely to have at home or in the community (Ahn et al., 2018; Clegg & Kolodner, 2014). Librarians can model such programs at their libraries to engage adult mentors to participate. Additionally, librarians should look out for new opportunities in the community that learners might be interested in to extend their learning. As librarians observe youths' developing interests and expertise, it becomes important that they link them to new programs that will enable them to further their development in those areas. Librarians can play key roles in helping community members take up these practices, to offer resources drawn from their own expertise, networks, and hobbies to young people.

Conclusion

Drawing from nonlibrary connected learning environments and research in learning sciences, this chapter presented types of help that young adults need and type of mentorships that librarians can provide in connected learning environments, with special emphasis on the skills and dispositions that librarians must possess. Knowing when to transition between these different types of mentorship and being comfortable in these diverse roles of mentorship calls for examining the strengths and needs of the youth and the community that librarians are serving. We encourage educators of youth and school librarianship in librarian preparation programs to cover these skills and dispositions in their core and required courses. We also urge professional organizations such as Young Adults Library Services Association, Association for Libraries Serving Children, and the American Association of School Librarians (divisions that serve youth librarians within the American Library Association) and state library agencies to include these skills in detail in their competencies for youth-serving librarians and to provide continuing education for in-service librarians. For small, rural, and tribal libraries that may not have a dedicated youth librarian, we encourage professional organizations such as Association for Rural and Small Libraries and Association of Tribal Archives, Libraries, and Museums to provide webinars and short professional development courses that will familiarize the library staff that work at these libraries on the forms of mentorships that they can offer to the youth that they serve. Through funding by the Institute of Museum and Library Services (IMLS), University of Maryland recently began a postmaster's certificate—the Graduate Certificate of Professional Studies in Youth Experience—for youth-serving librarians that dedicates a course to examining the various roles of mentorship that librarians can play in interest-driven connected learning environments. There is also a similar course for preservice librarians within the Master's in Library and Information Science program at the University of Maryland. In the upcoming year, a collaborative project between the University of Washington and the University of Maryland—ConnectedLib, funded by the IMLS—will allow public youth-serving librarians to explore various mentorship models through a comprehensive module on mentoring in connected learning environments. As participatory culture transforms the possibility of learning and engagement in the twenty-first-century, programs such as these that promote the development of connected learning mentorship skills for librarians are well on their way to situating libraries as hubs for interest-driven, peer-supported, and academically oriented connected learning.

References

Ahn, J., Clegg, T., Yip, J., Bonsignore, E., Pauw, D., Cabrera, L., Hernley, K., Pitt, C., Mills, K., Salazar, A., Griffing, D., Rick, J., & Marr, R. (2018). *Science Everywhere: Designing Public Tangible Displays to Connect Youth Learning Across Settings.* In the Proceedings of the 2018 SIGCHI Conference on Human Factors in Computing Systems (CHI '18). Montreal, Canada: ACM.

Ahn, J., Subramaniam, M., Bonsignore, B., Pellicone, A., Waugh, A., & Yip, J. (2014). 'I want to be a game designer or scientist': Connected learning and developing identities with urban, African American youth. In *Proceedings of the 11th International Conference of the Learning Sciences*, ICLS (pp. 657–664).

Barron, B., Gomez, K., Martin, C. K., & Pinkard, N. (2014). *The Digital Youth Network: Cultivating Digital Media Citizenship in Urban Communities.* Cambridge, MA: MIT Press.

Barton, A. C., & Tan, E. (2010). We be burnin'! Agency, identity, and science learning. *The Journal of the Learning Sciences, 19*(2), 187–229.

Braun, L., Ciotti, S., & Peterson, S. (2016). *Make do share: Our guide.* Retrieved from www.krl.org/makedoshare/ourguide

Braun, L. W., Harmant, M. L., Hughes-Hassell, S., & Kumasi, K. D. (2014). *The Future of Library Services for and with Teens: A Call to Action.* Chicago, IL: Young Adult Library Services Association.

Brown, T. (2009). *Change by Design.* New York, NY: Harper Collins.

Campbell, C., Haines, C., Koester, A., & Stoltz, D. (2015). *Media Mentorship in Libraries Serving Youth*. Washington, DC: American Library Association.

Ching, D., Santo, R., Hoadley, C., & Peppler, K. A. (2017, April). *Youth Signaling as a Means of Generating Social Support Around Interest-Driven Learning with Technology*. Paper presented at the AERA Conference, San Antonio, TX.

Clegg, T., Bonsignore, E., Ahn, J., Yip, J., Pauw, D., Gubbels, M., . . . Rhodes, E. (2014). Capturing personal and social science: Technology for integrating the building blocks of disposition. In *Proceedings of the Eleventh International Conference of the Learning Sciences (ICLS 2014)*, ICLS (pp. 455–462).

Clegg, T., Bonsignore, E., Yip, J., Gelderblom, H., Kuhn, A., Valenstein, T., . . . Druin, A. (2012, June). Technology for promoting scientific practice and personal meaning in life-relevant learning. In *Proceedings of the 11th International Conference on Interaction Design and Children* (pp. 152–161). New York, NY: ACM.

Clegg, T., & Kolodner, J. (2014). Scientizing and cooking: Helping middle-school learners develop scientific dispositions. *Science Education*, *98*(1), 36–63.

Clegg, T., Yip, J. C., Ahn, J., Bonsignore, E., Gubbels, M., Lewittes, B., & Rhodes, E. (2013, June). When face-to-face fails: Opportunities for social media to foster collaborative learning. In *Tenth International Conference on Computer Supported Collaborative Learning*, ICLS.

Clegg, T. L., Gardner, C., & Kolodner, J. (2011). Technology for supporting learners in out-of-school learning environments. In *Proceedings of the 9th International Conference of Computer-Supported Collaborative Learning*, ICLS (Vol. 1, pp. 248–255).

Connected Learning Alliance. (2018). Connected learning alliance. Retrieved from https://clalliance.org/

ConnectedLib. (in press). ConnectedLib project. Retrieved from: https://connectedlib.ischool.uw.edu/

Druin, A. (2002). The role of children in the design of new technology. *Behaviour and Information Technology*, *21*(1), 1–25.

Fails, J. A., Guha, M. L., & Druin, A. (2013). Methods and techniques for involving children in the design of new technology for children. *Foundations and Trends® in Human–Computer Interaction*, *6*(2), 85–166. doi:http://dx.doi.org/10.1561/1100000018

Gardner, C. M., Clegg, T. L., Williams, O. J., & Kolodner, J. L. (2006, June). Messy learning environments: Busy hands and less engaged minds. In *Proceedings of the 7th International Conference on Learning Sciences* (pp. 926–927). Bloomington, IN: International Society of the Learning Sciences.

Gardner, C. M., & Kolodner, J. L. (2007, July). Turning on minds with computers in the kitchen: Supporting group reflection in the midst of engaging in hands-on activities. In *Proceedings of the 8th International Conference on Computer Supported Collaborative Learning* (pp. 212–221). New Brunswick, NJ: International Society of the Learning Sciences.

Garmer, A. K. (2014). *Rising to the Challenge: Re-envisioning Public Libraries*. Washington, DC: Aspen Institute.

Gee, J. P. (2005). Semiotic social spaces and affinity spaces: From the age of mythology to today's schools. In D. Barton & K. Tusting (Eds.), *Beyond Communities of Practice: Language, Power and Social Context* (pp. 214–232). Cambridge, UK: Cambridge University Press.

Haines, C., & Campbell, C. (2016). *Becoming a Media Mentor: A Guide for Working with Children and Families*. Washington, DC: American Library Association.

Hill, C., Proffitt, M., & Streams, S. (eds.) (2015). *IMLS Focus: Learning in Libraries*. Kansas City, KS: Institute of Museum and Library Services. Retrieved from www.imls.gov/assets/1/AssetManager/IMLS_Focus_Learning_in_Libraries_Final_Report.pdf

Hoffman, K. M., Subramaniam, M., Kawas, S., Scaff, L., & Davis, K. (2016). *Connected Libraries: Surveying the Current Landscape and Charting a Path to the Future*. College Park, MD; Seattle, WA: ConnectedLib Project. Retrieved from http://go.umd.edu/5fh

Horrigan, J. B. (2016, September). Libraries 2016. *Pew Research Center*. Retrieved from www.pewinternet.org/2016/09/09/2016/Libraries-2016/

Ito, M., Baumer, S., Bittanti, M., boyd, d., Cody, R., Herr-Stephenson, B., Horst, H. A., Lange, P. G., Mahendran, D., Martínez, K. Z., Pascoe, C. J., Perkel, D., Robinson, L., Sims, C., & Tripp, L. (2009). *Hanging out, Messing Around, and Geeking out: Kids Living and Learning with New Media*. Cambridge, MA: MIT Press.

Ito, M., Gutiérrez, K., Livingstone, S., Penuel, B., Rhodes, J., Salen, K., Schor, J., Sefton-Green, J., & Watkins, S. C. (2013). *Connected Learning: An Agenda for Research and Design*. Irvine, CA: Digital Media and Learning Research Hub.

Jenkins, H., Purushotma, R., Weigel, M., Clinton, K., & Robison, A. J. (2009). *Confronting the Challenges of Participatory Culture: Media Education for the 21st Century*. A John D. and Catherine T. MacArthur Foundation Report on Digital Media and Learning. Cambridge, MA: MIT Press.

Larson, K., Ito, M., Brown, E., Hawkins, M., Pinkard, N., & Sebring, P. (2013). *Safe Space and Shared Interests: YOUMedia Chicago as a Laboratory for Connected Learning*. Irvine, CA: Digital Media and Learning Research Hub.

Nacu, D. C., Martin, C. K., Pinkard, N., & Gray, T. (2016). Analyzing educators' online interactions: A framework of online learning support roles. *Learning, Media and Technology, 41*(2), 283–305.

Nardi, B. A. (2005). Beyond bandwidth: Dimensions of connection in interpersonal communication. *Computer Supported Cooperative Work (CSCW), 14*(2), 91–130.

Nasir, N. I. S., & Hand, V. (2008). From the court to the classroom: Opportunities for engagement, learning, and identity in basketball and classroom mathematics. *The Journal of the Learning Sciences, 17*(2), 143–179.

Ogilvie, T., & Liedtka, J. (2011). *Designing for Growth: A Design Thinking Toolkit for Managers*. New York, NY: Columbia University Press.

Sebring, P. B., Brown, E. R., Julian, K. M., Ehrlich, S. B., Sporte, S. E., Bradley, E., & Meyer, L. (2013, May). *Teens, Digital Media, and the Chicago Public Library*. The University of Chicago Consortium on Chicago School Research. Retrieved from https://consortium.uchicago.edu/sites/default/files/publications/YOUmedia%20Report%20-%20Final.pdf

St. Jean, B., Subramaniam, M., Taylor, N. G., Kodama, C., & Casciotti, D. (2015). Impacts of the HackHealth After-school Program: Motivating youth through personal relevance. *Proceedings of the 78th Annual American Society for Information Science & Technology Conference, 52*(1), 1–11.

Subramaniam, M., Scaff, L., Kawas, S., Hoffman, K. M., & Davis, K. (in press). Using technology to support equity and inclusion in youth library programming: Current practices and future opportunities. *Library Quarterly*.

Subramaniam, M., Taylor, N. G., St. Jean, B., Follman, R., Kodama, C., & Casciotti, D. (2015). As simple as that? Tween credibility assessment in a complex online world. *Journal of Documentation, 71*(3), 550–571.

Valenza, J. (2008, August 25). *Library as Domestic Metaphor*. Retrieved from http://blogs.slj.com/neverendingsearch/2008/08/25/library'as'domestic'metaphor/

Walsh, G., Foss, E., Yip, J., & Druin, A. (2013, April). Facit PD: A framework for analysis and creation of intergenerational techniques for participatory design. In *Proceedings of the SIGCHI Conference on Human Factors in Computing Systems* (pp. 2893–2902). New York, NY: ACM.

Yip, J., Ahn, J., Clegg, T., Bonsignore, E., Pauw, D., & Gubbels, M. (2014, June). It helped me do my science: A case of designing social media technologies for children in science learning. In *Proceedings of the 2014 Conference on Interaction Design and Children* (pp. 155–164). New York, NY: ACM.

Yip, J., Clegg, T., Ahn, J., Uchidiuno, J., Bonsignore, E., Beck, A., Pauw, D., & Mills, K. (2016). The evolution of roles and social bonds during child-parent co-design. In *Proceedings of the 2016 SIGCHI Conference on Human Factors in Computing Systems (CHI '16)* (pp. 3607–3619). New York, NY: ACM.

Yip, J. C., Clegg, T. L., Bonsignore, E., Gelderblom, H., Lewittes, B., Guha, M. L., & Druin, A. (2012). Kitchen chemistry: Supporting learners' decisions in science. In J. van Aalst, K. Thompson, M. J. Jacobson, and P. Reimann, (Eds.), *The Future of Learning: Proceedings of the Tenth International Conference of the Learning Sciences*, ICLS '12 (Volume 1, Full Papers, pp. 103–110). Sydney, NSW, Australia: International Society of the Learning Sciences.

Yip, J. C., Foss, E., Bonsignore, E., Guha, M. L., Norooz, L., Rhodes, E., . . . Druin, A. (2013, June). Children initiating and leading cooperative inquiry sessions. In *Proceedings of the 12th International Conference on Interaction Design and Children* (pp. 293–296). New York, NY: ACM.

Yip, J. C., Gonzalez, C., & Katz, V. S. (2016). *The Learning Experiences of Youth Online Information Brokers*. In C. K. Looi, U. Cress, J. L. Polman, & P. Reimann (Eds.), *Transforming Learning, Empowering Learners: Proceedings of the 12th International Conference of the Learning Sciences*, ICLS '16 (Volume 2, pp. 362–369). Singapore: International Society of the Learning Sciences.

9

SMALL-TOWN LIBRARIANS AS EXPERIENCE ENGINEERS

Abigail L. Phillips, Victor R. Lee, and Mimi Recker

Introduction

With 80.5% of public library systems in the United States being composed of small and rural libraries, these libraries and the librarians who staff them play many important roles in communities across the country (Swan, Grimes, & Owen, 2013). From access to free and reliable broadband to early literacy education through lap sits and story times, small and rural libraries meet the need of populations who are typically underserved, impoverished, and inadequately educated (Alemanne, Mandel, & McClure, 2011). Because of the small-town environment, rural librarians and library staff are highly involved in their communities, paying close attention to regional events, local politics, and outreach opportunities.

Alongside public libraries, school libraries serve as another community anchor, particularly for students who do not have consistent transportation to the books, technology, and programming available at public libraries (Holland, 2015). By developing engaging and educative activities in collaboration with teachers, after-school programming, and a carefully selected collection, school librarians help in filling gaps existing between in and out of school learning and literacy education, and aid in bridging the digital divide (Hunsinger, 2015; Ito & Martin, 2013).

Much like urban school and public libraries, rural public and school libraries are providing innovative and engaging services. However, rural libraries are doing so without the budget, staffing, and other resources for large libraries and library systems (Flatley & Wyman, 2009). This chapter highlights two examples of small-town libraries that are breaking the mold for how youth can be served, engaged, and supported. Not only are these libraries helping meet the recreational and educational needs of youth, they are also acting as experience engineers. By "experience engineers," we are describing librarians who are patron centered and taking iterative approaches to developing services and programs and collections that reimagine what can happen in the library space. Finally, librarians as experience engineers include nontraditional services, ideas, and spontaneity.

Rural Libraries and Rural Librarianship

Like urban and suburban libraries, rural libraries can be supportive, nurturing, and welcoming environments for young adults (Jurkowski, 2006). In small rural communities, the public library is one of the only safe places for young adults to hang out after school, on weekends, and during school breaks (Smith, 2003). Public libraries function as a safe environment for young adults, where programming, materials, and services are available that encourage healthy behaviors.

School libraries in rural communities suffer from many of the same constraints as rural public libraries (Molnar, 2014). Inadequate funding, undertrained staff, and state and local politics place a limit on what services and materials school libraries can offer young patrons (Molnar, 2014 Rajput & Medley, 2003). In some religious and socially conservative communities, small and rural libraries face what may be seen as stricter parental, administrative, and community oversight. This limited access to libraries and library materials has an impact on an adolescent's "academic achievements and development of literacy skills" (Smith, 2014, p. 164).

Yet in small-town and rural communities, school libraries are a critical information and technology resource for young adults (Digital Literacy Task Force, 2013). Along with public libraries, school libraries offer students access to technology, active and passive programming, and education on literacy alongside that found in the classroom (American Association of School Librarians [AASL], 2017).

Despite the number of small-town and rural libraries, research on these libraries is scarce and dated (Phillips, 2016). Within library and information science (LIS), the literature largely focuses on academic libraries and services for students and faculty. School and public libraries do have tailored scholarly journals (e.g., *Public Libraries Quarterly* and *School Library Research*), however. The literature that is available comes from practitioner journals and magazines—usually personal anecdotes and descriptions of library programs and other activities. This chapter is one contribution to the literature on small-town and rural public and school libraries and an effort to demonstrate how dynamic and imaginative they can truly be.

Introduction to the Two Small-Town Libraries

The two libraries, Autumn Falls Middle School Library and Northern Hollow Public Library (both pseudonyms, as are the names of individuals mentioned in this chapter), discussed in this chapter draw from a larger IMLS-funded study (RE-31-16-0013-16) of the instructional supports needed for rural school and public librarians to develop STEM-geared maker programs in their libraries. For nearly two years, we have followed, documented, interviewed, and observed the activities at multiple small-town and rural libraries to better inform our understanding of how library programs are developed and implemented in these settings. We identified these two focal libraries as hosting especially novel experiences for the area in ways that connect to the interests of the patrons and to bold new ideas for how libraries can serve their local communities. Other libraries in our project would often hear about and inquire about ways to emulate what these two libraries and their librarians were doing.

The first focal library was located at Autumn Falls Middle School. This school and its library were located in a semirural community within a large school district and served approximately 800 seventh- and eighth-grade students. The library was divided into three areas: the book collection, instructional space, and lounging. However, these areas can blend when formal teaching is not taking place. Students lounge on beanbag chairs among the bookshelves, play cooperative games on the long, hard-topped desks, and build cities on the Lego table near the comfortable couches and reclining chairs.

The second focal library, North Hollow Public Library, was a modestly sized, recently renovated building with a brightly colored and playful children's area, movable shelving to conserve space, a computer area with desktop computers, and a generous work space with a coffee shop atmosphere with booths and plentiful electrical outlets for patrons. A collaborative space in the back of the library offers additional work space and a meeting place for the library's Teen Advisory Board (TAB). The library draws youth patrons from several neighboring communities, including those that are too small to have their own public library.

Experience Engineering in the School Library

The library in Autumn Falls Middle School (seventh and eighth grades) is managed by Anna, a former language arts teacher who has only recently completed her school library media certification. Not only is the library offering unexpected experiences for the students, it is also offering unexpected experiences for Autumn Falls teachers and administrators.

Early in her first year (2016–2017) as a school librarian, Anna began to demonstrate her abilities as an experience engineer within her library. She reached out to the school's faculty and promoted the library as a place for both formal and informal learning. She shared with all the Autumn Falls teachers an online listing of topics she could teach in the library as part of library-based instruction. Her teaching schedule quickly became full and continues to be. Anna leads instruction for the majority of the day, although she goes beyond what would often be expected for humanities-based instruction and will also host units and lessons relating to physics or computer programming.

Part of how Anna makes this happen is by promoting partnerships in lesson conceptualization and generating ideas for where the library could provide new or underused resources. For example, Anna had means to obtain sewing machines for the library in an effort to make it a creation space in addition to an information search space. Through conversations with the school's art teacher, they developed a multiday lesson on the steampunk genre. (Steampunk is a form of speculative fiction that is set in or around the Victorian era that integrates technology with that time period as a form of alternative history.)

Through this collaboration, Anna introduced students to steampunk as a literary genre represented in the library's collections while working with the art teacher to demonstrate the artistic style of steampunk as curated from the resources that she could find. Over three days, the art class came into the library to design and then create either an article of a steampunk costume or an entire costume that involved pleather, gears, headbands, keys, and other common steampunk decor. The breaking down of standard literacy instruction into a fully formed lesson including books, design, and construction of crafts demonstrates some of her ingenuity as an experience engineer. Furthermore, Anna was highly resourceful in obtaining materials needed for this activity, leveraging contacts she had at the local university and her knowledge of shops around town and what they offered.

Another novel move at the Autumn Falls school library has been the creation of a Teen Advisory Board (TAB). While TABs are common in public libraries, they are less so in school libraries. In the 2017–2018 school year, Anna began a TAB in her library—the first one of any school library in the county—and

FIGURE 9.1   Students participating in the steampunk design activity developed by Anna and the art teacher at Autumn Falls Middle School

received more than 25 applicants before their first meeting. Many of the TAB members were regulars in the library who hung out before school, during lunch, and after school and informally helped publicize the unique activities that could be found at the school library. The TAB exists independent of any existing class or previous school club.

The creation of the TAB for the school library was itself a new experience that created a sense of belongingness and voice for the youth patrons. In typical TAB meetings, Anna asks members for input about book selection, library activities, popular trends, and other topics of teen interest. During the meetings, Anna is actively engaged with the students, asking questions, making comments, and generally acting as an empathetic and helpful adult. The students wear the official TAB t-shirts (featured in Figure 9.2) to the monthly meetings, which also helps raise awareness throughout the school that there is something exceptional happening at the library. In interviews, Anna commented to us that the TAB acts as a time for the "library regulars" to hang out and feel like they are part of something. Participation in the TAB is one experience that many of the members lack during the rest of the school day. They are respected for the insights and guidance that they can provide Anna. They are relied upon to share what they know about teen interests regarding books, programming, and entertainment. They have the experience of collaboration that has a positive impact on the school and library

FIGURE 9.2 TAB meeting in the library at Autumn Falls with TAB members helping to decide on what kinds of maker activities should be available to students

and have more say in what kinds of interest-based pursuits should be available when students are hanging out in the library after the school bus drops them off, during lunch hour, or while they wait for the school bus to return them home.

In her interactions with students, Anna highlights the library as an inviting, shared space. She knows the students on a first-name basis, is aware of students' home lives and extracurricular activities, and acknowledges student achievements and interests. While Jan sets rules for appropriate behavior in the library, she manages to be flexible with discipline. The library exists as a space where "permissible transgressions," such as using one's mobile phone at school or putting feet on the furniture, is possible (Lee et al., 2017). She intuits when to step in as an authority figure, hang back and allow her aides to respond, or redirect the misbehaving student's attention to more suitable activity. Her actions allow the nature of the library space to be fluid and largely determined by the youth patrons themselves.

Anna has also demonstrated that she is unafraid to alter the physical layout and bring in unexpected materials. In another collaboration with the school's art teacher, Anna opened up shelving that had previously contained the reference collection for an art project. Before school began that August, she dramatically reduced her reference collection. She then painted the shelves with blackboard paint, purchased colorful chalk, and designated this space as a loosely controlled art area. Quarterly during the year, the art teacher brings students into the library to draw murals and work on specific projects. When the shelving is not in use for

FIGURE 9.3   Year-long collaborative blackboard chalk art project

the art class, students can write or draw and leave messages to one another, making the library an asynchronous communication space and a space for self-expression.

Passive programming, activities provided in the library without direct instruction from the librarian, is popular in Anna's library (see Johnson-Kaiser, 2016). Before school, during lunch, and after school, she sets out games, maker activities, and puzzles on tables for the students to access. Anna is attuned to the fickle interests of her students and rotates the options regularly. To find ideas, she explores coursework, blogs, lists, and other materials for passive programming ideas. At the request of some of the teens, she had purchased Lego tape so that walls could be made into surfaces where Lego blocks could be attached. These small activities encourage collaboration and participation, particularly among the quieter and shyer students in the school.

Autumn Falls Middle School Library, with a librarian as energetic and bold as Anna, demonstrates that despite the semirural environment, this is a library that has taken unique steps to break with what some have expected to be small-town school library tradition. While in school library media (SLM) coursework, relationship building and collaboration between librarians and teachers discussed, the reality of how challenging and frustrating these relationships typically emerges while on the job. However, Anna has excelled at engineering a space where collaboration, spontaneity, and understanding work together in a way that is highly youth centered.

Experience Engineering in the Public Library

North Hollow Public Library, located a few cities north of Autumn Falls, draws many of its teen patrons from several local schools. There is not a formal youth services department in this small and rural, single-county library. However, the assistant director, John (one of two full-time employees), and two library assistants develop and lead the after library hours teen programming. All of the teen programs take place after the library is closed. As John had shared with us during an interview, this not only helped reduce any conflicts between patrons seeking a quiet space to read or study and the teens looking for programs but also cultivated a sense of ownership of the library amongst the teens that did come to the teen programs. It was a time and space for them to behave as they wished, thus enabling a range of permissible transgressions to take place as well. When we observed the teen programs, there was loud music (which involved John wheeling out a large speaker so the music could be even louder) and food (not allowed during regular hours) and youth walking barefoot in the aisles or running across the floor. This made the teens feel the Northern Hollow library was a space where they could feel respected and included and were not expected to conform to expectations of parents or teachers. To illustrate this, consider what is shown in Figure 9.4. That figure is an image taken from an after-hours teen program featuring a *Wheel of Fortune*–style game about popular young adult literature. Notice in that image that

FIGURE 9.4 After-hours teen program with furniture rearranged

the teens have moved around furniture, pushed away the usual movable book-shelves, and lounge comfortably on the floor or with feet up on chairs. Other activities included overnight lock-ins (sleepovers, with parent consent), board game nights, videogame nights, and forms of Nerf gun tag. These novel experiences then encouraged other libraries to get involved, with occasional "battles" between youth patrons from different libraries.

North Hollow Public Library has an established and well-attended TAB. Popular in public libraries, TABs can be challenging to form and maintain in rural communities because of transportation issues, after-school conflicts, and available library space. Despite these challenges, the TAB at North Hollow draws an energetic group of 10 to 15 teens to the monthly organizational meeting. Facilitated by a library staff member, these meetings provide the TAB an opportunity to plan teen programs and offer insights on emerging youth interests within the community and volunteer possibilities. A novel feature of the TAB is the officer position of social media specialist in which the youth's social media savviness is leveraged to report on teen events and to publicize upcoming activities and involved the teens in library activities in unique ways.

One growing trend in public libraries is stepping beyond the traditional circulation of print materials to more off-the-wall collections (Cruz, 2016; Giaimo, 2017). North Hollow Public Library, under the leadership of Abraham, the director and only other full-time employee, circulated GoPro cameras, kayaks, paddleboards, park passes, and other materials that reflect the outdoor-loving and athletic nature of the community it serves. These unique collections were well liked by local families and youth patrons and aid in presenting the library as a one-stop destination for educational, leisure, and social needs. Under Abraham's direction, changes also took place in library programming for the broader community beyond the teens. Abraham created a Saturday farmer's market on its grounds so that the trip to the library could be coupled with purchase of fresh produce and local crafts. A strategic move Abraham, John, and others at the library engineered was to maintain a booth at the farmer's market where the teens could showcase and teach various craft activities that they themselves had experienced to younger visitors when they visited on the weekends. Abraham also established yoga and Pilates classes during the daytime at the library to serve those adults who wanted recreation classes.

In the summertime, Abraham regularly organized a summer reading kickoff (Figure 9.5) complete with bounce houses, rides, vendors from the Farmer's Market, TAB members operating a snow-cone booth, and local markets providing free food samples. This becomes a large festival-like experience with bubble machines and a drone overhead taking video and demonstrating quadcopter technology to interested visitors. This reading kickoff also had reading incentives for local youth to encourage continued literacy engagement while school was out. During the year, Abraham and John also established a teen participation program in which a

FIGURE 9.5 North Hollow summer reading kickoff

blockbuster film would be privately screened at a teens-only reserved theater at the local movie complex for teens who were involved in library programs and service projects.

In summary, the staff at North Hollow Public Library, particularly those working with teens, have cultivated an environment in which young patrons' experience kinship with peers, mentorship, and service were prioritized. The administration advocates for and promotes the library as not only an information resource but a connection to community.

Features of Library-Based Experience Engineering

Autumn Falls Middle School library and North Hollow Public Library were highlighted in this chapter because of the unique experiences these libraries offer to their patrons, and especially to their youth patrons. Related to youth patronage, recent research into connected learning, making in the library, and libraries as sites for critical informal learning attest to the growing awareness of the continued importance of and need for school and public libraries (Martin, 2015; Lee et al., 2017; Rainie, 2016). These libraries appear to demonstrate how that can be made possible in small community settings. In the information sciences, youth experience within the library is a growing interest among researchers and librarians. For example, this is reflected by the College of Information Studies at the University of Maryland, which had recently developed a certificate program focusing on youth experience and librarianship (YX @ UMD, 2018). By disconnecting with traditional library practices and traditional youth services, small-town and rural libraries are helping shift the conversation from what these types of libraries have long been seen as offering to the wide range of possibilities for what rural libraries are capable of providing communities.

In reflecting on how the librarians at these two libraries engineered new experiences that have been positively received by patrons, we make a number of observations. First is that there was a continual *user-centeredness* in the programs and activities that were created. Excellent engineering practice considers the end users, which, in the case of libraries, are the patrons. In the past, those patrons may have sought information and a quiet place to access technology and work. That has changed dramatically, even in small towns like the ones in which we met these librarians. This is in part because the range of interests has expanded beyond seeking information and instead to finding a space that can provide visitors with ways to communicate, explore interests, take on more civic and service responsibilities, and learn more about the community around them. With Abraham, John, and Anna, this turned into making spaces for teens, developing a farmer's market, printing custom t-shirts for a new advisory group, and collaborating with others to devise new experiences that many in the small communities would not expect to happen at the library.

Second, these librarians were *connected to their communities*. Anna had an excellent rapport with the art teacher and used that connection to jointly establish new units and lessons that leveraged what both educators could offer. Beyond that, she made herself and her library visible to all the teachers and students so that they knew what she and her space had to offer. At North Hollow, connections with local farmers and craftspeople enabled the creation of a farmer's market, and familiarity with the local small businesses enabled there to be a festival-like experience, with samples and donations for local families to kickoff summer reading programs. The librarians presented their libraries as hubs within their larger community networks.

Finally, these librarians were *comfortable with risk*. They pursued what was unconventional for local libraries, but they did so without hesitation. While smaller towns may present themselves as having fewer resources and may be seen as exhibiting reluctance to change, they also have less bureaucracy and more people who are interested in seeing what is going on in the area. These forces can support innovation when there are figures comfortable taking the lead in ways that are almost unapologetic. The successes, be it in the form of turnout of patrons or continued public interest in what the library will do next, appeared to do a great deal to assuage the concerns of those who were uncertain about what to expect and encourage even more new kinds of experiences to be designed and implemented. While small libraries across the country routinely struggle with space, budgets, and political and social constraints, Autumn Falls Middle School library and North Hollow Public Library both serve as demonstration cases that show how unique and popular library services and programming can be engineered to serve youth and other patrons of library spaces.

References

Alemanne, N. D., Mandel, L. H., & McClure, C. R. (2011). The rural public library as leader in community broadband services. *Library Technology Reports*, 47(6), 19–28.

American Association of School Librarians. (2017). *Standards for the 21st-Century Learner* (pp. 1–8). Chicago, IL: American Library Association.

Cruz, R. (2016, August 3). State parks passes a hit in Colorado. *Public Libraries Online*. Retrieved from http://publiclibrariesonline.org/2016/08/state-parks-passes-a-hit-in-colorado/

Digital Literacy Task Force. (2013). *Digital Literacy, Libraries, and Public Policy* (pp. 1–27). Washington, D.C.: Office for Information Technology Policy.

Flatley, R., & Wyman, A. (2009). Changes in rural libraries and librarianship: A comparative survey. *Public Library Quarterly*, 28(1), 24–39.

Giaimo, C. (2017, April 7). From fine art to fishing poles, the most surprising things libraries are lending now. *Atlas Obscura*. Retrieved www.atlasobscura.com/articles/library-weird-collection-art-cake-pan-fishing-pole-umbrella

Holland, B. (2015, January 14). *21st-Century Libraries: The Learning Commons*. Retrieved 13 June 2017, from www.edutopia.org/blog/21st-century-libraries-learning-commons-beth-holland

Hunsinger, V. (2015). School librarians as equity warriors. *Knowledge Quest*, 44(1), E10. Retrieved from http://search.proquest.com/openview/84f4ec0b6026c3f049f20d811a5384c8/1?pq-origsite=gscholar&cbl=6154

Ito, M., & Martin, C. (2013). Connected learning and the future of libraries. *Young Adult Library Services, 12*(1), 29.

Johnson-Kaiser, K. (2016, April 23). Passive programs for school age kids. *Association of Library Services for Children Blog.* Retrieved from www.alsc.ala.org/blog/2016/04/passive-programs-school-age-kids/

Jurkowski, O. L. (2006). The library as a support system for students. *Intervention in School and Clinic, 42*(2), 78–83.

Lee, V. R., Lewis, W., Searle, K. A., Recker, M., Hansen, J., & Phillips, A. L. (2017). Supporting interactive youth maker programs in public and school libraries: Design hypotheses and first implementations. In P. Blikstein & D. Abrahamson (Eds.), *Proceedings of IDC 2017* (pp. 310–315). Stanford, CA: ACM.

Martin, C. (2015). Connected learning, librarians, and connecting youth interest. *Journal of Research on Libraries and Young Adults, 6.*

Molnar, M. (2014, October 27). Many rural schools, libraries could lose funds under new E-rate reform. *Education Week.* Retrieved from http://blogs.edweek.org/edweek/marketplacek12/2014/10/many_rural_schools_libraries_could_lose_funds_under_new_e-rate_reform.html?cmp=SOC-SHR-FB

Phillips, A. L. (2016). *The Empathetic Librarian: Rural Librarians as a Source of Support for Rural Cyberbullied Young Adults* (Order No. 10120555). Available from ProQuest Dissertations & Theses Global.

Rainie, L. (2016). *Libraries and Learning.* Washington, DC: Pew Research Center. Retrieved from www.pewinternet.org/2016/04/07/libraries-and-learning/

Rajput, T., & Medley, N. (2003). Urban vs rural. *Children and Libraries: The Journal of the Association for Library Service to Children, 1*(2), 49–58.

Smith, D. (2014). Collaboration between rural school and public youth services librarians. *New Library World, 115*(3), 160–174.

Smith, E. L. (2003). Why rural libraries should serve young adults. *Rural Libraries, 23*(2), 45–68.

Swan, D. W., Grimes, J., & Owen, T. (2013). *The State of Small and Rural Libraries in the United States.* Washington, DC: Institute of Museum and Library Services.

YX @ UMD. (2018). *YX@UMD—Youth Experience.* Retrieved from https://yx.umd.edu/

10

CULTIVATING SCHOOL LIBRARIAN DISCERNMENT AS E-LEARNING TECHNOLOGY STEWARDS OF THE FUTURE

Rebecca Reynolds and Chris Leeder

Introduction

The evidence base for the school librarian's positive influence on student learning outcomes and their role in cultivating a climate of inquiry and innovation in schools is substantial. For instance, significant links have long been documented through evidence-based practice research as well as evaluation studies between school librarians' active engagement, and their students' learning outcomes in the core disciplinary subject domains (e.g., Scholastic, 2008; Lance, 2001; Lance, Rodney, & Russell, 2007; Todd & Kuhlthau, 2004; Callison, 2004; Small & Snyder, 2009, Library Research Service, 2011; Bailey & Paul, 2012; DiScala & Subramaniam, 2011). Studies conducted in three states (Pennsylvania, Colorado, and Oregon) indicate that participating library media programs' level of development in staffing, resources, and funding were predictors of student academic achievement outcomes (Lance, 2001; Lance & Rodney, 2014). A study in California found a significant correlation between school library services and student test scores across all student performance areas (Achterman, 2008). Subramaniam et al. (2015) found that school librarians are a strong asset in science learning, as they foster youth engagement in authentic inquiry practices and engage young people's everyday life interests in science learning.

School librarians have maintained a longstanding and integral instructional role in the school environment, especially as it relates to student literacy, reading, writing, and information seeking, which is traditionally seen as their primary instructional function. A wide variety of evidence-based models for school librarians' pedagogy in the areas of literacy, reading, writing, inquiry, and information literacy exists. For instance, with regard to research and inquiry skills, one study in New Jersey built upon the guided inquiry model (per Kuhlthau, 2004) and examined ways in which students build knowledge of a topic through intensive engagement in inquiry and information seeking using principles of Guided Inquiry. In this work, as teams of librarians and teachers guided students through the specified stages of guided inquiry, students were found to proceed far beyond mere fact finding in their inquiry, moving into personal understanding, meaning making, and transformative knowledge building (Todd, 2006).

What is more, school librarians of today wear many additional hats in teaching and learning involving digital technologies (Everhart, Mardis, & Johnston, 2011). Library and information sciences (LIS) scholarship increasingly positions the school library as the physical and virtual learning commons of the school environment—a locus for technology innovation, with a focus on students' creative engagement with information resources and knowledge building with digital tools (Todd, 2012; Kuhlthau, 2010; Kuhlthau, Maniotes, & Caspari, 2012; 2015). In New Jersey, Todd, Gordon, and Lu (2011) conducted an extensive mixed-methods empirical study of innovations in school librarianship, collecting 765 survey responses and conducting interviews and observations with 30 participants. Findings show that school librarians' practices with technologies contribute in rich and diverse ways to the intellectual life of a school and also to students' development of fluency in navigating their complex and increasingly digital information environments. Success factors for greater student knowledge production with digital tools included school librarians' leadership in forging strong instructional collaborations with classroom teachers; offering of direct instructional interventions and time on task with digital information resource use exercises; actively engaging students directly in meaningful and creative projects using digital resources; school librarians' embrace of new technologies and information systems, and librarians' role as technology innovation advocates, leaders, and pioneers, vis-a-vis the school administration and other teachers (2011). (See Chapter 9, this volume.)

As e-learning technologies continue to advance and evolve, the school librarian's role as an innovator is growing (Everhart et al., 2011; Johnston, 2012; Wine, 2016; Wolf, Jones, & Gilbert, 2014). Given the rigid accountability and testing goals that regular classroom educators are increasingly tasked with, school librarians have the potential to contribute to a greater climate of innovation and responsiveness to technological changes in ways that may be beyond the capacity of the average teacher. Such responsiveness will necessarily include school librarians' and administrators' attention to the growth and expansion of computer science education (CSE) in K–12 public school settings in the U.S. context as well, such as the priorities initially signaled by Obama administration's "CS for All" initiative and a growing national education policy agenda to offer high-quality, engaging, and research-driven computer science (CS) and computational thinking (CT) learning opportunities in the lower grade levels (Wilson, Sudol, Stephenson, & Stehlik, 2010). School librarians will need to consider where and how they fit within this expanding computer science educational mix.

School librarians have long been trained to adapt, self-advocate, and make themselves necessary in step with the times; this is even more important in today's environment of budget cuts, rapid technological evolution, and changing roles (Loertscher, 2003; Lonsdale, 2003; Oberg, 2006). With the growth of computer science educational priorities, digital literacy instructional imperatives, and calls to action by policy makers toward preparing the youth of today for the digital economy, we propose that the school librarian of today has significant and timely opportunities to become a key school leader and stakeholder in the delivery of computing-based instructional interventions that are (a) culturally responsive to youth cultures of today and (b) that can help develop students' dispositions, practices, and expertise in twenty-first-century skills they will need in future professional settings and, indeed, to be active, participatory citizens (Chu et al., 2016). In such a leadership role, school librarians will be tasked with key decisions regarding defining instructional goals and objectives, selecting effective e-learning solutions, and implementing curriculum for twenty-first-century skills (2016).

This chapter aims to empower such leadership in today's school librarians, offering a set of guidelines and strategies for choosing *effective* e-learning and curricular solutions to support positive learning outcomes among students in newly prioritized knowledge and practice domains involving technology and computing. The chapter first offers strategies for school librarians' technology decision making and implementation, building on Wenger, White, and Smith's (2009) framework for "technology stewardship," which applies in a broad range of professional climates, including schools. We then provide a case study example of e-learning solution decision making from the standpoint of the school librarian. In the case study example, we focus on reviewing the features, affordances, and evidence base for one particular e-learning solution. To demonstrate how such a review is necessary, we propose, in establishing sufficient justification for expenditure of time and resources to commit to implementation. We develop and offer selection criteria specific to K–12 school-based e-learning goals and objectives, considering "acquisition strategies" such as "use what you have," "build your own," "go for the free stuff," etc. (Wenger et al., 2009). Overall, the case study example can be used as a template to set a benchmark for school librarians' discernment, supporting responsibility to choose credible, evidence-based products and solutions that present greater likelihood to bear out success outcomes, in K–12 student e-learning.

Background

E-Learning Innovations

A wide array of options exists for school librarians who wish to initiate e-learning innovation in their schools, libraries, and classroom settings. Haythornthwaite and Andrews (2011) define e-learning quite broadly, as a transformative movement in learning, not just the transfer of learning to an online stage. The authors embrace the ways in which learning flows across physical, geographical, and disciplinary borders (2011). They describe e-learning as perpetual, sustained over a lifetime, and enacted in multiple daily occurrences as individuals search for information to satisfy their learning needs and contribute content that promotes their and others' understanding (2011). They state that in e-learning, teachers and learners use technology to create the social space in which learning occurs, which includes psychological space that is sustained across multiple devices and activities; cyberspace; and physical space, for instance using technology to connect learning to locations or objects in cities and museums (2011, p. 2). This broad definition highlights the ways in which e-learning options are expanding, making this concept inclusive of the existing and future range of innovations.

An earlier and narrower conceptualization of e-learning was focused on the "learning management system" or "LMS" (acronym not to be confused with the library media specialist). LMSs are web-based technologies that provide instructors with a way to create and deliver content, to monitor student participation and engagement, and to assess student performance online (Venter, van Rensburg, & Davis, 2012). Such platforms are making increasing headway in the K–12 marketplace, and many middle schools and high schools use such platforms to manage grades and their home/school parent/teacher relationships and scheduling, as well as some blended learning curriculum offerings involving e-textbooks. LMS platforms produced by commercial technology vendors are ubiquitous in higher education, with 99% of institutions having an LMS in place (Dahlstrom et al., 2011; Lang & Pirani, 2014). In addition, an ECAR study found that 85% of higher education faculty use an LMS, and 56% of faculty use it daily; 83% of students use an LMS, and 56% say they use it in most or all courses (Dahlstrom, Brooks, & Bichsel, 2014).

Much of the available data on learning management system prevalence in K–12 derives from industry data reports sequestered behind steep paywalls inaccessible to libraries. Culling together freely available data, we note that the K–12 LMS market represents almost 100,000 individual U.S. schools, compared to higher education's smaller market of ~7,000, which presents steep revenue opportunities for LMS providers pursuing K–12 ("LMS Data," 2015). Upside Learning (2016) predicts that "between the years 2017 and 2018, the LMS market will grow by about 23.17%, with an estimate of growth from $2.65 billion in 2013 to $7.8 billion in 2018, which is roughly an annual growth rate of 25.2%." Books are becoming augmented by electronic texts as well. Among eighty-six educational publishing companies analyzed in one market survey, the most frequently cited product medium for delivering instructional materials was online/digital delivery (82.6%), followed by print (65.2%), showing that electronic formats are increasing in prevalence (Simba, 2015).

Given these growth opportunities, Blackboard is actively expanding its LMS products and services into K–12 ("LMS Data," 2015). Similarly, Google is expanding upon its G Suite for Education, placing emphasis on the reach of Google Classroom into K–12 schools, a product that serves as a front end to their productivity suite, which includes Google Docs and Google Drive (Fenton, 2017). Publishing giant Pearson, which for a decade had worked to advance the LMS platform eCollege, has withdrawn from the LMS marketplace due to the growing competition, in favor of focusing on its digitized curricular content product offerings. Because traditional curriculum publishing companies like Pearson hold valuable longstanding ties to school districts and state-level departments of education, we may increasingly see LMS platform providers partnering with publishing companies on electronic content delivery for curriculum materials for use in K–12 classrooms in the core subject domains.

Critiquing the rapid advance of digitized book materials through commercial LMS infrastructure, Humphreys (2012) challenges the focus of LMS companies and publishers on reaching and serving greater numbers of students in a given program offering quickly rather than addressing *quality* of the learning experience and improvement of teaching strategies and learning outcomes (both the *what* and *how* students are learning with these digital tools). When considering learning affordances, we must consider the ways in which e-learning technologies are tailored, structured, and scaffolded to suit the given learning task, as well as the given learners and communities. At the K–12 level especially, where public education is a mandate, effective and personalized design and structure becomes an equity issue in that requiring use of an e-learning system that is unsuitable to particular learners restricts their equitable access to learning.

Research, Innovation, Customization

Expanding beyond more generic learning management systems to the broader definition of e-learning that we started with in this section, in an updated volume, Haythornthwaite, Andrews, Fransman, and Meyers (2016) highlight newer e-learning developments that have garnered recent attention. These include the following:

- Video-based resources for teaching and learning;
- Games and gamification of learning;
- Massive open online courses (MOOCs);
- Enhanced means of helping learners navigate through materials, such as lecture recordings that can be annotated;
- Adaptive learning systems that determine next steps according to learner progress and types of errors;
- Dashboards that show progress or effort in comparison to other learners; and
- Embedded tutors.

If well conceived, designed, and researched, as well as executed and implemented, e-learning offerings such as those discussed by Haythornthwaite et al. (2016) have potential to be tailored and customized to meet curricular learning goals and to be more adaptable to learner differences. Varying needs of student learners at the community, classroom, and individual levels may be addressed in more customized and tailored design approaches, taking into consideration factors such as grade level, reading levels, and individual differences in prior knowledge, motivation, self-regulation, and other dispositions.

Tailored and research-supported innovation in instructional design and e-learning development is occurring in arenas such as learning sciences, computer-supported collaborative learning, networked learning, educational data mining, learning@scale, and learning analytics (Haythornthwaite et al., 2016). These research domains often reside within university and nonprofit educational technology innovation hubs funded by entities like the National Science Foundation, focusing on human–computer interaction (HCI) research, design-based research (DBR), and learning sciences instructional theory and learning theory. Project materials and curricula that result from such endeavors are often made available for free online (but with few ongoing support services or resources for educators in their implementation once generated and published). Results of such research and development efforts can be found by school librarians in the proceedings of the International Conference of the Learning Sciences (ICLS), the *Journal of the Learning Sciences* (JLS), and the Computer-Supported Collaborative Learning (CSCL) conference and journal by the same name.

Culturally Responsive Teaching

Further, research on computer science education and e-learning increasingly acknowledges the need for curriculum that is culturally responsive to diverse student backgrounds, interests, and community needs stemming from racial, ethnic, and socioeconomic diversities. Culturally responsive teaching (CRT) recognizes the importance of including students' cultural references in all aspects of learning (Ladson-Billings, 1995). Vavrus (2008) proposes that such a reform measure in instructional design seeks to increase the engagement, motivation, and achievement of lower-socioeconomic status students and students of color who historically experience less academic success and greater alienation within public schools—by validating and infusing students' own cultures into the curriculum (2008). While much of the originating work in this arena has been developed in the traditional K–12 core curriculum subject domains, a number of K–12 computer science education experts have adapted culturally responsive *computing* (CRC) pedagogy (e.g., Pinkard, Erete, Martin, McKinney& de Royston, 2017; Scott, Sheridan, & Clark, 2015; Eglash, Gilbert, Taylor, & Geier, 2013; Margolis et al., 2012; Goode & Margolis, 2011; Henderson, 1996, 2007; Eisenhart & Edwards, 2004; Lee, 2003; Pinkard, 2001; McLoughlin, 1999).

Decisions about participation in STEM are frequently made prior to high school, and these decisions are impacted by prior experience, interest, and sense of fit with community (Pinkard et al., 2017). The cultural responsiveness of a CS education program has been found to contribute to its success (2017). Research indicates three distinct features that characterize a successful culturally responsive computing project (Scott et al., 2015):

- The learning experience engages program designers, educators, and students to *collaboratively reflect* on the intersection of their *experiences* and *identities* with digital technologies;
- Within these experiences, participants' discovery processes and building of artifacts reach beyond school; and
- Participants foster new *connections* with each other and their outside communities.

These scholars propose that digital learning projects may be particularly successful when the design artifacts created by students address issues facing members of their local community. The authors suggest that school decision makers should conceive of digital access in terms of students' availability of opportunity to engage in creation and innovation with digital technologies in a way that is culturally responsive to their local situation in order to support a pathway to greater digital equity (2015). It is important that e-learning solutions be culturally responsive and adaptive to the needs of different student, teacher, and school communities.

Overall, given new opportunities for e-learning developers to design and develop customized, tailored, and well-researched e-learning solutions being met with scholarly research and funding support from agencies such as NSF in the United States, better and more effective solutions are reaching the hands of educators of today in greater numbers. The opportunity to introduce more *effective* e-learning and computing education options into K–12 is exciting, but at the same time, all these choices should give education leaders pause.

Discernment among education decision makers and practitioners such as school librarians about the customization and fit of a given e-learning solution to their unique local context is key to the success of such initiatives. Next we provide some guidelines for technology decision makers such as school librarians, drawing upon a framework for "technology stewardship" from the field of organizational studies and management. This framework offers helpful guidelines for cultivating a closer attunement to the nuances and needs of one's local community setting for innovation—in this case between the school librarian and the school environment.

Technology Stewardship

Technology stewardship is a concept that is broad enough to encompass the types of decision making school librarian leaders are and will be faced with in choosing to deploy digital technologies to meet particular learning and teaching goals and objectives in their schools. In their book entitled *Digital Habitats: Stewarding Technologies for Communities*, Wenger, White, and Smith (2009) discuss the role of a technology steward as one who adopts a community's perspective (such as a local school community) to help the community choose, configure, and use technologies to best suit its needs. As both a *perspective* and a *practice*, technology stewardship involves a key stakeholder individual, such as a school librarian, taking on a responsible and committed role and mindset as a leader and acting with *initiative* to facilitate and guide technology solutions' selection and use, considering the unique needs and context of the given community and its goals, norms, and values (2009). The technology steward facilitates decision making, implementation, and ongoing adoption and usage of a given technology based on contingencies and constraints presented (2009).

A technology steward attends to both what happens spontaneously in the organization and what can happen purposefully, through planning and cultivation of insights in the lead-up to technology decision making. According to Wenger et al. (2009), those in the technology stewardship role must balance technological determinism (a view in which technology imposes influence and change upon human practice) with a more humanistic approach allowing the community needs to drive technology choices, proposing adoption of a pragmatic stance. One must consider questions such as: How should the community's norms, values, and practices shape technology decision making and integration? How can a given technology solution as it is designed (and as it may be customized) shape and improve practices and processes in the community? Technology stewardship can be applied in a broad array of communities including formal settings such as businesses, departments within a company, nonprofit organizations, and so on or informal settings such as hobby groups, citizen networks, political spheres of engagement, and the like. In the case of schools and educational settings, one can imagine a school librarian identifying a learning goal or need in a new computing curricular domain, perhaps in consultation with a classroom teacher and/or administrator, and then initiating a search and review process for an e-learning solution that can help facilitate the learning goal, through provision of platforms and/or curriculum content and activities. Such a decision might involve short-term educational interventions and/or more long-term formal curriculum experiences. Technology stewardship responsibilities are not undertaken alone but in concert with other experts in the local environment (2009), including perhaps a technology specialist who knows the school infrastructure, administrators, and so forth. For smaller cross-sectional learning activities, it may be that a school librarian will operate alone or in partnership with a teacher.

Wenger et al. (2009) provide a set of seven technology acquisition strategies that can be used by technology stewards in selecting a technology to meet the given community context. These are all quite pertinent to a school librarian technology steward and decision maker:

- Use what you have
- Build your own

- Go for the free stuff
- Patch elements together
- Get a commercial platform
- Build on an enterprise platform
- Use open-source tools

Given one's consideration of these acquisition strategies, the following framework is adapted from Wenger et al. (2009) and highlights the specific tasks engaged by the technology steward as they consider options, decide upon solutions, and deploy implementation of the given technology. Interwoven throughout these streams of activity (2009) are examples we have generated, contextualizing the technology stewardship model in choice and selection of solutions specifically within the sphere of e-learning.

These are just some initial guidelines, strategies, and questions for school librarians to consider as they grow and evolve to identify with the role as a technology steward for e-learning solutions in their local school setting. While these practices may seem new and different to some, this role can be quite gratifying, creative, and enjoyable. Wenger et al. (2009) discuss the very question of *why* someone would want to take

TABLE 10.1 The main tasks of technology stewardship, vis-à-vis decision making in the e-learning context

Key tasks of the technology steward, per Wenger et al. (2009)	For each dimension, the *e-learning technology steward* must consider the following questions, and more:
Understanding the community and local context needs (2009). These include the community's activities, member characteristics, subgroups, boundaries, aspirations, potentials, limitations, context.	• What are the learning goals and objectives, specific to student population and grade level? • What is the project scope (project timeline including development and deployment schedule, number of students/educators, grade level, time-on-task availability for students and teacher, etc.)? • What resources are available and needed (financial/infrastructure/curriculum/ teaching/aides)? • What are the unique needs of the student population, culture, individuals, classes, etc.? How do the students differ and vary, and how must the system adapt to this? • What is the level of expertise of the school librarian and/or teacher(s)? • What professional development is needed? • How long will it take students to acclimate and orient to the system? What are the knowledge prerequisites for students? What preteaching might be necessary before they start to ensure greater success? What peripheral skills may be needed that we will need to augment with supplemental instruction?

Having awareness of the technology options (2009). Keeping updated on technology trends, landscape, opportunities.	• Who are the leading experts in developing innovations for this particular learning knowledge domain? (This will require some research legwork on your behalf to develop a list of providers and options.)
	• What kinds of evaluation research backup the offerings' effectiveness? (See section following on evidence-based practice.)
	• What is the nature and quality of the content in the curriculum material, in the primary knowledge domain for the learning objectives (e.g., science, digital skills, information literacy skills)? How well does the content provided in this knowledge domain by vendor/source fit our learning goals and objectives, and unique student population's interests?
	• What are the e-learning technological delivery mechanisms for the learning experience (e.g., a learning game; an LMS already stocked with curriculum resources such as e-texts, tutorials, activities)? Is it a hosted solution that lives on the company's servers? Software as a service (SAAS)? Local client software requiring installation on the school's computers? Learning object delivered via a web browser? Content management system (CMS), e.g., a blog creation platform? Learning management system (LMS), e.g., Blackboard? Online database? Screen-capture recorder? Cloud computing solution requiring individual student accounts, e.g., online collaborative concept-mapping platform? Software vs. browser-based game system? Social media platform? E-learning portfolio archive of students' digital creative work files? A combination? Etc.
	• To what extent does the existing infrastructure in school support the technology requirements of the e-learning solution provider (e.g., internet speed, computer processors, operating system versions, browsers, etc.)? What additional infrastructure might be needed?
	• What privacy, security, and terms of service considerations are offered by the solution provider, and are these fair to you and your students?
	• What parental permissions will be needed?
	• What kind of features are offered, allowing teacher oversight and moderation of student comments? What permissions features are built into the platform to facilitate oversight and monitoring of student engagement?
	• What is the pricing model (e.g., per student? Site license? Volume discounts, across years?), and how does the cost fit our budget in the near and long term?

(Continued)

TABLE 10.1 (Continued)

Selection and installation of the given solution (2009). Help make informed choices such as selecting a whole new platform, upgrading existing systems, receiving advising on what features are requisite, sufficient, or optional but nice to have.	• How many different solutions have I researched, vetted, and reviewed to make sure I have a thorough understanding of the landscape of options and have exhausted all the best options? • Who will manage the installation and deployment, and how long will this take? Do we have staffing to make the installation and implementation feasible? Depending on the type and scope of the e-learning technology, this may entail need for more specialized technology director leadership/support. • How long into the future do I plan to utilize this version of the technology solution? How does pricing change over time? • What happens to legacy accounts from a prior year's students/teachers/classes? How long is data kept, if hosted? How can I save hosted data if we discontinue with license in the future? Is it possible to receive backup files in archive? • Is it possible to receive hard copies and/or PDFs of all curriculum content and/or professional development documentation for local and future use? • What is our data management and data ownership plan? Can my school "own" our own data? • How is data input into the system used by the company? • When is a new version of the solution going to be released, and what does it entail? • How long will the present version be supported? • Should we wait for a newer version to implement? • Are there components we can integrate with our existing systems? • What other systems does the product integrate with (e.g., grading system) that we might want to look into?
Adoption and transition (2009). Shepherding the community through the process of adopting or rejecting the new technology. Planning and facilitating this can be a substantial task for the technology steward.	• What product and customer support is provided by the e-learning solution provider to help manage the rollout and deployment's success? • What training is available for local educator/administrator constituents? • What is the timeframe for deployment, and what tasks must be accomplished on each day to meet deadlines? • What content/features/affordances should we preserve from older curriculum and/or systems? • How will we populate any user data and/or self-generated curriculum content into the system most effectively? E.g., will students create their own accounts, or will we create them and hand out access info? Etc.

Supporting everyday use (2009). Integrating the use of technology into the everyday practice of the community as it evolves. Includes everything from tool management, upgrades, access and security, backups. Onboarding newcomers, discovering and spreading new practices, helping craft agreements, building capacity.

- How will we track and monitor success and make improvements on the fly, especially in the early stages?
- How will we conduct iterative research on the rollout and schedule time for subsequent implementations to improve on early-phase rollout?
- What is an appropriate benchmark for evaluating the success of an implementation?
- What do I observe over time about student and teacher uses of the system to help me improve upon deployment?
- What changes/updates do I want to make to the curriculum content as time passes, and how often will I change this? How can I do this systematically so it is manageable?
- How often will I run interventions? Will the system be available for formal instructional purposes (e.g., lessons with a class) as well as for singular students (e.g., one of my after-school or lunch-time frequent visitors)?
- What alternative uses for the system emerge?
- How can I become a closer observer of student uses of the e-learning solution and develop strategies supporting them in maximizing their experiences learning with it?
- How do I need to personalize the implementation myself to make it better in ways the affordances of the e-learning solution do not address?
- How can I share these best practices with others in my setting (ongoing review meetings, etc.)?

on this role given how much work it may entail. They offer the following reasons (2009): because no one else is doing it, for the satisfaction in serving, for the leadership opportunities, to learn and grow in new directions, and for reputation building.

The main factors that can determine a technology steward's success include the following (2009):

- The steward's control of resources (negotiating with those in control to gain buy-in for the implementation);
- Their capacity for standard setting (do the standards and practices you introduce suit or not suit the given community?)
    - In school settings, this will include suitability for teachers, administrators, technology directors, and students who may use the e-learning solution, as well as perhaps the wider community depending on your goals;

- The interplay between the organization and community (reporting of community activity to the organization, etc.)

  - In the case of a school, this could be the communication between you and a teacher collaborator and your administration such as the principal or curriculum director as to successful buy-in, implementation, evaluation, and reporting. It may also be relevant to your communication with parents and other community members outside of school.

The more one anticipates and plans ahead, however, using the guidelines given, the sooner one will encounter approaches and solutions that are feasible in your given context, so a school librarian does not choose a path or option that exceeds their or their school's capacity. Wenger et al.'s (2009) book *Digital Habitats*, while slightly dated at this point in terms of its technology examples, offers keen insights for the school librarian who is engaging in technology decision making, and we recommend it as a source to explore this framework in more detail.

A Few Broad E-Learning Technological Modalities

When adapting the technology stewardship model for the e-learning context, we need to consider some of the hallmarks of e-learning solutions. Here we broadly frame some key e-learning modalities for consideration when defining and categorizing the range of offerings in this space.

One basic framing parameter in choosing e-learning is whether the e-learning activities are instructor led or learner led. According to Horton (2012), advantages to instructor-led e-learning include the following:

- Instructors can answer questions and solve problems that arise and provide the authority that some need for motivation;
- They can grade activities too subtle for automated scoring;
- They can provide personalized assistance to individuals in the learning process; and
- They serve in the capacity to sympathize, urge, empathize, cajole, and inspire.

For older and more expert learners who have a solid base of prior knowledge, learner-led instruction may be appropriate (Horton, 2012). It is important to note that more self-guided activities require greater self-regulation and thus are more appropriate for learners who are not novice in the given knowledge domain but have an established base of understanding from which to operate with the e-learning solution. Some advantages of such self-guided activities include:

- Learners are not bound to a specific schedule;
- They are empowered with agency;
- Learners may develop self-reliance;

- All learners get the same quality of materials/experience and can make of it what they will; and
- Learners won't be intimidated by the instructor or feel judged.

On another continuum, one might also consider the timescale of the e-learning solution, whether synchronous, blended, or asynchronous. In synchronous experiences, everyone learns at the same place, at the same time, in the same shared curriculum. Such contexts can be used when real-time discussion and discourse are required and learners need the addition of motivation that comes from group participation. In such settings, learners share many of the same needs/questions (Horton, 2012).

In blended learning contexts, learning is scheduled and instructor led and students meet face to face, but such experiences involve some uses of e-learning solution affordances asynchronously reflecting a mix of classroom, virtual classroom, and standalone e-learning. Instructors may mix informational, behavioral, cognitive, and constructive strategies, as well as material formats (web, online video, DVD, email, discussion boards, video conferencing, mobile apps, etc.) (2012).

In distance learning interventions, students share a certain timeframe in which to interact with materials, respond to posts, and interact with others enrolled. In asynchronous experiences, everybody is at a different point. Learners may come from a wide span of time zones and so on. This is beneficial for those with inflexible/unpredictable work schedules and at times when the content originator cannot wait for an entire class to form (2012).

School librarians will want to consider the particulars of their given learning objectives as they consider the modality of the e-learning solutions they explore to meet their learning goals.

School Librarians and Evidence-Based Practice

Earlier, we highlight the importance of school librarians choosing e-learning solutions that have empirical evaluation research support and cite a range of research and development communities in which deep innovation in e-learning technology development is occurring, such as the learning sciences. We highlight research and development communities in which more structured and scaffolded e-learning solutions are being developed that have strong research support as to their usability and effectiveness. The recommendation of choosing *research-supported* e-learning interventions follows Wenger's guideline for technology stewardship in maintaining awareness of the range of available technology solutions. Here we shine a light on another type of evidence usage that can be engaged by school librarians as they enter the implementation stage of their e-learning solution technology stewardship. That is the task of *evidence-based practice*.

Evidence-based practice is an area of active scholarly publication within school librarianship research. Through evidence-based practice, school librarians collect evidence from their own students and staff to shape and plan teaching and learning initiatives and programs at the school library (DiScala & Subramaniam, 2011). School librarians who engage in evidence-based practice can engage in ongoing iterative refinement and improvement of their local implementation. The evidence-based practice literature invites school librarians into engaging in a reflective practice that charts, measures, documents, and makes visible the impact of school libraries on learning outcomes (Todd, 2015). The focus is placed on improving one's own practice as well as demonstrating the effect of a school librarian's contributions to student achievement in the school community to advocate for their role. Evidence-based practice literature encourages school librarians to work with three types of evidence (2015):

- Evidence for practice: using high-quality existing empirical research on best practices that have been tested and validated to decide which practices one wishes to try out;
- Evidence in practice (applications/actions): engaging in research during one's own implementation and considering results vis-à-vis existing, prior research evidence base;
- Evidence in practice (results/impacts/outcomes): user-reported evidence shows that the learner changes as a result of inputs, interventions, activities, and processes.

Those who engage in this practice can utilize strategies from the *action research method* that links the theory and practice of school library instruction. This includes adopting self-reflection and continuous improvement (Gordon, 2009). Data collection methods can range from simple tools such as surveys, checklists, comment cards, and rubrics to more advanced diagnostic tools, perhaps including assessments embedded in the technology solutions of your choosing. The focus for reflective practice should reside in the particular learning objectives and knowledge domain specified. The use of diagnostics is recommended to contribute to the following roles of school librarians (DiScala & Subramaniam, 2011):

1. Their key role in increasing student achievement in high-stakes testing by presenting evidence that exemplifies the link between mastery of information literacy skills and high academic achievement;
2. Their capability as model collaborators in schools through practice of collaborative leadership with teachers and students; and
3. Their inherent quality of transformational leadership in schools by serving as the model teacher who listens and acts upon ideas and feedback from students through the assessments administered to students (2011).

One diagnostic tool for evidence-based practice includes the Tool for Real Time Assessment of Information Literacy Skills (TRAILS, 2017). Focused on the knowledge domain of information literacy, the TRAILS system covers five categories of information literacy skills: develop topic; identify potential sources; develop, use, and revise search strategies; evaluate sources and information; and recognize how to use information responsibly, ethically, and legally. Each of these categories are evaluated by ten-item assessments (Schloman & Gedeon, 2007). Another example of a diagnostic available for school librarians' evidence-based practice is the Perceived Competence in Information Skills (PCIS) measure developed by Arnone, Small, and Reynolds (2010). Educators can use this attitudinal measure to support student inquiry by identifying and addressing gaps in student confidence in their information skills. If a school librarian is engaging in technology stewardship of an e-learning solution or instructional project that focuses on information literacy as the knowledge domain, such diagnostics may be appropriate to help you measure student learning outcomes.

Evidence-based practice guidelines support school librarians as technology stewards exploring, selecting, and implementing a given e-learning solution successfully. Using evidence-based practice, school librarians can identify weaknesses in the implementation and apply improvement strategies. One may also want to offer feedback to the e-learning solution provider for improvements needed in the given design and instructional features.

Bringing It All Together

Overall, technology stewardship offers key guidelines and parameters for e-learning solution decision makers such as school librarians to encourage critical thinking and discernment in school librarians' choices of technology offerings for students. As technology stewards, librarians may choose solutions as well as implement them through direct instruction. As one introduces new research-driven e-learning technologies into the school community, we encourage engaging in evidence-based practice, involving ongoing refinement and iterative improvement of the e-learning implementation.

The goal of these guidelines is to place agency in the hands of school librarians in initiating innovation in their communities. That starts first and foremost with clearly identifying your prioritized learning objectives and instructional goals as key drivers of decisions and the fit and feasibility of the solutions sought. Making the effort to look to the research and development communities discussed for research-driven e-learning options that have an evidence base for their effectiveness will afford school librarians with access to cutting-edge, closely scaffolded innovations that lead to deeper learning outcomes in students.

Case Study

Considerations for School Decision Makers in Choosing an E-Learning Solution Provider

Now we turn to a case example of a research-driven e-learning solution in order to demonstrate types of attributes, affordances, and features one may consider during e-learning technology stewardship. In the context of this specific case, the e-learning solution we consider falls into the knowledge domain of students' "social constructivist digital literacy."

Game design has been recognized as a promising approach for engaging students in computer science education by allowing students to explore challenging CT and CS principles in a creative context that captures their imagination and enables student expression (e.g., Grover & Pea, 2013; Kafai & Burke, 2015; Harel, 1991; Harel Caperton, 2010; Reppening, Webb, & Ioannidou, 2010). In addition to computational programming, game design involves development of game message/content and mechanics, the expression of which give students a purpose driving their coding: publishing and sharing an interactive artifact that conveys meaning that can be made personal to them (Harel Caperton, 2010). Game design approaches can make thinking visible and create a "need to know" among students and have been found to engender students' systems-based thinking, interdisciplinary thinking, user-centered design, specialist language, metacognitive reflection, network literacy, and literacy with creative productivity tools (Salen et al., 2010).

The e-learning solution presented in what follows is called Globaloria, and aims to foster students' social constructivist digital literacy development through the activity of game design. The solution provider has been iterating a blended e-learning game design-based solution for CS education for more than ten years. Founded and led by Dr. Idit Harel and initially called the World Wide Workshop, the Globaloria program has been designed, scoped, and sequenced through ongoing design-based research by the founder and academic research partners including the lead author. The e-learning solution features a full curriculum and platform of services that is offered to schools as a game design course for integration in the block schedule, daily, for credit and a grade, for a single semester or full year.

In the 2016/2017 school year, the program was implemented in eighty-five active school locations across several U.S. states, totaling 570 classes across both fall/spring semesters, with 185 teachers and ~10,000 students, at the middle school and high school levels. A small number of schools in Texas are piloting the program's new elementary-level curriculum. Code.org in 2015 identified Globaloria as one of its featured CS learning providers and advocates for U.S. schools' utilization of this offering. In the last three years, Globaloria has also received a Microsoft Education Award and a Google Rise Award in recognition of its strong developments in advancing innovations in CS pedagogy for K–12.

Elements of School Librarian Decision Making

Establishing Learning Objectives and Learning Goals   Fundamental to school librarian decision makers' initial selection of an e-learning solution is the establishment of prioritized learning goals and objectives. We might imagine a school librarian choosing and establishing a learning objective of "social constructivist digital literacy" as a knowledge domain we wish to cultivate in their students. Here we outline the ways in which the e-learning solution providers themselves have clearly articulated and specified the learning objectives that underscore their instructional design. A school librarian can mesh their own goals with those specified by the provider to identify fit.

In outlining these learning objectives, Reynolds (2016a) maps a framework of the "6 Contemporary Learning Practices" that the program aims to cultivate. This article also identifies the instructional design attributes that connect to these practices as goals and means deployed in the instruction to inculcate these outcomes. The six dimensions that are targeted in the activities the program offers are described in brief as: create, manage, publish, socialize/collaborate, research, and surf/play. These dimensions are presented in Column 1 in Table 10.2. Reynolds (2016a) argues that these practices are epistemic and authentic to much of our real-world purposive engagement with technology, for instance in the professional world. If expertise within these practice dimensions is cultivated among middle school and high school learners through innovative educational interventions *in a coordinated way*, toward the productive development of a complex digital artifact, such an experience may better prepare students for concurrent and future engagement and participation in digital cultures, citizenship, and workplaces. Reynolds (2016a) outlines the scholarly rationale for the importance of learning in each dimension.

Understanding How the E-Learning Solution Meets Learning Objectives   Table 10.2, Column 2 specifies some of the Globaloria instructional design features that aim to support students' development of the social constructivist digital literacy learning objectives. Such a table was shared by the organization in earlier years to prospective school partners to demonstrate thoughtful and research-driven planning in instructional design. We might imagine a school librarian asking an e-learning solution provider, "How does your e-learning solution's design and implementation model meet our established learning goals and objectives?" One might expect an evidence-based provider to be able to provide such details. Different e-learning solution providers

TABLE 10.2 6 Contemporary Learning Practices Framework as learning objectives for Globaloria instructional design (circa 2016) (Reynolds 2016a)

The 6 Contemporary Learning Practices (6-CLPs) comprising "Social Constructivist Digital Literacy"	TECHNOLOGY ACTIVITIES/ INSTRUCTIONAL DESIGN AFFORDANCES e.g., in Globaloria, circa 2009–2015
1: CREATE Invention, creation, and completion of a digital project stemming from an original idea	• Brainstorm, develop game and simulation ideas and storylines using Web 2.0 tools • Generate creative ideas for designs to express the subject of the game and user experience • Write an original game narrative and a proposal to explain it • Plan/program/complete a game file representing the original game design functionality • Create a blog for the team project
2: MANAGE Project planning, project management, teamwork (e.g., role-taking, task delegation), problem solving	• Coordinate and manage the design/creation/ programming of game elements • Manage the project's execution by creating/ organizing a wiki and by sharing project assets and progress updates • Manage teamwork by defining and assigning team roles, coordinating/executing tasks • Use a sequence of online curriculum to learn programming
3: PUBLISH Publishing, distribution of self-created digital artifacts to an audience/community of peers	• Creating wiki profile page and project pages • Posting in-progress and completed text/video/ photos/audio/programming code/animations/ digital designs on wiki pages
4: SOCIALIZE Giving and getting feedback about project through social interaction, participation, exchange	• Collaborating by using social media tools such as posting to wikis/blogs/open source help forums/instant messaging • Exchanging/sharing feedback and resources by posting information/links/source code/ questions/answers • Reading and commenting on others' blogs and wiki pages • Presenting final digital projects for others both virtually in game galleries and in person in live game demonstrations
5: RESEARCH Inquiry, information seeking, searching to support the artifact's topic, message, design, execution	• Searching the Web for answers and help on specific issues related to programming games • Searching and finding resources on Globaloria. com network, website, e-learning platform • Searching the Web for new Flash design, animation, and programming resources • Searching for information in support of the game's educational subject and storyline

The 6 Contemporary Learning Practices (6-CLPs) comprising "Social Constructivist Digital Literacy"	TECHNOLOGY ACTIVITIES/ INSTRUCTIONAL DESIGN AFFORDANCES e.g., in Globaloria, circa 2009–2015
6: SURF/PLAY Surfing, experimentation, and play with existing networked Web applications and tools	• Surfing to MyGLife.org starter kit site and other game sites and playing games online • Keeping track of and bookmarking surfing results that are relevant to projects • Browsing Web 2.0 content sites such as YouTube, Flickr, blogs, Google tools

will have varying ways of meeting learning objectives in their system design. During the product review phase, you will need to further gain deeper understanding and demonstration of e-learning solution instructional features, perhaps a live demonstration.

Demonstration of Key Features by the E-Learning Solution Provider The following figures, provided by Globaloria circa 2017, demonstrate the platforms, instructional supports, and variety of courses in several computing subject domains available to Globaloria's participating schools at the time the figures were provided. The Globaloria.com website features additional details on each of the courses, including the game design and programming skills supported by the curricula and other choices that can be further personalized to the local school's agenda and goals.

Exploring Sample Curriculum Content Figure 10.3 presents a range of different levels of game design coursework made available by the organization. Each shield reflects a different course in the learning sequence. This is just the tip of the iceberg; a school librarian reviewing courseware will need specific samples of curriculum in such a context to assess the quality of the material and the activities your students will engage in and its feasibility given your local infrastructure and constraints.

Professional Development Supports In the case of Globaloria, in addition to the curriculum and e-learning platforms, the provider also offers a host of additional ongoing training, educator professional development, and support services to school partners. They recognize that many schools and teachers are new to implementing formal technology education. These consultative services offer ongoing supports to help empower schools and educators in these launch efforts. Some of these supports are outlined in Figure 10.4. These include trainings as well as real-time interventions in moments of both student and educator learning needs as the curriculum is delivered.

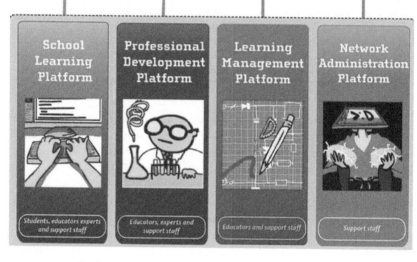

FIGURE 10.1   The four e-learning solution platforms in Globaloria offered to administrators, teachers, and students (circa 2017)

Selected Technology Platforms and Tools

Students	Faculty
• Project-based digital textbooks • Project-based digital workbooks • Help Center / Coding Coachers • Progress Tracker and Social Tools • Gamified Badges, Levels, Points • Portfolio-building Track	• Professional development courses • On-demand virtual and in-person support and co-teaching • Classroom management dashboard (individual and teams) • Grading and Evaluation rubrics

Account Management and Sales	Admin
• Proprietary license management platform • User data tracking and backend dashboards • Customized Salesforce platform • Robust reporting capabilities	• Fully hosted and secured • Account management tools • Classroom and student account creation tools • Competition management and judging tools

FIGURE 10.2   Services provided across these learning system affordances, by audience (circa 2017)

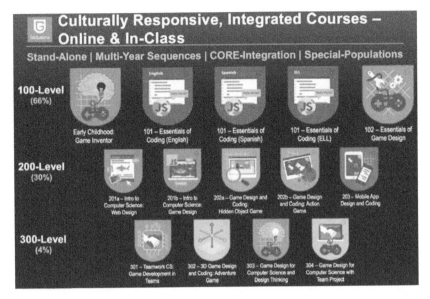

FIGURE 10.3   Coursework sequences in game design computing education in Globaloria (circa 2017)

Virtual Learning/Teaching Support Services

Educator Training	• Live, Virtual Help Sessions • Video Tutorials • Customized Dynamic Help Center Contet
Educator Support	• On-Platform Tracking and Support Systems (Salesforce and ZenDesk) • On-Site Ambassadors and Training Program (Globaloria Gurus)
Student Support	• On-Site Client-Trainers Programs • Professional Bootcamps on Demand

FIGURE 10.4   Virtual learning and teaching support services provided by Globaloria (circa 2017)

Establishing the Presence of a Research Evidence Base for the Given E-Learning Solution's Effectiveness   As discussed, a key consideration for your choice of an e-learning solution provider is the presence of a research evidence base that supports a given provider's instructional design effectiveness. A school librarian who inquires into the research evidence base for Globaloria's game design approach, for instance, would be met with a range of rigorous scholarly research studies offering support. The learning theories influencing the design of the program include social constructivism (Vygotsky, 1962) and constructionism (as defined by Papert & Harel, 1991). Research on Globaloria has been conducted by a network of more than fifteen academic research partner collaborators since 2008, with findings disseminated in peer-reviewed conferences, journals, and as third-party audited evaluation research. Findings, for instance, have shown positive effects of learner participation on student interest, engagement, and motivation in six digital learning domains, as well as measured game design knowledge outcomes (e.g., Reynolds & Harel Caperton, 2009; Reynolds & Chiu, 2012, 2013; Reynolds, 2016a). Findings with matched-case control groups also show significant increases in science, social studies, and English and language arts standardized test scores as a result of participation (Chadwick & Gore, 2010, 2011; Ho, Gore, & Chadwick, 2012). Participation was also shown to attenuate and eliminate known effects of the digital divide such as gender and socioeconomic status (Reynolds & Chiu, 2016). Copies of these articles and reports are available from the provider, as well as in journal article databases subscribed to by most public and academic libraries.

Culturally Responsive Computing   Local needs of the school community might include the socioeconomic status of the school population, the English language learning needs of students in diverse immigrant communities, and the racial, ethnic, and cultural characteristics of the student, teacher, and school communities. As Wenger et al.'s model encourages, as a technology steward a school librarian has keen insight into your community's own contingent needs. We also cited a range of literature on culturally responsive computing. In the case of Globaloria, these concerns and factors have been squarely addressed. For instance, the organization will be able to share with interested partners details reflecting a strong track record of history working with schools in diverse districts. The program has operated predominantly within rural low-income school communities in the states of West Virginia, Wyoming, and Oklahoma, as well as Hispanic immigrant and English language learner (ELL) communities in Austin, TX, Houston, TX, and San Jose, CA, and African-American and Hispanic students in Queens and the Bronx, NYC. The founder and staff help schools develop an implementation plan and choose relevant course offerings in a customized way to meet local predetermined needs specified by the e-learning technology steward; the organization has their own institutional knowledge around such needs, too. One responsive feature is Globaloria's ongoing work with Hispanic students who are English language learners, which led to the organization's creation of a specialized bilingual game design CS curriculum in Spanish, implemented in several Texas schools. Another cultural responsiveness feature is an extended mentor network of "Help Center Coding Coaches," employed full and part time, who are past Globaloria teachers and students and help schools onboard and manage the program, working hand in hand with educators new to the program, who can meet with their mentors via web conference weekly and in real time when needs surface.

TABLE 10.3 Globaloria principles guiding successful computer science learning culture

Facilitate learning the *actual* concepts and practices of computer science
Encourage everybody's participation, equity, and diversity
Focus on creating computational artifacts (i.e., software, websites, animated characters, games, simulations, mobile apps)
Support the study of computational thinking (CT) and algorithmic processes, as well as understanding their design, implementation, and impact on society
Emphasize how computing influences culture and culture shapes how people engage with computing
Facilitate CT central to the practices and concepts of computer science
Practice how to communicate about computing
Provide multiple pathways supporting a learning progression covering many CS concepts and principles

Towards the goal of cultural responsiveness, in December 2016, Harel developed and made available a framework of principles that have long guided the organization's efforts in offering a research-driven learning system for CS education through game design.

This framework demonstrates the organization's attention to the ways in which the implementation of their solution interplays with a culture's unique context factors. The organization you work with may specify detailed examples and provide references for existing school partners, enabling interested school librarians to initiate contact with other educators who are participating in the given provider's offerings.

Establishing the Technical Requirements for Participation   On a purely logistical level, the decision maker will need to consider the existing infrastructure available in one's setting and make sure the resources exist to make a given implementation feasible. In this case, Globaloria provides a detailed list of the technical requirements for schools' participation. While most U.S. schools have such affordances available, the school's unique customization will need to consider how many students can enroll in a given class based on the 1:1 computer requirement. Computer availability will influence how the course implementation is planned.

What About Cost?   As Wenger et al. (2009) indicate, cost and budgets are integral to your decision making. This commercial e-learning solution is available to schools as a licensed service. Their licensing models and costs vary and are flexible based on each location's budgets and the scope and scale of the effort in context. As of September 2017, the journalistic educational technology clearinghouse website EdSurge.com featured Globaloria as one among scores of e-learning solution providers. EdSurge.com published the following pricing details for Globaloria:

> An annual subscription fee includes a customized Digital Platform, Full Digital Course Curriculum, Blended Professional Development, and the

Virtual Learning and Expert Support, including a live instructional and coding help desk. Globaloria costs $75/student/year; volume and multi-year discounts are available. Interested schools must apply on Globaloria's site and provide comprehensive information about the school and faculty (including which faculty members can serve as Globaloria "facilitators").[1]

Overall, this case study provides just a few of the details a school librarian must aim to retrieve during the product-review phase of their e-learning technology stewardship process. For such an in-depth curriculum commitment and budgetary investment as the example provided represents, we must expect that the evidence base exists for its success. For more short-term and informal activities and interventions, the threshold and benchmarks for preselection criteria during product review may not need to be quite as high—again, it all depends on one's specification up front of those integral learning objectives. But in turn, one might expect that the depth and effect of the learning outcomes in short-term and less-intensive activities would not be expected to be as strong.

Conclusion

This chapter discusses the ways in which school librarians might continue in growing to think of themselves as innovation arbiters and decision makers in their school environments when it comes to e-learning solutions. We propose in the chapter that some school librarians may find gratification and opportunity in cultivating a role as discerning technology stewards. Implicitly, we also encourage school librarians to engage more and more in initiating and offering dedicated and deliberate direct instructional experiences to bring about digital and information literacy in their students. We encourage evidence-based practice, and we present a case study of an e-learning solution to demonstrate some of the key considerations a school librarian e-learning technology steward will need to address.

In this regard, Haythornthwaite, Andrews, Fransman, and Meyers (2016) discuss the ways in which the practices of educators and e-learners themselves are integral in the success of e-learning projects beyond the e-learning provider itself. They cite the work of Pollock and colleagues (2014), who identified roles for the teacher in e-learning settings as an explainer of technology, digesting, explaining, and extending new content through more integrated participatory engagement with the learner and their learning experience. The authors also highlight past findings that support greater attention to e-learners' roles and positions in their personal learning environments and networks, such that learners themselves can give greater context to relevant content that interests them, acting as peer supporters for other students (e.g., Haythornthwaite & Kazmer, 2004; Haythornthwaite et al., 2007). This call connects to the work on culturally responsive computing.

We started this chapter highlighting findings from an extensive study of NJ school libraries and librarians (Todd, 2012), which found that in the most active and productive settings, the school library served as a school's physical and virtual learning commons, providing a focus on creative engagement with information resources and knowledge building. Todd (2012) identified a set of core leadership dimensions for school librarians that will support a sustainable and high-impact school library for the future:

- Connected leadership through a collaborative team approach to inquiry-centered instruction, with school librarian as instructional partner (per Kuhlthau, 2010);
- Embedding of a range of digital and critical-thinking literacies into school librarian's repertoire;
- Encouraging students' creative engagement with new technology frontiers for deep learning, such as virtual learning worlds, online schooling, and virtual gaming and design.

To these leadership dimensions, we add discernment in decision making around e-learning solution choices and implementation of direct learning experiences that have higher potential for effectiveness and positive outcomes and that connect more closely to students' lives. We hope that the guidelines offered in this chapter will support school librarians' sound discernment towards engaging technology learning experiences founded on research-supported practices. School librarian leaders must be careful to establish a rigorous threshold and standard for the technology learning experiences introduced in their school settings. This practice hinges upon knowing and understanding the evolving needs of one's community of learners, heeding new standards for establishment of innovative learning objectives in computing arenas, and establishing quality benchmarks for sound and evidence-based e-learning solution choices to increase the likelihood of high-quality outcomes in these more future-forward knowledge domains.

Note

1 We note here the importance of including dates ("circa 2017") on a book chapter publication featuring details on a specific e-learning solution that predicates its curriculum model for student digital literacy development on its adaptability and ongoing system refinement year over year.

References

About TRAILS. (2017). *TRAILS Tool for Real-Time Assessment of Information Literacy Skills.* Retrieved from www.trails-9.org/about2.php?page=about

Achterman, D. L. (2008). *Haves, Halves, and Have-Nots: School Libraries and Student Achievement in California.* University of North Texas. ProQuest Dissertations Publishing.

Arnone, M. P., Small, R. V., & Reynolds, R. (2010). Supporting inquiry by identifying gaps in student confidence: Development of a measure of perceived competence. *School Libraries Worldwide, 16*(1), 47–60.

Bailey, G., & Paul, M. (2012). Report from the field: Outcome evaluation of the library media program on information literacy skills in Montgomery County Public Schools, Maryland. *Teacher Librarian, 39*(5), 46–49.

Callison, D. (2004). *Survey of Indiana School Library Media Programs: A Collaborative Project Between the Association for Indiana Media Educators & Indiana University-Indianapolis, School of Library and Information Science.* Presented at the 2004 AIME.

Chadwick, K., & Gore, J. (2010). *The Relationship of Globaloria Participation and Student Achievement.* Charleston, WV: Edvantia.

Chadwick, K., & Gore, J. (2011). *Globaloria Replication Study: Examining the Robustness of Relationships Between Globaloria Participation and Student Achievement.* Charleston, WV: Edvantia.

Chu, S., Reynolds, R., Notari, M., Taveres, N., & Lee, C. (2016, October). *21st Century Skills Development Through Inquiry Based Learning: From Theory to Practice.* Singapore: Springer Science.

Dahlstrom, E., Brooks, D. C., & Bichsel, J. (2014, September). *The Current Ecosystem of Learning Management Systems in Higher Education: Student, Faculty, and IT Perspectives.* Research report. Louisville, CO: ECAR. Retrieved from https://library.educause.edu/~/media/files/library/2014/9/ers1414-pdf.pdf

Dahlstrom, E., de Boor, T., Grunwald, P., & Vockley, M. (2011). *The ECAR National Study of Undergraduate Students and Information Technology.* Boulder, CO: Educause.

DiScala, J., & Subramaniam, M. (2011). Evidence-based practice: A practice towards leadership credibility among school librarians. *School Libraries Worldwide, 17*(2), 59–70.

Eglash, R., Gilbert, J. E., Taylor, V., & Geier, S. R. (2013). Culturally responsive computing in urban, after-school contexts: Two approaches. *Urban Education, 48*(5), 629–656.

Eisenhart, M., & Edwards, L. (2004). Red-eared sliders and neighborhood dogs: Creating third spaces to support ethnic girls' interests in technological and scientific expertise. *Children Youth and Environments, 14*(2), 156–177.

Everhart, N., Mardis, M. A., & Johnston, M. (2011). National Board certified school librarians' leadership in technology integration: Results of a national survey. *School Library Media Research, 14.*

Fenton, W. (2017, June 21). Google classroom absent from college courses. *Inside Higher Ed.* Retrieved from www.insidehighered.com/digital-learning/article/2017/06/21/google-classroom-not-college-classroom

Goode, J., & Margolis, J. (2011). Exploring computer science: A case study of school reform. *ACM Transactions on Computing Education (TOCE), 11*(2), 12.

Gordon, C. (2009). An emerging theory for evidence based information literacy instruction in school libraries, Part 2. *Evidence Based Library and Information Practice, 4*(3).

Grover, S., & Pea, R. D. (2013). Computational thinking in K–12: A review of the state of the field. *Educational Researcher, 42*(1), 38–43.

Harel, I. (1991). *Children Designers: Interdisciplinary Constructions for Learning and Knowing Mathematics in a Computer-Rich School.* Norwood, NJ: Ablex Publishing.

Harel Caperton, I. (2010). Toward a theory of game-media literacy: Playing and building as reading and writing. *International Journal of Gaming and Computer-Mediated Simulations, 2*(1), 1–16.

Haythornthwaite, C., & Andrews, R. N. L. (2011). *E-learning Theory and Practice.* London: Sage Publications.

Haythornthwaite, C., Andrews, R., Fransman, J., & Meyers, E. (2016). *SAGE Handbook of E-Learning Research, 2nd edition.* London: Sage Publications.

Haythornthwaite, C., Andrews, R., Kazmer, M. M., Bruce, B. C., Montague, R.-A., & Preston, C. (2007). New theories and models of and for online learning. *First Monday*, *12*(8). Retrieved 14 September 2015, from http://firstmonday.org/ojs/index.php/fm/article/view/1976

Haythornthwaite, C., & Kazmer, M. M. (eds.). (2004). *Learning, Culture and Community in Online Education: Research and Practice.* New York, NY: Peter Lang.

Henderson, L. (1996). Instructional design of interactive multimedia: A cultural critique. *Educational Technology Research and Development, 44*(4), 85–104.

Henderson, L. (2007). Theorizing a multiple cultures instructional design model for e-learning and e-teaching. In A. Edmundson (Ed.), *Globalized E-learning Cultural Challenges* (pp. 130–153). Hershey, PA: Information Science Publishing.

Ho, H., Gore, J., & Chadwick, K. (2012). *Globaloria Replication Study: An Examination of the Relationships Between Globaloria Participation and Student Achievement in Year 4 of the West Virginia Pilot Implementation.* Charleston, WV: Edvantia.

Horton, W. (2012). *E-Learning by Design* (2nd edition). San Francisco, CA: Wiley.

Humphreys, D. (2012). The questions we need to ask first. In D.G. Oblinger's *Game Changers: Education and Information Technologies.* Boulder, CO: Educause.

Johnston, M. P. (2012). Connecting teacher librarians for technology integration leadership. *School Libraries Worldwide, 18*(1), 18.

Kafai, Y. B., & Burke, Q. (2015). Constructionist gaming: Understanding the benefits of making games for learning. *Educational Psychologist, 50*(4), 313–334.

Kuhlthau, C. (2004). *Seeking Meaning: A Process Approach to Library and Information Services* (2nd edition). Westport, CT: Libraries Unlimited.

Kuhlthau, C. C. (2010). Guided inquiry: School libraries in the 21st century. *School Libraries Worldwide, 16*(1), 1.

Kuhlthau, C. C., Maniotes, L. K., & Caspari, A. K. (2012). *Guided Inquiry Design: A Framework for Inquiry in Your School.* Westport, CT: Libraries Unlimited.

Kuhlthau, C. C., Maniotes, L. K., & Caspari, A. K. (2015). *Guided Inquiry: Learning in the 21st Century.* Santa Barbara, CA: ABC-CLIO.

Ladson-Billings, G. (1995). Toward a theory of culturally relevant pedagogy. *American Educational Research Journal, 32*(3), 465–491.

Lance, K. C. (2001). Proof of the power: Quality library media programs affect academic achievement. *MultiMedia Schools, 8*(4), 14–16, 18, 20.

Lance, K. C., & Rodney, M. J. (2014). Teaching information literacy is the key to academic achievement: The success story of Oregon library media programs. *OLA Quarterly, 7*(2), 21–22.

Lance, K. C., Rodney, M. J., & Russell, B. (2007). *How Students, Teachers & Principals Benefit from Strong School Libraries: The Indiana Study.* Indianapolis, IN: Association for Indiana Media Educators.

Lang, L., & Pirani, J. (2014, May 20). *The Learning Management System Evolution.* Research bulletin. Louisville, CO: ECAR. Retrieved from www.educause.edu/ecar

Lee, C. D. (2003). Toward a framework for culturally responsive design in multimedia computer environments: Cultural modeling as a case. *Mind, Culture, and Activity, 10*(1), 42–61.

Library Research Service. (2011). *School Library Impact Studies.* Retrieved from www.lrs.org/impact.php

LMS Data Spring 2015 Updates. (2015). *Edutechnica.com.* Retrieved from http://edutechnica.com/2015/03/08/lms-data-spring-2015-updates/

Loertscher, D.V. (2003.) *We Boost Achievement! Evidence-based Practice for School Library Media Specialists, Facet*. Salt Lake City, UT: Libraries Unlimited/Distributed Products.

Lonsdale, M. (2003). *Impact of School Libraries on Student Achievement: A Review of the Research*. Report for the Australian School Library Association. Australian Council for Educational Research, Camberwell, Victoria, Australia.

Margolis, J., Ryoo, J. J., Sandoval, C. D., Lee, C., Goode, J., & Chapman, G. (2012). Beyond access: Broadening participation in high school computer science. *ACM Inroads, 3*(4), 72–78.

McLoughlin, C. (1999). Culturally responsive technology use: Developing an on-line community of learners. *British Journal of Educational Technology, 30*(3), 231–243.

Oberg, D. (2006). Developing the respect and support of school administrators. *Teacher Librarian, 33*(3), 13–18.

Papert, S., & Harel, I. (1991). *Constructionism*. Norwood, NJ: Ablex Publishing.

Pinkard, N. (2001). *Lyric Reader: Creating Intrinsically Motivating and Culturally Responsive Reading Environments*. Ann Arbor, MI: Center for the Improvement of Early Reading Achievement, University of Michigan.

Pinkard, N., Erete, S., Martin, C. K., McKinney DeRoysten, M. (2017). Digital youth divas: Exploring narrative-driven curriculum to trigger middle school girls? Interest in computational activities. *Journal of the Learning Sciences: Special Issue: Designing Learning Environments for Disciplinary Identification, 26*(3), 477–516.

Pollock, M., Yonezawa, S., Gay, H., Rodriguez, L., Garcia, G., & Qassimyar, M., with Gilkison, T., Hernandez, R., and the Early Academic Outreach Program. (2014). Innovating toward equity with online courses: Testing the optimal 'blend' of in-person human supports with low-income youth and teachers in California. *CREATE Equity Research Report 1*, March. Retrieved 14 August 2015, from https://create.ucsd.edu/research/CREATE%20Equity%20RR_1Mar2014.pdf

Reppening, A., Webb, D., & Ioannidou, A. (2010). Scalable game design and the development of a checklist for getting computational thinking into public schools. In *The 41st ACM Technical Symposium on Computer Science Education, SIGCSE 2010*. Milwaukee, WI: ACM Press.

Reynolds, R. (2016a). Defining, designing for, and measuring 'digital literacy' development in learners: A proposed framework. *Educational Technology Research & Development, 64*(1).

Reynolds, R., & Chiu, M. (2012, July). Contribution of motivational orientations to student outcomes in a discovery-based program of game design learning. *Proceedings of the International Conference of the Learning Sciences (ICLS)*, Sydney, Australia.

Reynolds, R., & Chiu, M. (2013). Formal and informal context factors as contributors to student engagement in a guided discovery-based program of game design learning. *Journal of Learning, Media & Technology, 38*(4), 429–462.

Reynolds, R., & Chiu, M. (2016). Reducing digital divide effects through student engagement in coordinated game design, online resource uses, and social computing activities in school. *Journal of the Association for Information Science and Technology (JASIST), 67*(8), 1822–1835.

Reynolds, R., & Harel Caperton, I. (2009, April). *The Emergence of 6 Contemporary Learning Abilities in High School Students As They Develop and Design Interactive Games*. Paper presented at AERA.

Salen, K., Torres, R., Rufo-Tepper, R., Shapiro, A., & Wolozin, L. (2010). *Quest to Learn: Growing a School for Digital Kids*. Cambridge, MA: MIT Press.

Schloman, B. F., & Gedeon, J. A. (2007). Creating TRAILS tool for real-time assessment of standards for the 21st-century learner (2017). *AASL American Association of School Librarians*. Retrieved from www.ala.org/aasl/standards/learning(2006)

Scholastic Research Foundation. (2008). *'School Libraries Work!' Report*. Scholastic. Retrieved from http://www2.scholastic.com/content/collateral_resources/pdf/s/slw3_2008.pdf

Scott, K., Sheridan, K., & Clark, K. (2015). Culturally responsive computing: A theory revisited. *Learning, Media and Technology, 40*(4), 412–436.

Simba Information. (2015). *The Complete K–12 Report 2015*. Retrieved from www.simbainformation.com/Complete-9588037/

Small, R. V., & Snyder, J. (2009). The impact of New York's school libraries on student achievement and motivation: Phase II—In-depth study. *School Library Media Research, 12*.

Subramaniam, M., Ahn, J., Waugh, A., Taylor, N. G., Druin, A., Fleischmann, K. R., & Walsh, G. (2015). The role of school librarians in enhancing science learning. *Journal of Librarianship and Information Science, 47*(1), 3–16.

Todd, R. J. (2006). From information to knowledge: Charting and measuring changes in students' knowledge of a curriculum topic. *Information Research, 11*(4). Retrieved from www.informationr.net/ir/11-4/paper264.html

Todd, R. J. (2012, November 11–15). *The Shifting Sands of School Libraries: Sustaining the Next Gen School Libraries*. Paper presented at the International Association of School Librarianship Annual Conference, Doha, Qatar.

Todd, R. J. (2015). Evidence-based practice and school libraries: Interconnections of evidence, advocacy, & actions. *Knowledge Quest, 43*(3), 8.

Todd, R. J., & Kuhlthau, C. C. (2004). *Student learning through Ohio school libraries*. Columbus, OH: OELMA.

Todd, R. J., Gordon, C. A., and Lu, Y.-L. (2011). *One Common Goal: Student Learning*. Report on Findings and Recommendations of the New Jersey School Library Study Phase 2.

TRAILS Development Timeline. (2017). *Trails-9.org*. Retrieved from www.trails-9.org/history2.php?page=about

Upside Learning. (2016). *LMS Selection Guide for SMBs*. Retrieved from www.upsidelms.com/free-ebook-lms-selection-guide-for-smbs.asp

Vavrus, M. (2008). Culturally responsive teaching. In T. L. Good (Ed.), *21st Century Education: A Reference Handbook* (Vol. 2, pp. 49–57). Los Angeles, CA: Sage Publications.

Venter, P., van Rensburg, M. J., & Davis, A. (2012). Drivers of learning management system use in a South African open and distance learning institution. *Australasian Journal of Educational Technology, 28*(2), 183–198.

Vygotsky, L. S. (1962). *Thought and Language*. Cambridge, MA: MIT Press.

Wenger, E., White, N., & Smith, J. (2009). *Digital Habitats: Stewarding Technology for Communities*. Portland, OR: CPsquare.

Wilson, C., Sudol, L., Stephenson, C., & Stehlik, M. (2010). Running on empty: The failure to teach K–12 computer science in the digital age. *Association for Computing Machinery Report*. Retrieved February 2015, from http://csta.acm.org/runningonempty/fullreport.pdf

Wine, L. D. (2016). School librarians as technology leaders: An evolution in practice. *Journal of Education for Library and Information Science, 57*(2), 207.

Wolf, M. A., Jones, R., & Gilbert, D. (2014). *Leading in and Beyond the Library*. Alliance for Excellent Education. Retrieved from https://all4ed.org/reports-factsheets/leading-in-and-beyond-the-library/

PART IV

Reconceptualizing Library Research

11

THE DESIGN OF DIGITAL LEARNING ACTIVITIES FOR LIBRARIES THROUGH PARTICIPATORY DESIGN

Jason Yip and Kung Jin Lee

Introduction

Libraries have always been the hub for knowledge and information collections. However, the space and the priorities of the library have to change to meet the growing needs of the patrons. One such change, as indicated by the authors of this book, is the needs of learners in the digital revolution. The growth of technology often means new learning opportunities are waiting to happen. New participatory, ubiquitous, and maker technologies are now pervasive and designed to support creative learning for children (Larson et al., 2013). In order to promote such creativity there is a need to think about how learning spaces with technology should be designed (Tevaniemi, Poutanen, & Lähdemäki, 2015).

Designing digital learning spaces and activities for users is not an easy task. One of the main problems is that designers do not think like users. Specifically, adults have a particularly hard time understanding the knowledge, values, and perspectives of youth. This can be especially problematic for librarians serving youth patrons with diverse needs. Specifically, for learning spaces with new technology, many librarians are not trained as educators or instructional designers. For these librarians, encountering new digital technologies and having to design learning activities associated with them can be overwhelming. With all these factors, it can be difficult for librarians to meet the needs of patrons looking to engage in digital learning in a library.

To address these design concerns, participatory design can be a way to solve the problem by working together with designers and patrons (Kensing & Blomberg, 1998). Participatory design is a method of design that focuses on close democratic collaboration with users and designers (Ehn, 1993). Because participatory design focuses on bringing designers and stakeholders closer together, each group of people can develop stronger relationships with and understanding of each other (Yip et al., 2016). We believe there is potential for participatory design to bring librarians and youth together in designing new digital learning spaces. However, to date, there have only been a few opportunities in which librarians have engaged in the codesign of learning spaces with youth. More research in this area needs to take place to recognize what tensions and opportunities exist and how librarians and designers can leverage this knowledge for truly collaborative and democratic designs.

In this chapter, we document a case study of an intergenerational design team of adults and ethnically diverse children (ages 7–11) called KidsTeam UW and their codesign collaboration with a librarian at The Seattle Public Library (SPL). Specifically, we describe an exploratory study of six codesign sessions between KidsTeam UW and SPL that occurred from fall 2015 to spring 2016. The goal of these codesign sessions was to collaborative work with the digital program manager (Javier, pseudonym) to create new digital learning activities for SPL and their librarians and communities.

Background

Participatory Design and Libraries

Participatory design is an overarching design methodology that involves users in the technology design process. During the mid 1970s, workers in Scandinavia began to feel threatened in their work environment. As computer-based technologies began to be introduced to the workplace in Europe, a feeling of losing control loomed upon work environments. This feeling of loss and lack of control lead to concerns of democracy in the workplace (Ehn, 1993), which lead to the UTOPIA project. This project began the participatory design movement, in which newspaper workers in Sweden started designing new computer-based tools for their work in the 1980s. Since then, the spirit of participatory design as a method of democratic design has influenced many researchers to work together with end users.

Using participatory design in libraries to design solutions for patrons is not new. Libraries have utilized participatory design methods to codesign functional use of the library for the community (Somerville & Collins, 2008). For instance, codesign work with libraries includes designing learning commons together with students, faculty members, campus stakeholders, and librarians (Somerville & Collins, 2008), cocreating organizational structures and communication systems with library employees (Somerville & Howard, 2010), engaging in the participatory action research and codesign approach to creating library spaces (Somerville & Brown-Sica, 2011), involving university students and librarians in coconceptualizing libraries of the future (Somerville, 2007), and coconstructing digital portals with academic teaching faculty and subject specialist librarians (Somerville & Vuotto, 2005).

Designers and researchers have also used participatory design methods to create new learning technologies for libraries. For example, Druin (2001) focused on how children searched for books in the International Children's Digital Library (www.childrenslibrary.org), a collection of digital books from all across the world. The children in the study could not use a library catalog system that was intended for adults, such as keyword boxes and drop-down menus asking for authors, titles, and subjects. Instead, using participatory design methods, Druin and her researchers worked closely together with children to create a system to find digital books by color, size of book, and themes. Participatory design has also been used for creating learning programs for teens, with teens. Subramaniam (2016) introduces different techniques within participatory design to capture the voice of teens and to shift the power dimension that is focused on librarians being the only expert.

Participatory Design and Children

Designing for children is no easy task; adults simply cannot try to think like a child because the world changes so quickly within technological contexts. Therefore, starting in the late 1990s, child–computer interaction researchers began employing participatory design as a way to work with children (Druin, 1999). Research in participatory design and children is robust, from the design techniques used in codesign (Walsh, Foss, Yip, & Druin, 2013), the products of children's codesign (Druin, 2001; Banerjee, Yip, Lee, & Popovic, 2016), to the challenges of codesign with children (Van Mechelen, Zaman, Laenen, & Vanden Abeele, 2015) and to new perspectives of the roles of children in codesign (Iversen, Smith, & Dindler, 2017; Yip et al., 2017).

The perspective that participatory design can help youth have an equal opportunity for design is an important argument for this chapter. Under participatory design there are different philosophical methods that provide a diverse way in which codesign is undertaken. Specifically, Druin (1999, Druin et al., 2001) states that children can be equal design partners through a participatory design method called cooperative inquiry. Cooperative inquiry emphasizes a more democratic space to hear more diverse voices. We cannot ignore what it means to be design partners with children and what it means to be equal design partners. Creating positive relationships among different stakeholders is emphasized when working together (Hoffman et al., 2016).

Yip et al. (2017) made an effort in unpacking what it takes to create the equal partnership by unpacking the meaning of equal partnerships and how equity plays a role. The researchers looked at the different dimensions of design partnerships in cooperative inquiry. The four dimensions are *facilitation, relationship building, design by doing,* and *elaborating together.* Facilitation refers to how much support and mediation takes place between the adults and children during codesign activities. Relationship building looks at how much social interaction occurs in the codesign group. Design by doing highlights how design activities take place and how collaborative building and designing artifacts are between children and adults. Elaboration looks at how adults and children generate and contribute ideas together. These four dimensions occur in a spectrum of unbalanced and balanced interaction. Unbalanced refers to a dominant amount of interaction by either children or adults, while balance occurs when equal distribution of interactions between children and adults exists. Our analysis of the video recordings of the design sessions focus on these different dimensions happening and offers insights on how this framework aids in understanding utilizing the participatory design (PD) method for librarians.

Methods

For this chapter, we look closely at a case of an intergenerational partnership among the University of Washington's KidsTeam UW and the Seattle Public Library. KidsTeam UW is a codesign group of children (ages 7–11) and adults that consult and work closely as equal design partners in the creation of new technologies and digital learning activities. KidsTeam UW worked in the project with the Seattle Public Library in creating a series of learning activities for youth to learn about new technologies in the library space. For this study, we examined a total of six codesign sessions from fall 2015 to summer 2016. The participants in this intergenerational codesign group are ten children and UW undergraduate and graduate students and professors with librarians from SPL (Table 11.1).

The design sessions incorporated different cooperative inquiry design techniques such as low-tech prototyping, using sticky notes to evaluate certain technology and collaboratively working on an idea using big paper (Walsh et al., 2013). For each codesign session (90 minutes), we recorded videos and took pictures to understand what was happening. Researchers on our team have also written journal reflections and memos that occurred after the design sessions.

TABLE 11.1 Demographics of child participants

Child name	Age	Gender	Ethnicity
Gina	11	Female	Asian
Aileen	11	Female	White
Athena	7	Female	Asian/Black
Austin	11	Male	Asian
Riku	9	Female	Asian/White
Anishinaabe	9	Female	Native
Animikiik	11	Male	Native
Simon	9	Male	White
Marlene	7	Female	White
Winston	7	Male	White

TABLE 11.2 Session descriptions

Codesign sessions	Technology	Description
Finch Robots (Three sessions)	Finch Robots are small robots that are tethered to a laptop and controlled through block programming. www.finchrobot.com/	The first session focused on evaluating the Finch Robots. The second session examined how to create an obstacle course for the robots. The last session examined how to create help and guidance for using a Finch Robot.
Little Bits (Two sessions)	Little Bits are electronic blocks that snap together to create programmable circuits. https://littlebits.cc/	The first session was an evaluation of Little Bits. The second session examined how children could use Lego blocks and other materials with Little Bits.
TaleBlazer	TaleBlazer is a programing environment that allows youth to build location-based augmented-reality games. http://taleblazer.org/	The session was an evaluation of TaleBlazer.

Additionally, we interviewed Javier (pseudonym) at SPL, who worked in all six codesign sessions with KidsTeam UW. Javier is the digital program manager and learning specialist at SPL. He participated in the six codesign sessions (Table 11.1) with KidsTeam UW and created the associated learning activities. First, we conducted an overall interview on reflecting in general on the experience of working with KidsTeam UW. For the next interview, we showed video clips of specific moments in the codesign session to do a reflection with Javier on what was happening during each session. We asked Javier to reflect on how the KidsTeam UW children were influencing the design of the learning activities and the interactions and relationships happening among the people in the design group.

Findings

Children as Codesigners Compared to Children as Users

For librarians (both MLIS-degreed professionals and library staff members), there are affordances and constraints when it comes to observing children using digital technologies with learning activities and partnering with children to codesign such activities. First, we have to consider the goal of librarians as they run learning activities in the library. When a librarian is observing children, they have to watch children interact with the technology and run the learning program. Javier noted that often librarians are seeking to know what to do with the learning activity and are not able to observe:

Interviewer: Is there, is there a feeling that people want things scaffolded in the libraries, or is that just something that like you observed?

Javier: Yeah, I think people want that. People want to know step 1, step 2, step 3.

Interviewer: The librarians or the kids?

Javier: The librarians. I think usually they want to know, okay, what am I going to do first, and what am I going to do next and next, right. So like lead me kind of things.

Because librarians may feel like they have to run a structured program, it can be difficult for library staff to run the program and make detailed usability observations of the learning activity for later design. For instance, Javier noted that even if librarians were to just observe the activities, without close design discussions, they may forget details and not take time to process their observations. This can make it difficult to integrate observations into design. We believe that observing children in the learning activities can be tricky for librarians who may be inexperienced at both running the activities and making detailed observations. When the goal of the librarian is observing children, there can be limited interaction happening. As the goal is not learning together, conversation may not arise easily during the design session.

However, when a librarian is codesigning with the children, the goal is for both adults and children to learn together about the new technology and the activities that can support such learning. Druin (1999, 2002) argues that children are capable and can be partners throughout the codesign process. Codesigning together allows librarians to focus on the design of learning activities with children, without pressure. For instance, Javier noted that codesign sessions provide a way for discussion to occur with children about design ideas and changes:

So if I go and I observe (a learning activity) I will just observe it. But then I may forget and it's not processed. But when I come and do the work with you (codesign) the observations are discussed at the end. So it's like a concrete result. So I have something concrete with our discussion.

Javier also noted that codesigning with children is not only about learning what children are thinking but also for adults to actively put their ideas out.

Right, so I think that what you're learning over here, right, is to how to like design with kids, work with them, bounce ideas, be open to collaborate with them. Like, you can . . . for me, some of the things that I learned the most about in KidsTeam is the fact *that the adult has a voice*, that usually

I think that kid's voice or youth voice, I used to have this concept that, that the voice meant that the adult didn't have one. Like, oh kid's voice mean, you're supposed to disappear in the room, right. I think that one of the things that I learned here by working with you is that the adult's voice is very valuable, right. Like you can say adults get to contribute to it, right. Because it pushes mostly forward, right.

Similarly, the goals of the children also differ based on whether the children are codesigning or being observed. Children who are engaged in learning activities are more focused on designing for themselves. For instance, children who come are expecting to try out the digital technologies and activities, not provide suggestions or design ideas. They may come only once to the library or multiple times, but children's goals in learning activities are not designing for others but designing for themselves.

However, in codesigning with librarians, creating a positive longer-term relationship with children is a priority (Yip et al., 2017). Javier gave a clear distinction between children being codesigners to observing children on their own designing.

The fact that they (children in codesign) are a group that comes every week for a long period of time and they are practicing the same kind of things like the thinking about designing and technology for the most part. And then they come in and they somehow already have an understanding of what is going to happen in that room. So, they come and I am going to say prepared but they have it's almost have like an expectation. They are not expecting. But you know what I mean. They are coming in and they have an understanding of what's going to happen there because they done it for so many times. With teens or with other kids that I see like at the library for example where the retention or the frequency of the workshops is not so often you haven't built that sort of muscle well for kids to work in a room and then say okay I know what I am here to do because you have to remind them or you have to bring them back to that mental state.

The limitation of simply observing children is that the ideas made are not pushed forward. Often children have ideas that are random, fun, and out of the box. The role of the librarian is to think how the ideas fit into the real world and how the design serves for more children in the future. Being codesigners means that the librarian needs to toss the ideas back and forth by asking critical questions of whether such design will play the intended role or adults suggesting and adding on to the idea.

A benefit of librarians codesigning with children compared to observing is that they do not have to know all the answers to a problem. To elaborate, in designing learning curriculums the instructor usually implements a problem a learner should figure out. However, codesign differs in that the child consistently participates in the design sessions, which allows a space for the child to interact with the adult.

For instance, Marlene (age 7) was a member of KidsTeam UW since Year 1 and was interacting with a technology called Little Bits, an electronic building blocks set with which children can make inventions. Javier was interested in cocreating a Little Bits learning curriculum using for future workshops in the library with Marlene and other children. Marlene wanted to create a hummingbird with the electronic blocks she had. The problem was that she did not have the equipment to make the sound. The librarian reflects on this scene as being worried about not having the answers to how to make the sound of a hummingbird. The first few thoughts that Javier had were about downloading a module of creating sounds or thinking about recording sounds. However, in this session the child was able to figure out how to make a sound using a fan electronic block by putting a paper inside the fan to make noise.

We suggest from the prior codesign example that librarians do not always have to have all the answers to the design problems children encounter. This is particularly true for some reference librarians, who may be used to being the helper for patrons seeking information. Librarians are used to having the answers to problems and to lead the lost patrons. However, from the codesign sessions with children, we are able to learn that the librarian does not always have to have all the answers, but when libraries provide the open space to explore, children are able to be codesigners with the librarian. This example may have occurred in the same setting without codesign. However, as children developed relationships with us, we were able to understand the reasoning behind such designs. Children in our codesign team have been trained to actively search for answers when encountering a problem. We argue that it is important for the library to create such space to happen too.

Why the Freedom to Design With Less Risk Matters for Learning Activities

Our reflection on these codesign sessions also revealed another benefit for the librarians adopting codesign. We believe codesign opportunities present less risk in trying out new learning activities. Libraries are informal learning spaces that do not necessarily fit into the constraints of formal education. It can be challenging to develop new learning activities and to convince patrons to come and to get other librarians' buy-in. However, codesign differs in that there is less risk in trying out new designs, as there is more flexibility and adaptation during codesign sessions. In codesign, adults and children are learning together and can realize that design failures are an option and quite welcome. In codesign, the adult and the child learn from the failure, whereas a failure of a digital learning program means losing patrons and wasting resources.

Javier called the codesign sessions an "experimenting space" in which it is safe to see a learning design fail. For instance, in a codesign session, we attempted to use TaleBlazer, a platform through which children can create location-based augmented-reality games. During the session, children worked with adults to evaluate this digital platform. However, we did not anticipate how difficult the platform was for younger children (ages 7–11). Based on what we learned in the codesign session, Javier was able to adjust the details of the curriculum for older children instead.

Working with children to codesign and evaluate TaleBlazer proved to benefit Javier and the library program. Here, having a safe space to try out new technologies and codesign the activities allowed us to make readjustments to our design. If the librarian is not able to oversee the problems that may occur, such as not allocating the right time for a session or not knowing the level of expertise of the child, the final implementation of the design to patrons could be troublesome. Difficult and frustration with digital learning designs can make is hard for child patrons to want to come back to future sessions. As digital media learning in libraries is a place of informal learning and is not pervasive in libraries yet, there is a need to be mindful about the perceptions the librarians have in implementing such activities. In what follows, Javier reflected on the design session.

Interviewer: Would you have found this out without the KidsTeam UW, like in trying it in the library, or was it something different about using codesign that like gave you a little more insight into this?

Javier: Well, I think . . . I don't know if codesign per se but the fact that it's an experimenting space, that it's safe to see something fail.

Interviewer: Can you talk about that?

Javier: Like if you go to the library . . . let's say I say, okay guys, we're going to have a 90-minute workshop on TaleBlazer on like this day, and bring 10 kids, and they come. It goes like this where it's like a complete mess, and I'm like, well it failed. So, and it would be hard to justify doing it again or programs that are better.

Interviewer: Yeah, or just the investment that it takes to get 10 kids there.

Javier: Yeah, right, like you have to work with the librarian. You've got to reserve the space.

Javier notes potential issues with difficult learning designs, such as the investment to get patrons to come, to train librarians, and to reserve the space.

In case of design sessions, there is no need for perfection, as the adults and the children are exploring the new technology together. The children and the adults have the freedom to try out different experiments using the technology. The process is messy in that there may not be a clear outcome, as the children and the adults are not following a structured curriculum. However, in this space there is no concern about failing, as it is more about exploring. Thinking about the population the public library serves as being diverse in age, interest, and expertise, the task for a librarian creating a curriculum that meets all the following needs is very challenging. The reflection from the codesign session shows how participatory design creates a space in which the librarian can experiment with new technology with children in a loose structure.

The Tensions and Affordances of Adult–Child Design Partnerships in Libraries

The motivation to create equal partnerships with children, librarians, and designers in codesign sessions is to create a democratic process that empowers our participants (Ehn, 1993). However, giving children autonomy and agency is not easy in the context of libraries for many reasons. We argue the need of still adopting such mentality, as libraries are independent learning places where democracy in action can take place. We believe our process of design follows the foundational principles of the libraries.

Within the traditional role of a librarian, there may be a need to want to help patrons find the answer they are seeking. However, this role can seep into codesign groups and can be antithetical toward children developing their own agency and autonomy in design. For instance, Javier reflected on a moment in codesign in which a child was having difficulty using a computer keyboard. During this time, Javier took over the keyboard to help the child.

> I would say, you know, don't stand behind them and take over the keyboard for them. Maybe come up front or stand next to them, lower yourself, and try for them to continue having control over the program and the keyboard, and to actually guide them as opposed to take over. I mean like, I took over the keyboard.

In his reflection, Javier noted that he should not have taken over the keyboard in solving the problem. He emphasized that what he has learned is that once he took over in solving the problem, he was the one answering the questions rather than letting the child solve the problem on their own.

Likewise, when children are stuck on a design problem, it can be easy for an adult to step in and help. However, it takes an effort to step back and allow the child to figure out the problem when the adult knows all the answers and sees the child is frustrated. This differs from simply observing children but is more about guiding the children to solve certain problems on their own. In codesign, there is an emphasis on *facilitation*, which is one of the dimensions in equal design partnerships. An unbalanced partnership is when adults only facilitate the session, whereas a balanced partnership is more about an adult and a child facilitating together (Yip et al., 2017). Javier noted how he could have situated himself, such as coming up front, standing next to the child, or lowering himself to encourage the child to work together with him.

Codesign for libraries can also be chaotic and messy. Librarians attempting to work with children in codesign need to anticipate their antics and rambunctious nature. For instance, in the Little Bits design session, children discovered that the wireless remotes were paired with a specific channel setting. For instance, Wireless Remote A controlled Receptor A and Wireless Remote B controlled Receptor B. However, there is a setting in Wireless Remote A that can switch it to B. Children determined that even though they have Wireless Remote A, they could change the frequency of it to become Wireless Remote B. This meant that children could secretly try to control another child's design without them knowing it. Needless to say, this created all kinds of chaos and disorderliness in the codesign session. Javier, however, saw this as an opportunity:

> I'm like oh no. So . . . but I mean for me, I think about, it was like okay, at first it was like oh, no, they, they made these . . . didn't make, you know, they just made it more chaotic and difficult like, but you could you know, make the argument that they were learning about you know, channels and transmission, you know. It was like, oh, okay, now you know that there are, you communicate through things in a certain way, you know like they need to match.

For Javier, this is a moment of both difficulty and learning. The difficulty is in managing and working through the disturbances the codesign children created as they "trolled" each other's designs. The learning portion comes in two parts. First, children in the codesign settings do learn and are known to understand new content and integrate it into their designs (McNally, Mauriello, Guha, & Druin, 2017). Second, this is a learning moment for Javier, as he has just learned to avoid this kind of channel switching that could have created more headaches for librarians.

Despite the tensions in codesign for librarians, we believe there is much potential for librarians to work together with child patrons in the design of new learning activities for digital technologies. The early stages of codesign can be difficult, with many logistics that need to be considered (e.g., time, investment of resource, role of librarians, etc.). Javier noted though:

> I hope that the librarians become better at facilitating design workshops for kids. You know like they are able to become design partners, and that they learn some practices about how you design together with kids, that they feel more at ease with that with things that emerge rather than that are prescribed. That will be an amazing thing.

Implications and Future Work

Libraries serve a fundamental institutional role in supporting democracy and schooling citizens in the conduct of democratic practices (Kranich, 2001). Democracy is not a simple concept to implement. It is an opportunity for everyone to participate in all aspects of society, but this is not always easy. We believe that through design-thinking principles, practices, and opportunities in libraries (Clarke, 2018), we can demonstrate democracy and collaboration to youth and family patrons. Participatory design was born out of the need for democratic engagement in design (Ehn, 1993). We argue that it is not just the product that is important (the need for digital learning activities in libraries); the process in design is just as important.

Our codesign sessions with the Seattle Public Library revealed many of the challenges and opportunities for librarians when it comes to designing learning environments around digital technologies. First, we recognize codesigning together with librarians is not easy and presents many logistical challenges. The role of the librarian is multifaceted and ever increasing. Asking librarians to take on the task of instructional designers and digital media specialists can be a burden on this overly committed job. Similarly, how librarians find and recruit youth and designers to join a codesign is also a logistical challenge. Second, there is risk whenever design is considered. Even though libraries present more different opportunities for learning with digital technologies than formal classrooms, there are still issues of getting patrons to come, developing buy-in from librarians, determining resource allocation, and examining the scale at which learning innovations are implemented. In short, while codesign provides opportunities for librarians to empathize, ideate, define, test, and evaluate with youth, we must still consider the local contextual hurdles to creating an intergenerational design team for libraries.

Our codesign team is privileged to be base in a university research setting that allows for support, such as access to student volunteers, material resources, and space. And yet we have attempted to demonstrate in this chapter that codesign can be a viable and productive way for librarians to design learning activities for their local contexts. Codesign provides a safe and experimental space to try out new ideas and designs, with little risk involved in terms of youth engagement and failed designs.

Based on this early preliminary research, we recommend university researchers engage in human-centered design and instructional design work together with libraries to set up codesign. Libraries themselves often have neighborhood youth boards or volunteers that could be potential codesigners. Universities have design students that could potentially collaborate with librarians. At the University of Washington, we have created LIS 598: Participatory Design for Libraries. LIS 598 is an academically based community service (ABCS) course (Benson & Harkavy, 2000). We are running this ABCS course with half of the class meeting for discussion and the other half of the class codesigning with youth and families at the Seattle Public Library. By developing university and library partnerships through codesign, we are attempting to support the democratic mission of the university (Harkavy, Benson, Hartley, & Hodges, 2017).

Overall, the insights we have gained through participatory design with youth and librarians inform our understanding of the diverse contexts and challenges that come with designing learning activities for libraries. Our findings suggest that while logistical challenges exist for librarians to implement codesign, a partnership between universities and libraries can be a starting point form which consider participatory design as part of design thinking in libraries. We know that participatory design as a design process can support learning for youth (McNally et al., 2017) and social bonding and collaboration within and between families (Yip et al., 2016). We believe because libraries are neighborhood institutions with strong ties to communities, participatory design can generate a process that is beneficial to patrons and a product that can engage learners in technology at the library.

References

Banerjee, R., Yip, J., Lee, K. J., & Popović, Z. (2016). Empowering children to rapidly author games and animations without writing code. In *Proceedings of the 15th International Conference on Interaction Design and Children* (pp. 230–237). New York, NY: ACM. doi:https://doi.org/10.1145/2930674.2930688

Benson, L., & Harkavy, I. (2000). Higher education's third revolution: The emergence of the democratic cosmopolitan civic university. *Cityscape*, 47–57.

Clarke, R. (2018). Toward a design epistemology for librarianship. *The Library Quarterly*.

Druin, A. (1999). Cooperative inquiry: Developing new technologies for children with children. In *Proceedings of the SIGCHI Conference on Human Factors in Computing Systems* (pp. 592–599). New York, NY: ACM.

Druin, A., (2002). *The role of children in the design of new technology. Behaviour & Information Technology, 21*(1), pp. 1–25.

Druin, A., Bederson, B. B., Hourcade, J. P., Sherman, L., Revelle, G., Platner, M., & Weng, S. (2001). Designing a digital library for young children. In *Proceedings of the 1st ACM/IEEE-CS Joint Conference on Digital Libraries* (pp. 398–405). New York, NY: ACM.

Ehn, P. (1993). Scandinavian design: On participation and skill. *Participatory Design: Principles and Practices*, 41–77.

Harkavy, I., Benson, L., Hartley, M., & Hodges, R. A. (2017). *Knowledge for Social Change: Bacon, Dewey, and the Revolutionary Transformation of Research Universities in the Twenty-First Century*. Philadelphia, PA: Temple University Press.

Hoffman, K. M., Subramaniam, M., Kawas, S., Scaff, L., & Davis, K. (2016). *Connected Libraries: Surveying the Current Landscape and Charting a Path to the Future*. College Park, MD; Seattle, WA: ConnectedLib Project.

Iversen, O. S., Smith, R. C., & Dindler, C. (2017). Child as protagonist: Expanding the role of children in participatory design. In *Proceedings of the 2017 Conference on Interaction Design and Children* (IDC '17) (pp. 27–37). New York, NY: ACM. doi:https://doi.org/10.1145/3078072.3079725

Kensing, F., & Blomberg, J. (1998). Participatory design: Issues and concerns. *Computer Supported Cooperative Work (CSCW)*, 7(3–4), 167–185.

Kranich, N. (2001). *Libraries and Democracy: The Cornerstones of Liberty*. Chicago, IL: American Library Association.

Larson, K., Ito, M., Brown, E., Hawkins, M., Pinkard, N., & Sebring, P. (2013). *Safe Space and Shared Interests: YOUMedia Chicago as a Laboratory for Connected Learning*. Pennsauken, NJ: BookBaby.

McNally, B., Mauriello, M. L., Guha, M. L., & Druin, A. (2017). Gains from participatory design team membership as perceived by child alumni and their parents. In *Proceedings of the 2017 CHI Conference on Human Factors in Computing Systems* (pp. 5730–5741). New York, NY: ACM.

Somerville, M. M. (2007). Participatory co-design: A relationship building approach for co-creating libraries of the future. In *Libraries for the Future: Progress, Development and Partnerships-Proceedings of the 73rd International Federation of Library Associations (IFLA) Conference*, Durban, South Africa. Retrieved from www.ifla.org/IV/ifla73/papers/122-Somerville-en.pdf

Somerville, M. M., & Brown-Sica, M. (2011). Library space planning: A participatory action research approach. *The Electronic Library*, *29*(5), 669–681.

Somerville, M. M., & Collins, L. (2008). Collaborative design: A learner-centered library planning approach. *The Electronic Library*, *26*(6), 803–820.

Somerville, M. M., & Howard, Z. (2010). 'Information in context': Co-designing workplace structures and systems for organizational learning. *Information Research*, *15*(4), 10.

Somerville, M. M., & Vuotto, F. (2005). If you build it with them, they will come: Digital research portal design and development strategies. *Internet Reference Services Quarterly*, *10*(1), 77–94.

Subramaniam, M. (2016). Designing the library of the future for and with teens: Librarians as the 'connector' in connected learning. *Journal of Research on Libraries and Young Adults*, *7*(2), 1–18.

Tevaniemi, J., Poutanen, J., & Lähdemäki, R. (2015). Library as a partner in co-designing learning spaces: A case study at Tampere University of Technology, Finland. *New Review of Academic Librarianship*, *21*(3), 304–324.

Van Mechelen, M., Zaman, B., Laenen, A., & Vanden Abeele, V. (2015). Challenging group dynamics in participatory design with children: Lessons from social interdependence theory. In *Proceedings of the 14th International Conference on Interaction Design and Children* (IDC '15) (pp. 219–228). New York, NY: ACM. doi:http://dx.doi.org/10.1145/2771839.2771862

Walsh, G., Foss, E., Yip, J., & Druin, A. (2013, April). FACIT PD: A framework for analysis and creation of intergenerational techniques for participatory design. In *Proceedings of the SIGCHI Conference on Human Factors in Computing Systems* (pp. 2893–2902). New York, NY: ACM.

Yip, J. C., Clegg, T., Ahn, J., Uchidiuno, J. O., Bonsignore, E., Beck, A., . . . & Mills, K. (2016, May). The evolution of engagements and social bonds during child-parent co-design. In *Proceedings of the 2016 CHI Conference on Human Factors in Computing Systems* (pp. 3607–3619). New York, NY: ACM.

Yip, J. C., Sobel, K., Pitt, C., Lee, K. J., Chen, S., Nasu, K., & Pina, L. R. (2017). Examining adult-child interactions in intergenerational participatory design. In *Proceedings of the 2017 CHI Conference on Human Factors in Computing Systems* (pp. 5742–5754). New York, NY: ACM.

12

PROBING CAUSAL RELATIONSHIPS BETWEEN WHAT SCHOOL LIBRARIANS DO AND WHAT LEARNERS GAIN IN SCHOOL LIBRARIES

A Reconceptualization of the Profession's Research Agenda

Marcia A. Mardis, Faye R. Jones, Lenese Colson, Shana Pribesh, Sue Kimmel, Barbara Schultz-Jones, Laura Pasquini, and Laura Gogia

Introduction

Learning is a self-directed, ongoing, transferrable, and social process of applying understanding; information, a core element of this process, is reported to be a significant contributing cause of learning (National Research Council [NRC], 2000). Like nurses (e.g., Spence Laschinger, 2008) and social workers (e.g., Rubin & Parrish, 2012), school librarians contribute to learners' outcomes through direct and indirect contact and collaborative relationships with other professionals; as with these fields, school librarianship has a strong anecdotal evidence base, but few researchers have attempted to document causal relationships between what professionals do and what beneficiaries gain (Morris & Cahill, 2016). Numerous local, state, and federal education policies tie educators' financial and technical support to their abilities to document cause/effect relationships between their practice and learner outcomes. For the school librarianship community, then, a high priority is to reconceptualize the profession's research agenda toward one which builds causal understanding. However, this shift may be daunting because, as Morrison and van der Werf (2016) pointed out, "To search for causality in educational research is to search for the holy grail. Causality is elusive" (p. 1). In this chapter, we share the foundation and current state of school librarianship as well as the research agenda we developed and have begun to enact. We conclude with a look into future research directions, potential challenges, and implications for researchers, practitioners, and policy makers.

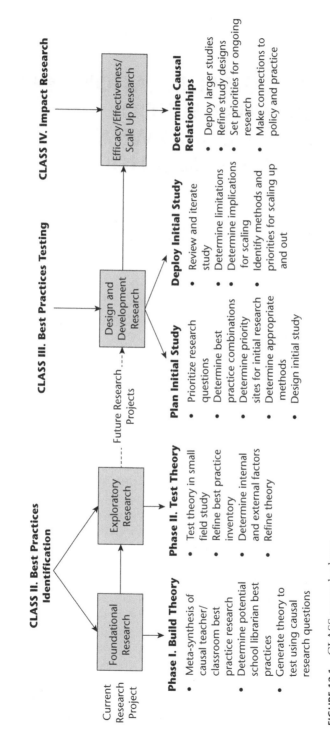

FIGURE 12.1 CLASS research phases

Research Heritage

In 2014, the American Association of School Librarians (AASL) was awarded Causality: School Libraries and Student Success (CLASS), an Institute of Museum and Library Services (IMLS) National Forum grant. The purpose of the CLASS forum was to bring together leaders in school library research and related fields to build consensus on a national agenda for school library researchers to move to from correlational studies conducted by a variety of research teams and individual researchers to a planned and coordinated causal research agenda for the profession. CLASS was highly successful in outlining next steps for a decade of progressive research, as Figure 12.1 shows.

Figure 12.1 illustrates the causal evidence development process outlined in *Common Guidelines for Education Research and Development* (Institute of Education Sciences & National Science Foundation, 2013) and affirmed by the CLASS forum participants (AASL, 2014). This agenda builds carefully toward a thorough and elaborate approach to causal research that will ultimately place school library research in line with federally recognized scientifically based empirical research. Each part of the research agenda builds on the one before, all leading to the ultimate goal of research that documents the causal implications of school library practice.

The purpose of Phase I of the CLASS research trajectory illustrated in Figure 12.1 is to generate theory about how school librarians relate to learners' outcomes; this process is designed to be initially operationalized through rigorous meta-analysis of best practice research relating to educators and student achievement. To conduct the research specified in Phase I of Figure 12.1, AASL engaged the CLASS II research team, that is, the chapter authors from Florida State University (FSU), Old Dominion University (ODU), and University of North Texas (UNT). In the research presented in this chapter, we addressed the first part of Phase I of that agenda by using meta-syntheses; our goal was to distill a working theory that will be tested and refined through the second part of Phase I, field studies that are currently underway.

Research Purpose and Question

The purpose of the research described in this chapter was to employ meta-synthesis to surface educators' effective practices that school librarians can also use to benefit learners. We pursued this objective in the context of the research question "What causal relationships between school-based malleable factors and student learning are present in published research?" We defined "school-based factors" as learning activities that occur within a school, such as aspects of classroom instruction or other malleable factors.

To provide a foundation upon which to understand this work, in this chapter, we begin by exploring the challenges of causal research in education as well as the correlational research relating to school librarians, school libraries, and student learning. Then we describe our process for identifying best practices by exploring previous research connecting what teachers do, the contexts in which they engage with learners, and student learning outcomes. We conclude by outlining our research in process and the next steps for the CLASS research agenda.

Literature Review

Today's students must navigate an information terrain that demands sophisticated information discovery, creation, and communication skills. To be prepared for the demands of tomorrow's workforce and higher education, learners must make many ethical and safety decisions related to information and technology (Cooper & Bray, 2011). Myriad forces such as the common standards movement's emphasis on conceptual application; growing global needs for dynamic, innovative, and flexible workplace readiness skills; and ubiquitous information and technology heighten the demands on educators responsible for students' success (AASL, 2016).

School librarians are educators, information specialists, and leaders. They possess the expertise, knowledge, and influence to ensure students' mastery of a wide range of cognitive, interpersonal, and intrapersonal skills (AASL, 2009; AASL, 2018). However, some states have fewer than half of their schools with a full-time certified school librarian, and the school library field has made little progress in changing that, despite active support in some areas (United States Department of Education, National Center for Education Statistics, 2016). Research is needed to demonstrate what kinds of the effects a quality school library program, defined as a fully funded and fully staffed learning space led by a state-certified school librarian, has on student learning and success.

Causality in Education Research

An intervention such as a curricular innovation can be viewed as the cause of an effect, such as improved student learning, according to philosopher John Locke: "A cause is that which makes any other thing, either simple idea, substance, or mode, begin to be; and an effect is that which had its beginning from some other thing" (as quoted in Yolton, 1977, p. 325). As Shadish, Cook, and Campbell (2002) observed, we rarely know all of the causes of observed effects or how they relate to one another. Holland (1986) pointed out that a definite cause cannot be determined unequivocally; rather, causal studies establish the probability that an effect will occur.

The strongest causal research design, theoretically, is an experimental design such as a randomized control trial (RCT) (Morgan & Winship, 2014; Murnane & Willett, 2011), in which units are randomly assigned to either a treatment or a control condition. Random assignment probabilistically controls for confounding variables other than the presence/absence of the treatment. However, randomized control trial studies both are expensive and have major feasibility problems in education research; randomly assigning learners to educational interventions is difficult and even undesirable to implement (Thomas, 2016). The alternative would be to use one of the stronger, viable nonrandomized experimental designs, generally known as quasi-experimental designs, such as a time-series design or matched samples design (Shadish et al., 2002).

While experimental and quasi-experimental designs are optimal for summative evaluation (determining *whether* the intervention had an effect), they are not as useful for formative assessment (understanding how to *improve* existing programs). As Pawson (2006) argued,

> The nature of causality in social programmes is such that any synthesis of evidence on whether they work will need to investigate how they work. This requires unearthing information on mechanisms, contexts, and outcomes. The central quest is to understand the conditions of programme efficacy and this will involve the synthesis in investigating for whom, in what circumstances, and in what respects a family of programmes work.
>
> *(p. 25)*

Building these connections requires using methods that can elucidate contextual influences and the processes by which these operate; these are particular strengths of qualitative, rather than quantitative, research. However, in the current policy landscape, qualitative and descriptive studies are not as valued as sources of evidence for education intervention choices (U.S. Department of Education, 2016).

Current Social and Education Challenges Demand Causal Research

Causal research is also warranted by two intertwined current trends:

Broadening Ideas of Student Learning

While standardized test scores dominate the current discourse surrounding measuring student achievement, current federal education policy allows for the consideration of discipline referrals, attendance, parental involvement, graduation rates, and college application rates—as long as these considerations can be measured and their use is evidence based. Other areas of education have already moved to causal studies focusing on the degree to which educational practices, policies, teaching interventions, or out-of-school factors relate to student achievement. Examples of these recent studies include the effects of class size reductions (Shin & Raudenbush, 2011); home environment disruption (Hanscombe, Haworth, Davis,

Jaffee & Plimin, 2011); socio-economic status (Schubert & Becker, 2010); family involvement (Evans, Kelley, Sikora, & Trieman, 2010), and principal leadership (Tubin, 2011). Because students' in-school and out-of-school learning experiences include the school library, education research that does not consider the school library's contribution is providing an incomplete, and possibly misleading, view of student learning.

Every Student Succeeds Act and Evidence-Based Interventions

The major federal funding bill for public education, the Every Student Succeeds Act (ESSA), was signed into law on December 10, 2015 (United States Department of Education, 2016). As state education policy makers consider accessing ESSA funds for public education, they must prepare an implementation plan that includes proposed interventions for student improvement that are evidence-based. These interventions must demonstrate a statistically significant effect on improving student outcomes or other relevant outcomes based on strong evidence from at least one well-designed and well-implemented experimental study; moderate evidence from at least one well-designed and well-implemented quasi-experimental study; or promising evidence from at least one well-designed and well-implemented correlational study with statistical controls for selection bias. Policy makers may also select interventions that have been proven to demonstrate a rationale based on high-quality research findings or positive evaluation that such activity, strategy, or intervention is likely to improve student outcomes or other relevant outcomes; and includes ongoing efforts to examine the effects of such activity, strategy, or intervention.

Foundational Research on School Librarians' Effectiveness

For decades, researchers interested in school libraries have explored the relationship of school-level characteristics of libraries, such as the size of school library collections or the qualifications of school library staff, and student achievement. Additionally, there have been numerous case studies examining various aspects of school library practice.

Researchers began undertaking studies designed to measure the impact of school libraries and school librarians on student performance as early as the 1960s, when Gaver (1963) found higher average test score gains among students in elementary schools with centralized school libraries staffed by certified school librarians than in the other groups. In the five decades since Gaver's (1963) study, several researchers have suggested correlational relationships between school library program elements and academic achievement without a centralized collection and a school librarian. Lance and a team of researchers (Lance, Wellborn, & Hamilton-Pennell, 1993) published the first study that reported a correlation between school library program components and student achievement in Colorado; this study has become known as the "Colorado Study." In the ensuing correlational studies, researchers consistently reported a significant positive correlation between reading test achievement and particular elements of school library programs (Scholastic, 2016). These studies used factor analysis and regression modeling to isolate external variables, such as poverty and parental educational attainment, that related to student achievement to claim statistical significance about the school library–related results.

In the Colorado Study and its replications, researchers reported significant correlational relationships between reading test scores and:

1. School library staff size (Baxter & Smalley, 2003; Baumbach, 2002; Lance, Rodney, & Hamilton-Pennell, 2001; Smith, 2001; Lance, Rodney, & Hamilton-Pennell, 2000; Lance et al., 1999);
2. Presence of full-time, certified school librarians (Callison, 2004; Rodney, Lance, Hamilton-Pennell, & Center, 2002; Lance et al., 1999, 2000);
3. Frequency of library-centered instruction (Lance et al., 1999) and collaborative instruction between school librarians and teachers (Lance, Rodney, & Hamilton-Pennell, 2001, 2005; Lance et al., 2000);
4. Size and currency of library collections (Burgin, Bracy, & Brown, 2003; Smith, 2001; Lance et al., 2000);
5. Networked library access to licensed databases (Lance, Rodney, & Hamilton-Pennell, 2002);
6. Flexible scheduling (Lance et al., 2005; Rodney, Lance, & Hamilton-Pennell, 2003); and
7. School library budget size (Baxter & Smalley, 2003; Lance et al., 2001).

Education researchers have expressed caution concerning the over-interpretation of correlational studies, finding that readers often mistake correlation for causation when interpreting findings (Bleske-Rechek, Morrison, & Heidtke, 2015). However, the correlational findings have strongly suggested that evolving research to focus on specific professional activities, program elements, and learning outcomes unique to the school library was a promising direction and one that requires testing causal structures that explain correlational data (Russo, 2011). Although these studies' correlational approaches do not causally isolate the effects of school libraries, in the same manner that experimental and quasi-experimental methods may allow, their results do warrant causal investigation. As Mardis (2007) suggested, "Correlation should be the starting point, not the focus of advocacy since it is so often misinterpreted or over-claimed" (p. 25).

Challenges to Causally Linking School Librarianship and Student Learning

While existing correlational studies are valuable in identifying possible effects and the features of school libraries and school librarians that may cause them, they are not able to credibly rule out plausible alternative explanations. Strong causal studies partnered with the existing body of correlational research would strengthen claims about the influence of school libraries and school librarians on student learning, but several challenges remain.

Interlocking and Overlapping Roles

School librarians' roles are teacher, instructional partner, leader, information specialist and program administrator (AASL, 2009). In these roles, the school librarian works with everyone in the school and in learning spaces that are inclusive but not limited to the designated school library facility. The school library is an open learning space in which school librarians, through their various roles, directly or indirectly affect student learning. The school librarian also frequently works with other educators including teachers and administrators through instructional or institutional planning, coteaching, or the identification and provision of high-quality resources.

Identifying the school librarian's direct effect on learning is therefore challenging; the interconnected nature of school librarianship makes it difficult to separate the actions of effective school librarians from the organizational function of effective school libraries. Without a clear distinction between the two areas, causal researchers are challenged to determine what phenomena to study, or to put it simply, for what school librarians should be held accountable or given credit for (DiScala & Subramaniam, 2011; Zmuda & Harada, 2008).

Common Standards

Recent standards for college and career readiness including the Common Core State Standards (CCSS) and the Next Generation Science Standards (NGSS) (Achieve & NRC, 2013) aim to more closely connect the relationship between education and student learning by emphasizing the discovery of causal relationships. Current common standards-based school reform efforts often include strong emphases on information literacy skills, knowledge, dispositions, and self-assessments that ensure college and career readiness. Qualities such as curiosity, creativity, and persistence that appear in college and career readiness standards (National Governors' Association & Council of State School Officers, 2010; National Research Council, 2013) and the National School Library Standards (AASL, 2018) are vital skills in which the school librarian may play a significant role in imparting and are not necessarily reflected by standardized tests.

Information literacy, a particular concern of school librarians in their intended outcomes, includes "including digital, visual, textual, and technological" (AASL, 2007, n.p.) competencies reflected in the CCSS and NGSS. The NRC (2013) maintained that children will meet future challenges and achieve their potential as adults only if they develop a range of transferable skills and knowledge that prepare them to use information, connect information to prior knowledge, ask questions about what is not known, investigate answers, construct new understandings, and communicate with others to share those new understandings. However, methods of reliably measuring school librarians' role in imparting information literacy skills have yet to be developed (Neumann, Finger, & Neumann, 2017).

Method

In line with the theory-building process outlined in the *Common Guidelines for Educational Research* and levels of evidence specified by ESSA, CLASS II researchers identified activities and characteristics that showed strong relationships with student learning using three independent concurrent syntheses of current education policy, theory, and best practices research. We integrated the syntheses results and refined a list of possible causal features that may be present in school librarians' actions and activities that occur within the school library.

Mixed Research Synthesis

For this study, researchers from FSU, ODU, and UNT looked to the causal determination efforts in parallel fields in which professionals perform their duties as well as collaborate with other professionals. We opted to use mixed research synthesis (MRS), a method often used in nursing and social work research (Sandelowski, Voils, & Barroso, 2006) to determine the contributions of independent professional actions as well as the effects of professionals working together. "Mixed" are the objects of studies (i.e., the findings appearing in empirical qualitative, quantitative, and mixed-methods studies) as well as the methods (i.e., the qualitative and quantitative approaches). The researchers chose MRS because it is a useful method to develop evidence summaries and to determine key factors in an implementation chain of interventions, programs, and policies (Pawson, 2006).

MRS Step 1. Aggregation

In this step, each team reviewed a different corpus of peer-reviewed published research on causes of student learning published between 1985 and 2015. Per the *Common Guidelines for Educational Research* (IES & NSF, 2013) section on foundational research, we conducted searches of periodical databases to identify relevant empirical research. To compile the initial corpus, we agreed upon an initial Boolean search phrase such as "cause and student and (learning or achievement)." Researchers kept track of the searches conducted by recording date, source, search string and filters, citation, and number of results. Publications were then reviewed for relevancy to the research question.

FSU Aggregation Data Collection and Analysis

The FSU team examined practice guides and studies included in the What Works Clearinghouse (WWC) database. Established in 2002, the Institute of Education Sciences (IES) oversees the WWC within the U.S. Department of Education. WWC staff conduct ongoing searches of education research sources to identify studies that use an eligible design (i.e., randomized controlled trial, quasi-experimental design, regression-discontinuity designs, or single-case design) (IES, 2014). WWC staff assess the quality of evidence the study provides on the effectiveness of an intervention and determine whether it "Meets WWC Design Standards Without Reservations," "Meets WWC Design Standards With Reservations," or "Does Not Meet WWC Design Standards" (IES, 2014). WWC staff then assign the study an ESSA level of evidence (i.e., strong, moderate, or promising).

The FSU team also examined the WWC Practice Guides as of July 2016 ($N = 19$), which provide topical syntheses of studies with a special emphasis on educator agency and actions that have been proven to have a positive effect on a range of student outcomes (IES, n.d.). Panels of education researchers conducted the syntheses and developed the practice guides. The practice guides available in July 2016 were:

- *Assisting Students Struggling with Mathematics* (Gersten et al., 2009)
- *Assisting Students Struggling with Reading* (Gersten et al., 2009)
- *Developing Effective Fractions Instruction for Kindergarten Through 8th Grade* (Siegler et al., 2010)
- *Dropout Prevention* (Dynarski et al., 2008)
- *Effective Literacy and English Language Instruction for English Learners in the Elementary Grades* (Gersten et al., 2007)
- *Encouraging Girls in Math and Science* (Halpern et al., 2007)
- *Helping Students Navigate the Path to College* (Tierney et al., 2009)
- *Improving Adolescent Literacy: Effective Classroom and Intervention Practices* (Kamil et al., 2008)
- *Improving Mathematical Problem Solving in Grades 4 Through 8* (Woodward et al., 2012)
- *Improving Reading Comprehension in Kindergarten Through 3rd Grade* (Shanahan et al., 2010)
- *Organizing Instruction and Study to Improve Student Learning* (Pashler et al., 2007)
- *Reducing Behavior Problems in the Elementary School Classroom* (Epstein et al., 2008)
- *Structuring Out-of-School Time to Improve Academic Achievement* (Beckett et al., 2009)

- *Teaching Academic Content and Literacy to English Learners in Elementary and Middle School* (Baker et al., 2014)
- *Teaching Elementary School Students to Be Effective Writers* (Graham et al., 2012)
- *Teaching Math to Young Children* (Frye et al., 2013)
- *Teaching Strategies for Improving Algebra Knowledge in Middle and High School Students* (Star et al., 2015)
- *Turning Around Chronically Low-Performing Schools* (Herman et al., 2008)
- *Using Student Achievement Data to Support Instructional Decision Making* (Hamilton et al., 2009)

For each WWC study and practice guide, the FSU researchers extracted the statistically significant effective practices noted in the studies. For this research, the FSU researchers only considered WWC studies that not only met the design standards without reservations but also constituted, according to the WWC, strong or moderate evidence of effectiveness. In all, FSU retrieved 407 unique studies, 168 of which were included in the team's analysis.

ODU Aggregation Data Collection and Analysis

ODU researchers created a conceptual map, based on the work of Hattie (2008) that illustrated the various broad domains that influence student achievement, and each domain was synthesized independently. To identify pertinent literature, the team first searched prominent databases that catalog peer-reviewed literature about educational issues such as EBSCO, Scopus, Google Scholar, and JSTOR. Selected articles had to meet certain criteria: available in English, peer reviewed, published after 1985, centered on school-aged children but not concentrated on students with disabilities. Using the ESSA guidance on using evidence to strengthen education investments (United States Department of Education, 2016), the ODU team members read each article and assigned an ESSA level. As an investigation into causal research, the team was most interested in randomized controlled trials; however, team members recognized the rigor of matching designs, propensity score matching, regression discontinuity, and other strong correlational designs. Meta-analyses that included correlational studies but use the power of aggregation to locate effective educational practices were culled from Hattie's (2008) *Visible Learning: A Synthesis of Over 800 Meta-Analyses Relating to Achievement.* An initial search resulted in approximately 159 articles from the databases as well as articles located through lists found in Hattie (2008). The team used these results to snowball—searching the reference lists for additional literature that added another 200 articles. Upon close examination, the team excluded articles that did not fit the inclusion criteria. Of the final 245 articles, 107 provided strong evidence, 135 provided moderate or promising evidence, and 3 demonstrated a rationale applying the ESSA levels of evidence criteria.

UNT Aggregation Data Collection and Analysis

UNT researchers conducted a literature discovery search using the Scopus database, the largest abstract and citation database of peer-reviewed literature: scientific journals, books, and conference proceedings. The team searched Scopus with a search string of

librar* AND caus* AND (school* OR learn* OR achiev*)

to retrieve 514 articles. From this initial search, the team conducted 89 separate searches using keyword "school librar*" with the relevant codes ($n = 105$) and themes ($n = 18$) related to school learning and/or achievement from the broad Scopus search. To be included in the corpus, each identified document was: focused on school libraries; reported empirical research; published in a peer-reviewed journal or in conference proceedings; published or available online as in press between January 1985 and March 2016; and written in English. The team defined empirical papers as those that gathered and analyzed primary or secondary data in their investigation. Conceptual and theoretical publications did not meet the inclusion criteria. The majority of the publications discovered in the literature search were not empirical and were excluded. Out of 330 results returned, 264 fit the inclusion criteria.

Following the ESSA standards, the UNT researchers kept seventy-six studies, with just over half (56.6%) published between 2010–2016. The majority were journal articles, as only 2 studies were from conference proceedings. The academic disciplines were limited to education ($n = 8$) and library and information sciences ($n = 68$); however, 22% ($n = 17$) included technology as a means for intervention for school librarians. The majority of the papers, 65.8% ($n = 50$) represented studies involving school librarians based in the United States. The papers that remained and added to the larger corpus included 1article (Shoham, 2001) that met ESSA's level of "strong evidence," 9 papers that reflected moderate evidence, 27 papers that had promising evidence, and 39 papers demonstrated a rationale.

MRS Step 2. Synthesis

To identify possible learning outcomes that directly result from library learning space activities, the researchers reviewed the corpus of studies aggregated in MRS Step 1 and applied the integrated MRS design with a top-down configuration synthesis method. In an integrated MRS, studies in a targeted domain are grouped by findings viewed as answering the same research questions or addressing the same aspects of a target phenomenon (Sandelowski et al., 2006). This MRS approach included top-down configuration such as counting, tabulating, diagramming, and narrating thematically diverse individual findings, or sets of aggregated findings, into a coherent theoretical rendering. Figure 12.2 depicts a sample analysis conducted with an Integrated MRS.

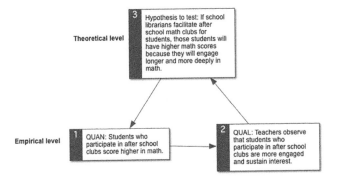

FIGURE 12.2 Sample integrated MRS with top-down configuration[1]

Findings in configuration syntheses may contradict, extend, explain, or otherwise modify each other. In configuration synthesis, researchers link findings, even though these links may not have been addressed in any of the primary studies reviewed. This particular approach is well suited for the proposed study because it can identify promising causal relationships that must be extrapolated from the original study context (Sandelowski, Voils, Leeman, & Crandell, 2012). This list will provide a foundation for subsequent systematic, causal investigations of school libraries as learning spaces. The meta-syntheses also screen for methodologies for discovering and documenting what works for the school library learning space.

Individual Team Synthesis Results

In this section, we present the results of each team's synthesis.

FSU Synthesis

As the FSU researchers examined their 168 studies that included strong evidence of the relationship between educational interventions and student learning, they distilled the following fifteen educator-led practices that related specifically to positive learner outcomes:

1. Linking new knowledge to prior knowledge;
2. Blending direct, explicit, and systematic instruction on new material with strategically timed small-group reinforcement activities;
3. Using hands-on experiences to connect learning with real-world or familiar content and experiences;
4. Employing contextual instruction in questioning and other metacognitive skills;
5. Providing formative, corrective feedback, including quizzes, which promotes and reinforces learning;
6. Exposing learners to vocabulary through reading and listening as well as explicit vocabulary instruction and acquisition strategies;

7. Prioritizing frequency of instruction over the total amount of instruction time;
8. Personalizing the amount and type of intervention or teaching to meet individual needs;
9. Modifying the learning environment to decrease problem behavior, although a positive learning environment may not be sufficient;
10. Using instructional prompts that encourage students to pose and answer deep questions;
11. Assisting students in monitoring and reflecting on the problem-solving processes;
12. Teaching students how to use visual representations;
13. Providing direct and explicit reading comprehension strategies;
14. Making available intensive and individualized interventions for struggling readers; and
15. Explicitly intensively teaching academic vocabulary words across several days using a variety of instructional activities.

In addition to these practices, the FSU researchers also noted that their body of reviewed literature consistently noted that teachers are most effective when they had advanced degrees, particularly in mathematics, followed traditional preparation paths, and had two to five years of teaching experience.

ODU Synthesis

After reviewing the 245 articles, the ODU researchers surfaced three educator best practices supported by strong evidence:

1. Teaching practices and strategies that include direct, explicit instruction;
2. Focusing on inquiry or questioning; and
3. Creating situations in which learners apply real-world content, materials or tasks.

In addition to these practices, the ODU also identified teacher characteristics that provided strong evidence of a relationship with student outcomes. The research in their corpus indicated that well-prepared teachers were especially important and had lasting effects for at-risk children. Principals appeared to have weak, indirect effects on student achievement, but embracing a constructivist approach in a learning environment is more important than teacher race or gender. The ODU corpus also indicated that while types of teacher preparation programs and certification paths suggested some links to student outcomes, teachers with Master's degrees only appeared to relate to student achievement in mathematics.

UNT Synthesis

Though the UNT team only identified one article that met the ESSA standard for strong evidence, their corpus ($N = 76$) indicated contextual considerations for translating educator practices to a school library environment in the following domains:

1. Learner Needs: Target demographics, characteristics, or perceptions of learners such as personal qualities (e.g., age, special needs) or contextual qualities (e.g., low socioeconomic status, rural/urban setting)
2. Learning Environment: Qualities of the context in which learning, intervention, or interactions take place, such as physical space and climate (e.g., libraries, classrooms, online) programs or services (e.g., disability accessibility, services, accelerated reading); types of collections; and workflow and policy (e.g., automated systems, staffing, circulation)
3. School Librarian: Perceptions of the school librarian role as they interact with professional identity or practice in contextual areas (e.g., school level, collaboration, staff/administrative interactions); behaviors and outcomes (e.g., self-censorship, technology use, reflective practice); perceptions of personal leadership skills, professional role, effectiveness, and student learning
4. Strategy: Includes pedagogical/theoretical frameworks (e.g., problem-based learning, inquiry-based learning, universal design for learning), practices or approaches, resources (e.g., audiobooks, consultations, workshops), and interventions (e.g., testing/surveys, professional development, evaluation, and action research)
5. Subject Area/Purpose: Relates to the content, area, or discipline of the intervention or program with a focus on biology, reading, and/or science; programs include professional development, research, evaluation and collaborative practices, disability education, information literacy, and digital/technology literacy
6. Nonschool Library Faculty and Administration: Target demographics, characteristics, or perceptions of nonschool library staff include personal qualities, professional identification (mainly teachers and administrators), community context, and strategic planning initiatives

Preliminary Integrated Syntheses Discussion

In response to widespread calls among the school librarian (AASL, 2014) and education policy maker (US Department of Education, 2016) communities to guide educator actions with evidence derived from causal studies, three teams of researchers investigated "What causal relationships between school-based malleable factors and student learning are present in published research?" We pursued this question by examining the combined corpus of empirical research ($N = 496$)

and synthesizing promising educator practices that not only appeared to have strong causal relationships with learner outcomes but that were also possible for school librarians to enact.

At the conclusion of each team's aggregation and review process, the three teams compared the results of the team syntheses and created an integrated synthesis. Through the integrated synthesis review, all researchers considered whether the educator practices common to the syntheses reflected activities that school librarians could:

1. *Lead or conduct individually.* In this instance, leadership is defined as "coaching others to do for themselves, acting as a sounding board for decision-makers bringing people together, and taking the risk of leading when the opportunity arises" (DiScala & Subramaniam, 2011, p. 60). Leadership is linked to accountability, and school librarians are best positioned to lead activities for which they are accountable (DiScala & Subramaniam, 2011), especially because they fall within their job roles.

2. *Participate and/or collaborate.* For these activities, school librarians are not positioned to colead or partner but are positioned to participate in a larger group that is conducting the activity. School librarians would not have accountability or get credit for these activities because they are tangentially related to their roles.

3. *Not be involved.* These are activities that fall outside of a school librarian's role and are the duties of other school personnel.

The integrated synthesis thus far suggests that school librarians have the potential to impact a causal relationship with student learning when they engage in:

- Direct, explicit, and systematic instruction on new material blended with strategically timed small-group reinforcement activities;
- Hands-on experiences in science and mathematics that connect learning with real-world or familiar content and experiences;
- Contextual instruction in questioning, problem-solving strategies, and other metacognitive skills;
- Formative, corrective feedback, including quizzes, that promotes and reinforces learning;
- Exposure to vocabulary through reading and listening as well as explicit vocabulary instruction and acquisition strategies;
- Frequent, short-burst instruction;
- Modifying the learning environment to decrease problem behavior, although a positive learning environment alone may not be sufficient;
- Creating visual representations; and
- Intensive and individualized interventions for struggling readers.

The research results included in each of the three data corpi also suggest that the amount and type of intervention or teaching is personalized to meet individual needs, and this tailored approach may have a causal effect on student learning, especially when instruction is conducted by teachers with two or more years of teaching experience.

Conclusion

The teams are still working together to distill themes that reflect activities that school librarians can lead or in which they can participate to positively affect student outcomes. Reviews to date suggest that these areas of classroom-based research are particularly promising for school librarians to identify practices that appear to have a causal relationship with learner outcomes. Our next steps are to have school librarians test the efficacy of the practices identified in this study in small scale causal design field studies which were initiated in fall 2017.

The purpose of the CLASS project (AASL, 2014) was to provide school library researchers with a new trajectory, from correlational studies conducted by a variety of research teams and individual researchers to a planned and coordinated causal research agenda for the profession. The national school library research agenda outlined in Figure 12.1 was designed to enable researchers to move toward the causal analyses that will elaborate and quantify the differences that certified school librarians could make for students from diverse backgrounds, in poverty, and with special needs (Pribesh, Gavigan, & Dickinson, 2011). Recent economic crises have devastated school libraries with job loss, the trend to measure teacher effectiveness by test scores, and several states' reclassification of librarians to support, not instructional, staff (United States Department of Education, National Center for Education Statistics, 2016). These factors point to the immediate need to understand, demonstrate, and promote the causal relationships between strong school libraries and measurable student achievement.

This study is a first step toward providing school librarians, at all levels and in all types of schools, with a voice, amplified by evidence-based and generalizable proof to advocate for adequate resources and equitable access to school library programs to help students be academically successful. Increasing the proliferation of causal school library research will provide cause–effect inferences to decision makers at all levels and will delineate the evidence that points to the causal effectiveness of the school library program. Through an examination of the methodological strengths and weaknesses of the studies, we have begun to surface evidence that will inform the next steps in evaluating the impact of school libraries on student achievement and help to determine what works for whom and under what conditions.

Acknowledgment

This research was supported, in part, by IMLS Grant RE-00-15-0114-15.

Note

1 Example findings from Herrera, Grossman, & Linden (2013) and Schlosser & Balzano
(2014).

References

Achieve & National Research Council [NRC]. (2013). *Topic Arrangements of the Next Generation Science Standards*. Retrieved from www.nextgenscience.org/sites/ngss/files/NGSS%20Combined%20Topics%2011.8.13.pdf

American Association of School Librarians [AASL]. (2007). *Standards for the 21st-Century Learner*. Chicago, IL: American Library Association.

American Association of School Librarians [AASL]. (2009). *Empowering Learners: Guidelines for School Library Media Programs*. Chicago, IL: American Library Association.

American Association of School Librarians [AASL]. (2014, December). *Causality: School Librarians and Student Success (CLASS): American Association of School Librarians National Research Forum White Paper*. Chicago, IL: American Library Association. Retrieved from www.ala.org/aasl/sites/ala.org.aasl/files/content/researchandstatistics/CLASSWhitePaperFINAL.pdf

American Association of School Librarians [AASL]. (2016, June 25). *Instructional Role of the School Librarian*. Retrieved from www.ala.org/aasl/sites/ala.org.aasl/files/content/aaslissues/positionstatements/AASL_Position_Statement_Instructional_Role_SL_2016-06-25.pdf

American Association of School Librarians [AASL]. (2018). *National School Library Standards for Learners, School Librarians and School Libraries*. Chicago, IL: American Library Association.

Baker, S., Lesaux, N., Jayanthi, M., Dimino, J., Proctor, C. P., Morris, J., . . . Newman-Gonchar, R. (2014). *Teaching Academic Content and Literacy to English Learners in Elementary and Middle School*. Retrieved from http://files.eric.ed.gov/fulltext/ED544783.pdf

Baumbach, D. (2002). *Making the Grade: The Status of School Library Media Centers in the Sunshine State and How They Contribute to Student Achievement*. Spring, TX: Hi Willow Research and Publishing.

Baxter, S. J., & Smalley, A. W. (2003). *Check It out! The Results of the School Library Media Program Census*. Final Report. Metronet.

Beckett, M., Borman, G., Capizzano, J., Parsley, D., Ross, S., Schirm, A., & Taylor, J. (2009). *Structuring out-of-school Time to Improve Academic Achievement*. Retrieved from http://files.eric.ed.gov/fulltext/ED505962.pdf

Bleske-Rechek, A., Morrison, K. M., & Heidtke, L. D. (2015). Causal inference from descriptions of experimental and non-experimental research: Public understanding of correlation-versus-causation. *The Journal of General Psychology, 142*(1), 48–70. doi:10.1080/00221309.2014.977216

Burgin, R., Bracy, P. B., & Brown, K. (2003). *An Essential Connection: How Quality School Library Media Programs Improve Student Achievement in North Carolina*. Greensboro, NC: RB Software & Consulting.

Callison, D. (2004). *Survey of Indiana School Library Media Programs: A Collaborative Project Between the Association for Indiana Media Educators & Indiana University-Indianapolis, School of Library and Information Science*. Retrieved from http://c.ymcdn.com/sites/www.ilfonline.org/resource/resmgr/aisle/infinalreportnextsteps.pdf

Cooper, O. P., & Bray, M. (2011). School library media specialist-teacher collaboration: Characteristics, challenges, opportunities. *TechTrends, 55*(4), 48–54. doi:10.1007/s11528–011–0511-y

DiScala, J., & Subramaniam, M. (2011). Evidence-based practice: A practice towards leadership credibility among school librarians. *School Libraries Worldwide, 17*(2), 59.

Dynarski, M., Clarke, L., Cobb, B., Finn, J., Rumberger, R., & Smink, J. (2008). *Dropout Prevention*. Retrieved from http://files.eric.ed.gov/fulltext/ED502502.pdf

Epstein, M., Atkins, M., Cullinan, D., Kutash, K., & Weaver, R. (2008). *Reducing Behavior Problems in the Elementary School Classroom*. Retrieved from http://files.eric.ed.gov/fulltext/ED502720.pdf

Evans, M. D., Kelley, J., Sikora, J., & Treiman, D. J. (2010). Family scholarly culture and educational success: Books and schooling in 27 nations. *Research in Social Stratification and Mobility, 28*(2), 171–197. doi:doi.org/10.1016/j.rssm.2010.01.002

Frye, D., Baroody, A. J., Burchinal, M., Carver, S. M., Jordan, N. C., & McDowell, J. (2013). *Teaching Math to Young Children*. Retrieved from http://files.eric.ed.gov/fulltext/ED544376.pdf

Gaver, M. V. (1963). *Effectiveness of Centralized Library Service in Elementary Schools* (2nd edition). New Brunswick, NJ: Rutgers University Press.

Gersten, R., Baker, S. K., Shanahan, T., Linan-Thompson, S., Collins, P., & Scarcella, R. (2007). *Effective Literacy and English Language Instruction for English Learners in the Elementary Grades*. Retrieved from http://files.eric.ed.gov/fulltext/ED497258.pdf

Gersten, R., Beckmann, S., Clarke, B., Foegen, A., Marsh, L., Star, J. R., & Witzel, B. (2009). *Assisting Students Struggling with Mathematics*. Retrieved from http://files.eric.ed.gov/fulltext/ED504995.pdf

Gersten, R., Compton, D., Connor, C. M., Dimino, J., Santoro, L., Linan-Thompson, S., & Tilly, W. D. (2009). *Assisting Students Struggling with Reading*. Retrieved from http://permanent.access.gpo.gov/lps120047/rti_reading_pg_021809.pdf

Graham, S., Bollinger, A., Olson, C. B., D'Aoust, C., MacArthur, C., McCutchen, D., & Olinghouse, N. (2012). *Teaching Elementary School Students to Be Effective Writers*. Retrieved from http://files.eric.ed.gov/fulltext/ED533112.pdf

Halpern, D. F., Aronson, J., Reimer, N., Simpkins, S., Star, J. R., & Wentzel, K. (2007, September). *Encouraging Girls in Math and Science*. Retrieved from http://files.eric.ed.gov/fulltext/ED498581.pdf

Hamilton, L., Halverson, R., Jackson, S. S., Mandinach, E., Supovitz, J. A., & Wayman, J. C. (2009). *Using Student Achievement Data to Support Instructional Decision Making*. Retrieved from http://files.eric.ed.gov/fulltext/ED506645.pdf

Hanscombe, K. B., Haworth, C., Davis, O. S., Jaffee, S. R., & Plomin, R. (2011). Chaotic homes and school achievement: A twin study. *Journal of Child Psychology and Psychiatry, 52*(11), 1212–1220. doi:10.1111/j.1469–7610.2011.02421.x

Hattie, J. (2008). *Visible Learning: A Synthesis of over 800 Meta-analyses Relating to Achievement*. New York, NY: Routledge.

Herman, R., Dawson, P., Dee, T., Greene, J., Maynard, R., Redding, S., & Darwin, M. (2008). *Turning Around Chronically Low-Performing Schools*. Retrieved from https://ies.ed.gov/ncee/wwc/Docs/PracticeGuide/Turnaround_pg_04181.pdf

Herrera, C., Grossman, J., & Linden, L. L. (2013, January). *Staying on Track: Testing Higher Achievement's Long-Term Impact on Academic Outcomes and High School Choice*. Retrieved from www.mdrc.org/publication/staying-track-testing-higher-achievement's-long-term-impact-academic-outcomes-and-high/file-full

Holland, P. (1986). Statistics and causal inference. *Journal of the American Statistical Association, 81*, 945–970.

Institute of Education Sciences [IES]. (n.d.). *Practice Guides*. Retrieved from https://ies.ed.gov/ncee/wwc/PracticeGuides

Institute of Education Sciences [IES]. (2014, March). *What Works Clearinghouse: Procedures and Standards Handbook*. Version 3.0.

Institute of Education Sciences [IES], & National Science Foundation [NSF]. (2013). *Common Guidelines for Education Research and Development*. Retrieved from http://ies.ed.gov/pdf/CommonGuidelines.pdfCommonGuidelines.pdf

Kamil, M. L., Borman, G. D., Dole, J., Kral, C. C., Salinger, T., & Torgesen, J. (2008). *Improving Adolescent Literacy*. Retrieved from http://files.eric.ed.gov/fulltext/ED502398.pdf

Lance, K. C., Hamilton-Pennell, C., Rodney, M. J., Petersen, L., & Sitter, C. (1999). *Information Empowered: The School Librarian as an Agent of Academic Achievement in Alaska Schools*. Anchorage, AK: Alaska State Library.

Lance, K. C., Rodney, M. J., & Hamilton-Pennell, C. (2000). *Measuring up to Standards: The Impact of School Library Programs and Information Literacy in Pennsylvania Schools*. Greensburg, PA: Pennsylvania Citizens for Better Libraries.

Lance, K. C., Rodney, M. J., & Hamilton-Pennell, C. (2001). *Good Schools Have School Librarians: Oregon School Librarians Collaborate to Improve Academic Achievement*. Salem, OR: Oregon Educational Media Association.

Lance, K. C., Rodney, M. J., & Hamilton-Pennell, C. (2002). *How School Libraries Improve Outcomes for Children: The New Mexico Study*. Santa Fe, NM: New Mexico State Library.

Lance, K. C., Rodney, M., & Hamilton-Pennell, C. (2005). *Powerful Libraries Make Powerful Learners: The Illinois Study*. Canton, IL: Illinois School Library Media Association.

Lance, K. C., Wellborn, L., & Hamilton-Pennell, C. (1993). *The Impact of School Library Media Centers on Academic Achievement*. Castle Rock, CO: Hi Willow Research and Publishing.

Mardis, M. A. (2007). School libraries and science achievement: A view from Michigan's middle schools. *School Library Media Research, 10*.

Morgan, S. L., & Winship, C. (2014). *Counterfactuals and Causal Inference: Methods and Principles for Social Research*. New York, NY: Cambridge University Press.

Morris, R. J., & Cahill, M. (2016). A study of how we study: Methodologies of school library research 2007 through July 2015. *School Library Research, 20*.

Morrison, K., & van der Werf, G. (2016). Searching for causality in educational research. *Educational Research and Evaluation, 22*(1–2), 1–5. doi:10.1080/13803611.2016.1195081

Murnane, R. J., & Willett, J. B. (2011). *Methods Matter: Improving Causal Inference in Educational and Social Science Research*. Oxford, UK; New York, NY: Oxford University Press.

National Governors' Association [NGA], & Council of Chief State School Officers [CCSSO]. (2010, June 2). *Common Core State Standards for English Language Arts & Literacy in History/Social Studies, Science, and Technical Subjects*. Retrieved from www.core-standards.org/assets/CCSSI_ELA%20Standards.pdf

National Research Council. (2000). *How People Learn: Brain, Mind, Experience, and School: Expanded Edition*. Washington, DC: National Academies Press.

National Research Council. (2013). *Education for Life and Work: Developing Transferable Knowledge and Skills in the 21st Century*. Washington, DC: National Academies Press.

Neumann, M. M., Finger, G., & Neumann, D. L. (2017). A conceptual framework for emergent digital literacy. *Early Childhood Education Journal, 45*(4), 471–479. doi:10.1007/s10643-016-0792-z

Pashler, H., Bain, P. M., Bottge, B. A., Graesser, A., Koedinger, K., McDaniel, M., & Metcalfe, J. (2007). *Organizing Instruction and Study to Improve Student Learning*. Retrieved from http://files.eric.ed.gov/fulltext/ED498555.pdf

Pawson, R. (2006). *Evidence-based Policy: A Realist Perspective*. Thousand Oaks, CA: Sage Publications.

Pribesh, S., Gavigan, K., & Dickinson, G. (2011). The access gap: Poverty and characteristics of school library media centers. *The Library Quarterly, 81*(2), 143–160. doi:10.1086/658868

Rodney, M. J., Lance, K. C., & Hamilton-Pennell, C. (2003). *The Impact of Michigan School Librarians on Academic Achievement: Kids Who Have Libraries Succeed*. Salt Lake City, UT: Library of Michigan.

Rodney, M. J., Lance, K. C., Hamilton-Pennell, C., & Center, M. (2002). *Make the Connection: Quality School Library Media Programs Impact Academic Achievement in Iowa*. Bettendorf, IA: Mississippi Bend Area Education Agency.

Rubin, A., & Parrish, D. E. (2012). Comparing social worker and non-social worker outcomes: A research review. *Social Work, 57*, 309+.

Russo, F. (2011). Correlational data, causal hypotheses, and validity. *Journal for General Philosophy of Science, 42*(1), 85–107.

Sandelowski, M., Voils, C. I., & Barroso, J. (2006). Defining and designing mixed research synthesis studies. *Research in the Schools, 13*(1), 29.

Sandelowski, M., Voils, C. I., Leeman, J., & Crandell, J. L. (2012). Mapping the mixed methods—mixed research synthesis terrain. *Journal of Mixed Methods Research, 6*(4), 317–331. doi:10.1177/1558689811427913

Schlosser, L. K., & Balzano, B. (2014). Playing to learn. *SAGE Open, 4*(4). Retrieved from http://journals.sagepub.com/doi/pdf/10.1177/2158244014558031 doi:10.1177/2158244014558031

Scholastic. (2016). *School Libraries Work!* A compendium of research supporting the effectiveness of school libraries. Retrieved from www.scholastic.com/SLW2016

Schubert, F., & Becker, R. (2010). Social inequality of reading literacy: A longitudinal analysis with cross-sectional data of PIRLS 2001 and PISA 2000 utilizing the pair wise matching procedure. *Research in Social Stratification and Mobility, 28*(1), 109–133. doi:doi.org/10.1016/j.rssm.2009.12.007

Shadish, W., Cook, T., & Campbell, D. T. (2002). *Experimental and Quasi-Experimental Designs for Generalized Causal Inference*. Boston, MS: Wadsworth Cengage Learning.

Shanahan, T., Callison, K., Carriere, C., Duke, N. K., Pearson, P. D., Schatschneider, C., & Torgesen, J. (2010). *Improving Reading Comprehension in Kindergarten Through 3rd Grade*. Retrieved from http://files.eric.ed.gov/fulltext/ED512029.pdf

Shin, Y., & Raudenbush, S. W. (2011). The causal effect of class size on academic achievement: Multivariate instrumental variable estimators with data missing at random. *Journal of Educational and Behavioral Statistics, 36*(2), 154–185. doi:10.3102/1076998610388632

Shoham, S. (2001). Evaluating the effectiveness of bibliographic information. *Journal of Librarianship and Information Science, 33*(1), 39–46. doi:10.1177/096100060103300105

Siegler, R., Carpenter, T., Fennell, F., Geary, D., Lewis, J., Okamoto, Y., . . . Wray, J. (2010, September). *Developing Effective Fractions Instruction for Kindergarten Through 8th Grade: NCEE 2010–4039*. Retrieved from http://files.eric.ed.gov/fulltext/ED512043.pdf

Smith, E. (2001). *Texas School Libraries: Standards, Resources, Services, and Students' Performance*. Austin, TX: Texas State Library and Archives Commission.

Spence Laschinger, H. K. (2008). Effect of empowerment on professional practice environments, work satisfaction, and patient care quality: Further testing the nursing worklife model. *Journal of Nursing Care Quality, 23*(4), 322–330. doi:10.1097/01. NCQ.0000318028.67910.6b

Star, J. R., Foegen, A., Larson, M. R., McCallum, W. G., Porath, J., Zbiek, R. M., . . . Lyskawa, J. (2015). *Teaching Strategies for Improving Algebra Knowledge in Middle and High School Students*. Retrieved from http://files.eric.ed.gov/fulltext/ED555576

Thomas, G. (2016). After the gold rush: Questioning the 'gold standard' and reappraising the status of experiment and randomized controlled trials in education. *Harvard Educational Review, 86*(3), 390–411. doi:10.17763/1943–5045–86.3.390

Tierney, W. G., Bailey, T., Constantine, J., Finkelstein, N., & Hurd, N. F. (2009). *Helping Students Navigate the Path to College*. Retrieved from http://files.eric.ed.gov/fulltext/ED506465.pdf

Tubin, D. (2011). From principals' actions to students' outcomes: An explanatory narrative approach to successful Israeli schools. *Leadership and Policy in Schools, 10*(4), 395–411. doi:doi.org/10.1080/15700763.2011.610556

United States Department of Education. (2016). *Non-regulatory Guidance: Using Evidence to Strengthen Education Investments*. Retrieved from https://www2.ed.gov/policy/elsec/leg/essa/guidanceuseseinvestment.pdf

United States Department of Education, National Center for Education Statistics. (2016). *Table 701.10: Selected Statistics on Public School Libraries/Media Centers, by Level of School: Selected Years, 1999–2000 Through 2011–12*. Retrieved from https://nces.ed.gov/programs/digest/d15/tables/dt15_701.10.asp

Woodward, J., Beckmann, S., Driscoll, M., Franke, M., Herzig, P., Jitendra, A., . . . Ogbuehi, P. (2012, May). *Improving Mathematical Problem Solving in Grades 4 Through 8*. Retrieved from http://files.eric.ed.gov/fulltext/ED532215.pdf

Yolton, J. W. (ed.). (1977). *The Locke Reader: Selections from the Works of John Locke with a General Introduction and Commentary*. Cambridge; New York: Cambridge University Press.

Zmuda, A., & Harada, V. H. (2008). *Librarians as Learning Specialists*. Westport, CT: Libraries Unlimited.

13

USING RESEARCH–PRACTICE PARTNERSHIPS TO SUPPORT INTEREST-RELATED LEARNING IN LIBRARIES

William R. Penuel, Josephina Chang-Order, and Vera Michalchik

Introduction

The public sphere is evolving with technology, and libraries are changing, too. Many of the ways libraries are changing represent their renewal as centers of community, especially among youth. Youth programming in libraries increasingly focuses on supporting learning related to young people's interests, aims, and concerns. This programming is significant, because libraries have freedom to support youth's own goals for learning in ways that differ from how students learn in school.

New, replicable models of learning in libraries have emerged in recent years that make use of new digital media, both emphasizing exploration and diving deep into specific areas of interest (Tripp, 2011). Research on these new sites for learning is just beginning to emerge, and much of it presents descriptive analyses of designs for programs and spaces (e.g., Subramaniam, Ahn, & Waugh, 2015). To support the ongoing improvement of these designs, though, more sustained research and evaluation activities are needed. Such activities are needed to identify what youth-aims libraries address successfully and unsuccessfully, and they also are needed to help libraries adjust programming to improve outcomes for youth.

This chapter describes research conducted over a five-year period in a single library on that library's efforts to design opportunities to support connected learning. Connected learning is a design framework emphasizing programming that is interest powered, production centered, peer supported, openly networked, oriented to shared purposes among learners, and meaningfully related to advancing personal goals in relation to careers, academics, or personal pursuits (Ito et al., 2013; Ito, Salen, Sefton-Green, in preparation). The research activities we have described here have been organized as a research–practice partnership between university researchers and librarians, involving multiple phases of mutually developed design and implementation. Here, we describe those different phases and what we have learned from each about how library programs and spaces can be organized to support connected learning.

The Connected Learning Framework for Supporting Interest-Related Learning

Connected learning is a synthetic model of learning that many libraries and other institutions have used to organize programs and spaces to support youth in discovering new pursuits and deepening existing ones. It is a synthetic model in that it draws from different strands of learning theory, from ecological theories of interest development (e.g., Barron, 2006) to sociocultural theories inspired by the writings of Lev Vygotsky (e.g., Cole, 1996; Rogoff, 2003; Wertsch, 1985) to the constructionist theories of Seymour Papert (1993). From these different theories, connected learning brings together insights regarding the key features of learning environments that can support interest-related learning, qualities of learning experiences that researchers and evaluators might look for in learning environments, and a set of design principles for connecting learning across different settings. Importantly, many of these principles were derived from studies of learning in library spaces that were intentionally designed to support youth in using digital media to explore different pursuits (e.g., Barron, Gomez, Pinkard, & Martin, 2014; Tripp, 2011).

Key Features of Learning Environments

There are three features of learning environments emphasized in the connected learning model: (1) peer supported, (2) interest powered, and (3) future oriented.

Peer Supported

A peer-supported environment is one in which peers play significant roles. They do so within activities by providing help and often by serving as coteachers within learning environments. Sometimes, peers are the same age with more experience in a pursuit; other times, they are older. In a library makerspace, for example, peers might be given roles to help others get started on or troubleshoot projects. Peers also play roles in connecting youth to opportunities, or what is sometimes called "brokering in" to a space (Ching et al., 2015). Youth can play significant roles in getting friends to try out a new activity, bringing them to a learning environment, and keeping them there (Cartun, Kirshner, Price, & York, 2014).

Interest Powered

To say an environment is interest powered is to say that it supports both the discovery of new pursuits and the deepening of existing pursuits that are enjoyable to youth. Interest-powered environments are ones that youth choose to spend time in partly, at least, because there is a particular combination of novelty and challenge that they are drawn to. These pursuits are often not limited to a particular setting, though, and a learning environment that is interest powered encourages youth to explore the pursuit elsewhere, often allowing it to "morph" over time. Pursuits might evolve into a "line of practice" (Azevedo, 2011) for youth in which their own roles and activities within a setting change. As a result, the settings themselves in which youth pursue these activities change as well.

Future Oriented

By being future oriented, connected learning environments offer and help youth cultivate their own images of possible futures for themselves and their communities. Some of these environments have an explicit academic orientation that can help youth connect interest-related pursuits to future opportunities in school (Ito et al., 2013). Others are oriented toward career-related pathways, supporting youth in envisioning futures in which their interests lead to future jobs and professions (Sefton-Green, Watkins, & Kirshner, 2018). Many connected learning environments include support for youth to envision and bring about new civic and public spaces (Ito et al., 2015).

Qualities of Connected Learning Experiences

One way to study or evaluate connected learning is to focus on the key qualities of youth experience and whether they are present for youth in an environment. Three key qualities of experiences are (1) production centered, (2) shared purpose, and (3) openly networked.

Production Centered

When youth experience environments as production centered, they have many opportunities to make things or perform publicly for others. Within those opportunities, they routinely ask for and receive feedback on ongoing work or performances, and they iterate on the basis of that feedback. They constantly apply a critical stance toward their own and others' designs, much as might happen within a professional community of creative artists (e.g., Soep, 2006). They circulate designs, too, to broad audiences outside a particular learning environment and seek to influence their audience's affect, thinking, and patterns of action.

Shared Purpose

In connected learning experiences, youth feel as though they have a say in the purposes of activity and what goes on in it. They may engage in solo activity, but there is some aspect of their engagement that is defined by a common purpose and supported by practices for promoting equitable participation. Youth feel that they have opportunities to make meaningful contributions toward common aims and also to lead activities.

Openly Networked

When youth experience learning as openly networked, it means they can follow a pursuit wherever it takes them and know that they will have the social support and resources to do so. Youth have access to digital tools they might use, as well as opportunities to move freely into new spaces where they can continue a pursuit or deepen it. Opening and making transparent pathways for youth can be challenging, especially when their pursuits do not follow institutionalized pathways. It is also challenging because pathways that are accessible to them may not exist within their community (Pinkard et al., 2016).

Design Principles for Connected Learning

Creating a connected learning environment requires attention to certain key design principles that can promote equity, engagement, growth, community, and new opportunities for youth. The design principles derive both from the work of the Connected Learning Research Network (CLRN) and other allied research in the field (Ito et al., 2013, in preparation).

Everyone Can Participate

Connected learning activities need to have multiple, accessible entry points for multiple learners, as well as support equitable participation for learners there. They also need "high ceilings," meaning opportunities for youth to explore more deeply pursuits that interest them, even when that means adults helping them find an activity at another program or site.

Learning by Doing

For youth to experience a learning environment as production centered requires that they be engaged in some form of learning by doing. In environments that promote connected learning, youth are often engaged in making and tinkering activities, writing and performing for others, or coding and creating games. Learning isn't just acquiring knowledge or even participating in valued activities; rather, it's a form of production (Soep, 2006).

Challenge Is Constant

One reason games provide such compelling learning opportunities for many youth is that they present constant challenges to players (Gee, 2007). It is indeed desirable for educators to design out-of-school learning environments to be free of the kind of challenges youth might expect to find in school that are "challenging" only because they require young people to apply their energy and attention to assignments. Connected learning experiences are designed to challenge youth as a means for propelling their development and learning. Another way to express this design principle is that the environments should support and encourage "leveling up" from time to time to deepen learning.

Everything Is Interconnected

Connected learning begins with the premise that learning is a cross-setting phenomenon (Barron, 2010). That is to say, when a young person engages in a pursuit they enjoy, they are likely to pursue it over time and across multiple settings. As such, a design principle for organizing connected learning is that educators should look for ways to connect different learning environments and to broker youths' access to learning environments other than their own. In today's resource-limited environment for community organizations, there are few incentives for this kind of collaboration (Russell, Knutson, & Crowley, 2013), but it is an essential feature of connected learning.

Why Organize Research on Connected Learning as a Research–Practice Partnership?

Research–practice partnerships are long-term collaborations between educational and cultural institutions (e.g., schools, museums, libraries) and researchers focused on investigating problems of practice and developing solutions for them (Bevan, Ryoo, Forrest, & Penuel, 2015; Coburn & Penuel, 2016). In being focused on problems of practice, researchers make practice the source of questions to be investigated. They seek to answer questions that focus on matters of concern to practitioners, participants, and other stakeholders in a setting or program rather than on questions that are primarily of interest to other researchers. Partnerships are long-term arrangements between researchers and practitioners, often spanning many different projects and forms of engagement. The open-endedness of the commitment of partners allows partners to follow the "contours of problems in order to identify systemically sustainable solutions" to them (Donovan, 2013, p. 318). Another commitment of partners is to mutualism, that is, to each partner benefiting from the collaboration. This commitment is typically realized through specific strategies to promote mutualism, such as formal processes for establishing long-term research agendas (Roderick, Easton, & Sebring, 2009), codesign of solutions to problems (Penuel & Gallagher, 2017), and engaging in forms of research that are participatory—that is, led or coled by members of the community being studied (Kirshner, Pacheco, Sifuentes, & Hildreth, 2018). Finally, researchers add value to extant administrative data available to practitioners (e.g., program attendance, circulation) by conducting original analyses that have potential to create new insights about successes and challenges in practice. For example, a partnership's analysis might show how program attendance is related to the content of programming or whether a friend is in attendance.

The potential benefits of research–practice partnerships are many (see Coburn & Penuel, 2016, for a complete review). Researchers and practitioners working together can diagnose problems more effectively, and they can also design, test, and develop evidence for solutions to those problems together. Importantly, in a partnership, researchers stick around also to help educators address the new problems that arise from implementation of potential solutions. In a partnership, researchers can help practitioners adapt programs that have worked elsewhere to the local setting and study their effects. Researchers can also examine whether the programs are having desired effects in the new contexts.

The participation of practitioners in research activities is also important. Stakeholder-based (e.g., Mark & Shotland, 1985) and participatory models (e.g., Cousins & Earl, 1992; Tzou et al., this volume) of research and evaluation help us as researchers be accountable to a wider diversity of interests and claims on what our libraries and other public institutions can and should be. As such, they help us identify outcomes and opportunities we might not otherwise see. Such models help us appreciate that there is often a diversity of pathways to success, not a single one captured by a single bank of measures. Fostering participation in research also supports a key experience of connected learning, namely shared purpose. In this way, research on connected learning can—in certain circumstances—become a form of it.

Research–practice partnerships are organized for and strive for equity. By "organized for," we mean that the commitment to mutualism and intentional strategies for promoting it foreground the need for equity between researchers and practitioners. But many partnerships also strive to promote more equitable opportunities and outcomes for participants (Barton & Bevan, 2016). Doing so requires partnerships to name and address specific historical and persisting inequalities associated with racism, classism, sexism, and heteronormativity (Politics of Learning Writing Collective, 2017; Philip & Azevedo, 2017).

Initiation of the Anythink–CU Boulder Partnership

The research–practice partnership between the University of Colorado Boulder (CU Boulder) and Anythink Libraries (Anythink, n.d.) began in fall 2012, when CU Boulder researchers approached the library about being part of a longer-term study of connected learning. The research team was part of the Connected Learning Research Network, which was studying different forms of connected learning in different settings—schools, community organizations, sharing economies, and libraries. They learned about Anythink from another member of the network.

For its part, Anythink was just getting off the ground as the newly contracted library services provider for Adams County, Colorado. During the Great

Recession, the county was in search of a novel solution to budget problems and contracted with Anythink as a private entity to build and manage nine libraries across the former Rangeview Library District. Their mission was to reimagine the library space as a site for both education and entertainment, that is, where their library patrons (called "customers") could discover new interests and experience "a new creative space that is more engaging than any library you have ever visited before" (Anythink website, "About" page).

When CU Boulder researchers approached Anythink, the libraries had already applied for and won a grant to develop a space that resembled another library space that had been an inspiration for developing the connected learning model—YOUMedia, housed at the Harold Washington Library in Chicago. The YOUMedia space was one that catered to youth and was organized into different zones that supported different kinds of activity—hanging out with friends, messing around with new digital tools, and "geeking out" through more intensive exploration of particular activities, such as music production or slam poetry. Anythink won a grant from the Institute of Museum and Library Services to replicate this model at their site. They were eager to collaborate with CU researchers, in part because they were interested in ideas the researchers might have about how to support them in setting up their new connected learning space for teens.

Anythink staff also resonated with the particular "ask" that CU researchers made of them, namely to collaborate in a youth participatory research study of connected learning. Anythink staff already had a commitment to youth voice in programming, embodied in a youth council they had set up to advise the adult staff at the Wright Farms branch of the library. They saw the research as one possible activity of the youth council, an activity that could gather useful data on what the library's teenaged customers wanted in the space. Findings from the study would inform the youth council and provide evidence for Anythink staff to use in setting program direction. The CU research team also asked Anythink to take part in a longitudinal survey study of connected learning as part of researchers' role in the Connected Learning Research Network, a study described later in this chapter.

As discussions continued, the research team learned of an enduring problem of practice for Anythink: matching program offerings for youth to what they wanted so that their customers would be satisfied and come back. This problem clearly was one that the partnership would need to investigate and address. For the researchers, a key step for promoting mutualism was fitting their own goals for research into the library's needs so that both the research team and library staff would benefit as fully as possible from the partnership.

Phase 1 of the Youth Research Partnership: Pilot

With the shared identification of a key challenge faced by Anythink—creating programming to better match the needs, interests, and concerns of local youth—the partnership was able to begin productive work. The alignment of the researchers' interest in connected learning with the youth council's charge to advise staff at the Anythink Wright Farms branch on programming made it possible for program coordinators to champion, develop, and help shepherd the partnership's efforts.

During a three-month pilot phase in early 2013, the participatory research team was composed of Anythink youth customers, CU researchers, and Anythink staff. The six youth researchers—four boys and two girls, ages 13 to 17—committed to 30 hours of work on the project, receiving an honorarium in appreciation for their time. Interview notes, transcripts, and other data were made available in between meetings via a shared wiki site. The youth at Anythink also met with other youth researchers at four additional sites around the country ($n = 22$) with whom they compared their experiences, data, and findings in five biweekly meetings.

The team's primary goal was to support the youth in conducting an ethnographic study to learn about their peers' experiences with connected learning at their library. The project used a "youth as coresearchers" approach (Kirshner, Mitra, O'Donoghue, 2001; Watson & Marciano, 2015), in which youth were introduced to the connected learning framework and then apprenticed as researchers of their own programs. Researchers engaged youth as coresearchers in order to enlist their support for goals that had already been established for the overall study, but with the idea that the inclusion of youths' voices could greatly enhance and shape the study's direction, both in the kinds of questions to be asked of other youth regarding their experiences of connected learning and in their insights and analysis. This approach is less youth-driven and intensive than youth participatory action research (YPAR), though it shares with YPAR a commitment to foreground issues of equity and access in their social world (cf., Cammarota & Fine, 2010).

Using self-ethnographic methods (Shadduck-Hernández, 2006), youth researchers created "interest stories" detailing the development of a pursuit and also created brief digital self-introductions. In addition, they mapped their daily routines, especially as these related to their interest-related pursuits, and they collected data through interviews with peers and library staff.

Youths' maps focused on their daily routines, particularly the activities they pursued across different settings. They mapped the key locations where they spent their time each day (such as home, school, and hangouts) and noted who and what (including objects, interests, and even emotions) traveled with them between sites. They developed field notes and reflections to go along with the maps, which they audio-recorded. The example shown in Figure 13.1 includes the youth researcher's home, school, and grandmother's house, noting interests and pathways among them.

The youth coresearchers also interviewed their peers using protocols codeveloped with the research team. They asked each other questions in three broad categories: the Anythink programs, a typical project they had undertaken at the

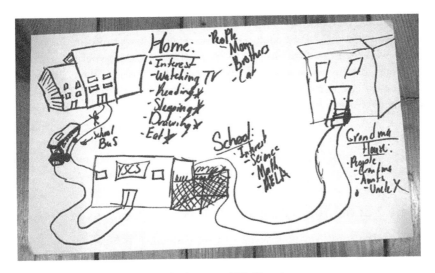

FIGURE 13.1 A Youth Coresearcher's Map of His Routine

site, and what they learned there. They sought to find out more about what makes activities and settings engaging (e.g., "What's the best thing about Anythink?"), how projects there developed (e.g., "How did your project get started?"), and where they see connections among interest-powered pursuits in their lives (e.g., "When the project was over, did you share it with anyone?" and "How does this place compare with school?"). Youth asked Anythink instructors about the activities they offered, the successes and challenges of their work, and the ways in which the learning environment and programs were designed to support youths' interests.

The youth researchers recognized the value of the mapping task for identifying the people and objects that travel between locations helping connect activities, noting the usefulness of this approach for encouraging conversation around connected learning principles and outcomes. The youth researchers further cultivated the insight that this task is particularly useful for young people to develop a critical awareness and analytical skills addressing the barriers and opportunities that young people face for connecting "out" from their sites—what CLRN researchers have termed the "last mile" of connection between youth development experiences and their next steps towards careers or college education (Sefton-Green et al., 2018). In thinking about the redesign of their methods, though, they also wanted to modify the task to ensure that the spaces within a site were represented in the maps and to be clear on where the youth themselves were "visible" in their pathways, seen by others as competent, engaged, reputable or whichever dimensions mattered in those pathways.

Open interchange between university-based researchers and the youth members of the research team regarding data collection, analysis, and interpretation led to insights carried forward from the pilot to the subsequent phase of the research. For example, youth helped adult researchers reinterpret what was meant by one youth who used the term "haters" to speak of social pressures related generally to interest-driven pursuits—not specific pressures from peers at the collaborating research site. Concerns about sufficient time to explore topics during interviews, sharing interpretations of the data with youth participants at the sites, helping students take next steps or broker "out" to new possibilities, and more emphasis on "action" in the action research—that is, designing and testing new approaches to creating programming that aligned with interests and needs within the community—all were areas considered for further development in the partners' work.

Phase 2 of the Youth Research Partnership: Pathways

Program leaders at Anythink Wright Farms continued to seek youth input on programming, to sponsor an active youth council, and to build the relationship with the CU research team. The second phase of the youth-as-coresearcher effort, called the Pathways Project, was undertaken in the summer of 2014. The Anythink and CU partners decided that an important focus for the work would be the ways in which connected learning programs supported postsecondary pathways into STEM or digital media arts fields for participating youth, depending on their interests and the supports provided in the library's programs. At this point, the collaboration between Anythink and CU was taking on more characteristics of a true research–practice partnership, spanning multiple, overlapping projects, serving the ongoing needs of each partner, and working to codesign systematic and sustainable means of addressing problems of practice.

Building on the methods tested in the pilot, youth at Anythink again conducted interviews, this time to learn about the perspectives of program alumni in addition to current youth customers and program staff. The alumni interviews focused on whether and how youth continued pursuing their interests once they graduated from the library's programs.

The youth researchers also expanded the mapping project tested in the pilot, using GPS data loggers to gather data and enter into Google Maps key sites in the community related to the interests of Anythink youth. They mapped places where they could find resources on a wide range of interests, including digital media, music production, sports, psychiatry, gaming, comics, and engineering. Their intent was to create a resource that could help other youth in the area pursue their connected learning interests by finding appropriate ways to build on experiences within the local system of opportunities. The youth researchers additionally pinned the locations they identified on custom maps and analyzed their accessibility by various forms of transportation. Because the Anythink branch was located in a suburb of Denver, the youth researchers noted that unless teens had access to personal vehicles, they would need to get to these locations on foot or by bus—which would be time consuming and potentially difficult for novice users of the bus system.

As in the first phase of youth research, the participating youth researchers engaged with the data during the analysis phase and offered views and counter-narratives that checked the interpretations of the university researchers. Findings from this phase indicated the importance of access to various forms of technology—including video and audio equipment, graphic arts, and 3D printing and other makerspace resources—for youth to develop skills that they might take into postsecondary education and work. The youth emphasized the value of these experiences in daily life as well. Two youth researchers stayed on with the Pathways Project in the fall of 2014 to do more analytical work on the interview and mapping data. They also proposed collecting interviews from people working in the fields they were interested in, and one of the Anythink youth copresented on the process and findings from the mapping project, emphasizing the use of Google Maps as a tool for exploring local opportunities, taking into account issues of accessibility and transportation, at the Digital Media and Learning conference in Los Angeles the following spring.

For the CU researchers, there were numerous valuable findings across the two phases of the youth research work. They were able to better conceptualize the relationship between spatially distributed resources within a community and the effects on "last mile" outcomes leading to college and career. They also were able to further document key characteristics of connected learning—validating, refining, or expanding their key categories for activities (e.g., tinkering, artistic performance, hanging out), interest development (e.g., gaining exposure, achieving levels of expertise, transferring into or out of a setting), identity outcomes (e.g., change vs. stability, self-representation, social differences), and connections (e.g., sharing with others, linkages across settings, obstacles, and barriers). The research team identified three important themes to investigate in how youth experience connected learning:

- Interplay of choice and obligation in connected learning
- Expanded access to connected learning opportunities through social ties
- Changes to self-representations through participation in activity.

The Anythink staff, on their part, maintained a commitment to addressing what had been for them an enduring problem of practice: matching program offerings for youth to what the youth wanted. What had originally been a problem to solve, however, became a practice to sustain. Over time, Anythink's agreement to participate in the original survey research and then the YPAR activities evolved into an ongoing collaboration, a more fully realized research–practice partnership, and, ultimately, what might be seen as practitioner appropriation of research methods for ongoing formative self-study, iterative program improvement, and continued organizational learning. This outcome coemerged with the development of the research–practice partnership and points to an encouraging phenomenon for potential replication among other library systems.

Anythink Participation in Longitudinal Study of Connected Learning

In parallel to the youth research effort, Anythink participated in a longitudinal study of connected learning jointly conducted by University of Colorado Boulder and SRI researchers. The research team's aims were to develop validity evidence for a survey of the core principles of connected learning, as well as to study the link between connected learning experiences and youth development outcomes, such as civic engagement and bonding to school. Anythink applied to be part of the study, and in their application wrote that participation fit within their strategic plan, stating that "ongoing research and review of our programs" was a priority. They were particularly interested in the "opportunity to work with researchers to evaluate program design" to better meet community needs and foster youth engagement. Further, Anythink had begun already to plan for expansions of the Wright Farms Studio model to all seven of the Anythink libraries in the district, and they saw the opportunity to participate in research to "help ensure that these expansions are successfully attuned to community needs."

It's noteworthy that the library's goals for participation were not fully consonant with the goals of the study. The researchers did not have intentions to evaluate program designs: ours was a descriptive, longitudinal study, and sites were chosen on the basis of the likelihood that youth there would be engaged in pursuits that reflected the principles of connected learning. At the same time, we knew that sites would likely be interested in participating because it might help them meet evaluation needs that are often difficult for community-based organizations to meet because of limited resources.

As an accommodation, we decided to provide sites with reports of the research that characterized not only the mix of activities students participated in, but also the "levels of depth" with which youth were engaged in those activities, according to the connected learning principles. We found that the youth at Anythink engaged in a wide variety of activities, and they mostly fell on the lower end of the scale for the "production centered" dimension. According to Anythink staff, these data helped spur them to "design [their] experiences to engage and encourage more in-depth work and learning from the students." Also noteworthy to Anythink staff for purposes of program improvement was the view of most youth that the content they produced at the site was only occasionally intended to or successful at reaching or influencing others.

The data on some of the other principles was more encouraging to staff. For example, most Anythink youth described their activities as high in being openly networked, indicating that they had access to the tools and resources they need to explore their interests. Most Anythink youth also said they had a say in the goals and structure of their interest-related pursuit and participated alongside adults, indicative of a high degree of shared purpose.

Coplanning Evaluation of Youth and Staff Experiences

The researchers working with Anythink built on their shared efforts to develop a new project, Capturing Connected Learning in Libraries (CCLL), that they undertook with a consortium of library networks.[1] CCLL was designed to enable libraries to document learning outcomes for youth participating in connected learning programs, to develop new ways to describe and improve these services, and to demonstrate their value to library funders and other stakeholders.

Anythink was a key partner in planning the project and has continued working within CCLL to develop an evaluation plan to use as a model for other library programs.

From the start of the project in 2016, it was clear that Anythink had as much to offer the researchers engaged in the project as the researchers had to offer the library to help with evaluation. Anythink had explored both informal ways of assessing youth engagement and formal mechanisms of program review that included a youth council of advisors. For example, prior to the collaborative work on the evaluation plan, Anythink had used a type of tool called "Talkback Boards" to quickly collect customers' "votes" on statements about their Studio experience that day. As the researchers collaborated with the library, they based their approach on what library staff were already doing, identifying ways to enhance the quality of information they were getting to improve their programming.

Anythink continued to seek useful ways of gathering evidence about the depth of customer engagement with Studio experiences and the support customers found for creating products related to their interests. Anythink staff also hoped to gain insight into how to adapt Studio experiences for spaces other than the Wright Farms branch of the local library consortium. To meet these goals, the research team adapted daily practical activities such as the Talk Back boards to include types of questions that we had successfully used to measure different connected learning principles. We worked collaboratively with library staff to construct questions for overarching evaluation plans that could identify how deep youth were going in their interest-related pursuits on site, as well as to discover youths' reasons for engaging in activities at the site.

What started off as a secondary goal in the evaluation became more important to staff as the project proceeded. Because Anythink was in the process of piloting new activities and expanding capacity at Wright Farms, staff members' own insights about these changes became vital for considering how to make future recommendations to the consortium as well as develop the Studio itself. Much of this planning turned on staffs' direct experience applying connected learning principles in the Studio. Thus, as the Studio space evolved in the early part of 2017, the staff-focused component of the evaluation took on greater importance for Anythink. One of the most useful evaluation practices codeveloped with researchers during this time was a daily staff survey, intended to capture the staff's observations about customer engagement and interests. The survey questions were

FIGURE 13.2 A Talkback Board from the Anythink Studio

written and adapted according to the activities offered each day in the three focal areas, 3D printing, textile design, and jewelry making. They addressed engagement across these activities, including in rapidly shifting makerspace trends (such as the sudden popularity of designing fidget spinners for 3D printing). Staff often found the space for open-ended reflection most valuable.

Guidance for Researchers Partnering with Libraries

Our work as university-based and nonprofit researchers with libraries over the past several years has been deeply rewarding to us. As scholars committed to libraries as spaces where all are welcome and can access cultural resources and activities that enrich lives, the opportunity to serve the research needs of libraries is an honor. We have also learned much about the potential for libraries as spaces for organizing learning in such a way that young people can discover new interests. We know—thanks to both the continued involvement of Anythink and their direct feedback—that libraries can and do value research and their partners who help meet those research and evaluation needs. But researchers who approach libraries as simply a "site for data collection" are likely to wind up unsatisfied, as are their prospective library partners. Therefore, in conclusion, we offer some advice for researchers on approaching libraries as prospective partners.

A Primary Concern of Library Staff Is Understanding How and Why Their Patrons Come and Return

Whereas researchers are often concerned with more traditional outcomes (e.g., "What did this young person learn about STEM when they came to a Maker program?"), library staff's primary concern is with drawing in and keeping the interest of patrons from all sectors of their communities. Researchers approaching libraries should seek to find questions related to engagement that align with their own questions and those of the field. How young people discover and pursue interests is one obvious focus for research, one in which choice about how to spend one's time and social supports are central concerns of theory and empirical study. In our view, connected learning resonates as a framework for practitioners in libraries precisely because it foregrounds issues they grapple with in designing programs, namely how to draw in patrons by appealing to their interests and by providing opportunities to discover new ones.

The Design of Spaces Is a Key Way Librarians Can Support Interest Discovery

Education researchers and evaluators often think of programs as an appropriate focus of research—that is, of organized activities, led by adult staff, to accomplish particular objectives that can be met through sustained participation in those activities. But libraries (and many other settings for learning outside of schools) are places where people drop in, where events are more common than ongoing programs for youth, and where volunteers and youth sometimes lead activities. What is distinctive about them is the possibilities for reorganizing spaces to support varied forms of participation. Again, these possibilities—realized in the example from Chicago's Harold Washington Library—are what have drawn librarians to the connected learning framework more broadly, and also to the HOMAGO framework ("hanging out, messing around, geeking out"; Ito, 2009) for characterizing different forms of engagement. The variety of library spaces designed to support connected learning makes it possible for young people to move fluidly between different activities that capture their attention or attract them to activities in which peers are deeply engaged. As education researchers, we are only beginning to explore the ways that spatial arrangements support and hinder different forms of learning. Much of the existing literature focuses not on the organization of activities but on environmental qualities, such as lighting and temperature, that affect learning in formal educational settings (e.g., Mott et al., 2012).

Focus on Data Collection That Is Easy to Implement and Integrate Into the Space, Providing Visibility for Patrons and Staff Alike

We have been struck by the uptake of talkback boards as a possible evaluation technique in our work with other libraries in our current project. We think the value of using talkback boards is that they give staff specific, timely, and potentially actionable feedback about program space. In the case of Anythink, the review of feedback from boards fits within a broader cycle of team meetings and reflection that exemplify ways sites can use informal evidence to guide efforts for improving programming. Researchers can help specifically by suggesting prompts that are provocative or that elicit aspects of participants' experience that are likely to be related to desired learning and developmental outcomes. Researchers can also help with analyzing data accumulated from boards over a longer period of time, yielding insights that would be difficult for staff to find time to develop on their own.

Our work with Anythink described here is intended to present just one case of how research–practice partnerships can support connected learning in libraries. Even within this one case, though, what we hope is clear is that research that follows the contours of problems of practice can take many forms and turns over time. Research that is mutualistic requires accommodation on both sides and responsiveness in the moment and over the long haul. This dynamism and responsiveness are precisely what attract many of us to this work, and it is also what makes it possible for research to be relevant to the ongoing work of libraries to serve their communities.

Note

1 The project is funded through a grant from the Institute for Museum and Library Services and includes the Los Angeles Public Library, the Young Adult Library Services Association, and the YOUMedia Community of Practice.

References

Anythink. (n.d.). *About Anythink*. Retrieved from www.anythinklibraries.org/

Azevedo, F. S. (2011). Lines of practice: A practice-centered theory of interest relationships. *Cognition and Instruction, 29*(2), 147–184.

Barron, B. (2006). Interest and self-sustained learning as catalysts of development: A learning ecology perspective. *Human Development, 49*(4), 193–224.

Barron, B. (2010). Conceptualizing and tracing learning pathways over time and setting. In W. R. Penuel & K. O'Connor (Eds.), *Learning Research as a Human Science: National Society for the Study of Education Yearbook, 109*(1), 113–127.

Barron, B., Gomez, K., Pinkard, N., & Martin, C. K. (2014). *The Digital Youth Network: Cultivating Digital Media Citizenship in Urban Communities*. Boston, MA: MIT Press.

Barton, A. C., & Bevan, B. (2016). *Leveraging RPPs to Address Racial Inequality in Urban School Districts*. Retrieved from http://wtgrantfoundation.org/leveraging-rpps-address-race-reduce-inequality-urban-school-districts

Bevan, B., Ryoo, J., Forrest, J., & Penuel, W. R. (2015). *Enriching and Expanding the Possibilities of Research-Practice Partnerships in Informal Science*. San Francisco, CA: Exploratorium.

Cammarota, J., & Fine, M. (eds.) (2010). *Revolutionizing Education: Youth Participatory Action Research in Motion*. New York, NY: Routledge.

Cartun, A., Kirshner, B., Price, E., & York, A. J. (2014). Friendship, participation, and site design in interest-driven learning among early adolescents. In J. L. Polman, E. A. Kyza, D. K. O'Neill, I. Tabak, W. R. Penuel, A. S. Jurow, K. O'Connor, T. F. Lee, & L. D'Amico (Eds.), *Proceedings of the 11th International Conference of the Learning Sciences* (Vol. 1, pp. 348–353). Boulder, CO: ISLS.

Ching, D., Santo, R., Hoadley, C., & Peppler, K. A. (2015). *On-ramps, Lane Changes, Detours and Destinations: Building Connected Learning Pathways in Hive NYC Through Brokering Future Learning Opportunities.* New York, NY: Hive Research Lab.

Coburn, C. E., & Penuel, W. R. (2016). Research-practice partnerships in education: Outcomes, dynamics, and open questions. *Educational Researcher, 45*(1), 48–54.

Cole, M. (1996). *Cultural Psychology: A Once and Future Discipline*. Cambridge, MA: Harvard University Press.

Cousins, J. B., & Earl, L. M. (1992). The case for participatory evaluation. *Educational Evaluation and Policy Analysis, 14*(4), 397–414.

Donovan, M. S. (2013). Generating improvement through research and development in educational systems. *Science, 340*, 317–319.

Gee, J. P. (2007). *Good Video Games and Good Learning: Collected Essays on Video Games, Learning, and Literacy*. London: Routledge.

Ito, M. (ed.). (2009). *Hanging out, Messing Around, and Geeking out: Kids Living and Learning with New Media*. Cambridge, MA: MIT Press.

Ito, M., Gutiérrez, K. D., Livingstone, S., Penuel, W. R., Rhodes, J. E., Salen, K., Schor, J., Sefton-Green, J., & Watkins, S. C. (2013). *Connected Learning: An Agenda for Research and Design*. Irvine, CA: Digital Media and Learning Research Hub.

Ito, M., Salen, K., & Sefton-Green, J. (in preparation). *Connected Learning: New Directions for Design, Research, and Practice*. Cambridge, MA: MIT Press.

Ito, M., Soep, E., Kligler-Vilenchik, N., Shresthova, S., Gamber-Thompson, L., & Zimmerman, A. M. (2015). Learning connected civics: Narratives, practices, infrastructures. *Curriculum Inquiry, 45*(1), 10–29.

Kirshner, B., Mitra, D., & O'Donoghue, J. L. (2001, April). *Youth as Researchers: Expanding Our Understandings of Expertise and Evidence.* Paper presented at the Annual Meeting of the American Research Association, Seattle, WA.

Kirshner, B., Pacheco, J., Sifuentes, M., & Hildreth, R. (2018). Rethinking 'the community' in university-community partnerships: Case studies from CU Engage. In B. Bevan & W. R. Penuel (Eds.), *Connecting Research and Practice: Developing New Models for Equity and Ethics.* New York, NY: Routledge.

Mark, M. M., & Shotland, R. L. (1985). Stakeholder-based evaluation and value judgments. *Evaluation Review, 9*(5), 605–626.

Mott, M. S., Robinson, D. H., Walden, A., Burnette, J., & Rutherford, A. S. (2012). Illuminating the effects of dynamic lighting on student learning. *Sage Open,* 1–12.

Papert, S. A. (1993). *Mindstorms: Children, Computers, and Powerful Ideas.* New York, NY: Basic Books.

Penuel, W. R., & Gallagher, D. (2017). *Creating Research-Practice Partnerships in Education.* Cambridge, MA: Harvard Education Press.

Philip, T. M., & Azevedo, F. S. (2017). Everyday science learning and equity: Mapping the contested terrain. *Science Education, 101*(4), 526–532.

Pinkard, N., Penuel, W. R., Dibi, O., Sultan, M. A., Quigley, D., Sumner, T., & Van Horne, K. (2016). *Mapping and Modeling the Abundance, Diversity, and Accessibility of Summer Learning Opportunities at the Scale of a City.* Paper presented at the Annual Meeting of the American Educational Research Association, Washington, DC.

Politics of Learning Writing Collective. (2017). The learning sciences in a new era of U.S. nationalism. *Cognition and Instruction, 35*(2), 91–102.

Roderick, M., Easton, J. Q., & Sebring, P. B. (2009). *The Consortium on Chicago School Research: A New Model for the Role of Research in Supporting Urban School Reform.* Chicago, IL: Consortium on Chicago School Research.

Rogoff, B. (2003). *The Cultural Nature of Human Development.* New York, NY: Oxford University Press.

Russell, J. L., Knutson, K., & Crowley, K. (2013). Informal learning organizations as part of an educational ecology: Lessons from collaboration across the formal-informal divide. *Journal of Educational Change, 14*(3), 259–281.

Sefton-Green, J., Watkins, C., & Kirshner, B. (2018). *Young People's Journeys into Creative Work: Challenges and Transitions into the Workforce.* New York, NY: Routledge.

Shadduck-Hernández, J. (2006). Here I am now! Critical ethnography and community service-learning with immigrant and refugee undergraduate students and youth. *Ethnography and Education, 1*(1), 67–86.

Soep, E. (2006). Critique: Assessment and the production of learning. *Teachers College Record, 108*(4), 748–777.

Subramaniam, M., Ahn, J., & Waugh, A. (2015). The role of school librarians in enhancing science learning. *Journal of Librarianship and Information Science, 47*(1), 3–16.

Tripp, L. (2011). Digital youth, libraries, and new media literacy. *The Reference Librarian, 52*(4), 329–341.

Watson, V. W. M., & Marciano, J. E. (2015). Examining a social-participatory youth co-researcher methodology: A cross-case analysis extending possibilities of literacy and research. *Literacy, 49*(1), 37–44.

Wertsch, J. V. (1985). *Vygotsky and the Social Formation of Mind.* Cambridge, MA: Harvard University Press.

14

LEARNING THROUGH NEW EXPERIENCES

A Researcher of Modern-Day Librarianship Discovers the Learning Sciences

Abigail L. Phillips

Introduction

The majority of my professional life has been spent within the realm of information science. During my Master's in library and information science (MLIS) coursework, I learned about information as a concept, information ethics as multifaceted and often contradictory (e.g., balancing privacy and access, determining professional boundaries), and the intricacies in helping individuals not only locate information but satisfy a larger need (e.g., the affective dimensions of information seeking). Postgraduation, my experiences as a librarian in a small, rural public library taught me what librarianship truly looks like and what library work entails, particularly when working with youth. My doctoral work narrowed my attention to a smaller area of information science (Phillips, 2016) while also expanding my understanding of the interdisciplinary nature of the field I have chosen to call home.

Information science has much to offer and learn from other fields. I concentrate on learning sciences in this essay for two key reasons: first, I have been a postdoctoral fellow in a department that has several active programs of learning sciences research. Second, I have encountered curiosity and enthusiasm from learning scientists when discussing my information science–focused research and collaborations with learning sciences and education scholars. With these collaborations is a recognition of librarians as educators has been emerging within learning sciences.

In this brief essay, I will highlight what learning sciences can learn from information science and what information science can learn from learning sciences. What has continued to surprise me since I began my fellowship has been the close connection between the two fields. I came to Utah State with little background in learning sciences—only recommended readings and participation in meetings, colloquia, and attending learning sciences–related conferences. Through a significant amount of reading and discussions with some of the people in the field, learning sciences is feeling more like a home for me as well—a different type of home but a welcoming environment for a young researcher.

Learning From Information Science

In my work, a major research strand is modern-day librarianship. With the ongoing shift in public perception of school and public libraries as "more than just books," librarians have taken on new and previously unrecognized roles and responsibilities. The Young Adult Library Services Association (YALSA) and American Association of School Librarians (AASL), two major divisions within the American Library Association (ALA), have produced recent publications, standards, and strategic plans that emphasize teaching and learning as librarian practices (AASL, 2014, 2017; Braun et al., 2014). As mentioned in the introduction to this volume by Lee and Phillips, scholars from learning sciences have begun to take note of the informal and even formal learning occurring in school and public libraries. However, there is still more to be discussed and examined.

Librarians as Learners

After leaving an MLIS or certification/endorsement program and entering the profession, librarians acquire roles and responsibilities the coursework may not have prepared them to do. School librarians are tasked with creating lessons outside of the more traditional information literacy instruction, developing strong relationships with teachers and administrators, and leading school clubs and activities (e.g., Student Council, Yearbook Club). Public librarians are increasingly pushed to develop STEM/STEAM-geared programming that may be outside of their comfort zone, collaborate with school systems to ensure students have needed resources in the public library, and fight for state, local, and federal funding.

For those in learning sciences, the number of roles and responsibilities librarians perform on a daily basis is probably surprising. Librarians manage more than books and other resources, often without helpful training or support. For learning sciences researchers and educators, this is an opportunity to fill existing education and information gaps. In a collaborative project with Victor Lee, Mimi Recker, and others, I have had the experience to learn how to address these gaps in librarian learning through a learning sciences lens. Our ongoing research seeks to better understand what instructional supports rural school and public librarians need to develop STEM-geared maker activities in their libraries (Lee et al., 2017). The research in learning sciences related to the design of learning environments and on teacher learning has relevant connections. Drawing on these literatures and connecting to librarianship could be one way that learning sciences and information sciences can mutually inform one another.

Library as an Informal Learning Space

The concept of "library as space" has been well researched in library and information science (LIS). Scholarship has been conducted on accessibility problems in academic libraries, school libraries as a learning environment, and public libraries as a shared community space (Audunson, Essmat, & Aabø, 2011; Lankes, 2012; Limberg & Alexandersson, 2003). Everything from decorations, layout, furniture, and book displays have an impact of how youth perceive the library (e.g., friendly and warm vs. quiet and rigid). The dispositions of the librarians maintaining these libraries have an important role in the library as a space and its overall feel. For some youth, libraries are a place of refuge from a difficult school day, being the outsider, or a rough home life. The librarian as empathetic and welcoming can do much to support the social, emotional, and psychological development of a youth (Phillips, 2017).

The library as an informal learning space has been a long-existing reality. School and public librarians provide print materials and online resources for curious young minds. But more and more librarians are turning to passive programming (e.g., computers for coding through Scratch, puzzles, K'Nex sets, and DIY activities) and community member–led events on everything from how to 3D print to graphic novel writing. Information science could contribute to existing conversations in learning sciences about space by highlighting research in the library as a physical learning space, different from a classroom or museums, with unique affordances, limitations, and roles (e.g., shared community space, programming space).

Learning From Learning Sciences

While still continuing to learn more about the field of learning sciences, slightly over 18 months into my fellowship, I continue to come across concepts, scholarship, and approaches to research that I believe should be shared with information science researchers and educators. Following are three examples that show the possible kinship between information science and learning sciences.

Teacher Learning

One interesting focus within learning sciences, which has implications for librarianship, is teacher learning. The coursework of various learning sciences programs demonstrates a commitment to increasing understanding of how people learn (Sommerhoff et al., 2018), particularly how teachers learn and how what teachers know impact the way in which they teach (Fishman & Davis, 2006). The attention to supporting ongoing professional learning of teachers and providing ways for analysis and reflection on teaching practices could easily fit into school library media coursework regarding instruction, evaluation, and assessment.

MLIS students interested in becoming public librarians frequently receive little or no education in information science programs about how to instruct patrons in a thoughtful and planned approach. With both school and public librarians taking on more instructional roles, there is an increased demand from librarians about how to teach effectively and efficiently. Time and staffing are often limited. Both school and public librarians are in need of information and instruction about how to help educate patrons of all ages, whether it is a series of sessions about digital literacy or a one-shot program on designing a website.

Design-Based Research (DBR)

First introduced to me through a series of articles and interactions at learning science–geared conferences (including the DBIR Workshop 2016), this methodology attempts to improve educational practices through an iterative process of analysis, design, development, and implementation (Design Based Research Collective, 2003; Penuel, Fishman, Haugan Cheng, & Sabelli, 2011). It requires the collaboration between researchers and practitioners in a learning setting. This collaboration is what has continued to interest me as I reevaluate how I conduct research and look for future directions.

Collaborating with researchers, inviting them to come into the library and work with librarians to aid in evaluating programs, services, or other aspects of librarianship would be a significant benefit to advancing library services. Both design-based research (DBR) and design-based implementation research (DBIR) efforts in libraries have been limited in the research literature (although a version of DBIR appears in Tzou et al., Chapter 10.), but there is hope for growth and continued interest. Although in practice DBR may pose challenges including confusions and misunderstandings, it provides valuable opportunities for research to impact practice and practice to impact research.

Different Forms of Empirical Research

When diving into the learning sciences literature, I noticed a contrast in the type of research conducted within learning sciences versus some of the research from information science. Learning sciences displays a broad set of systematic methodology that I have not seen consistently within information science. In the conclusion of this volume, Beth Yoke comments on the need for research that propels librarianship forward. Especially when looking at public library and youth services research, readers encounter anecdotes, how-to guides, and best practices reflections. These are worthwhile resources for librarians and other library staff, but this does little to provide meaningful and lasting contribution to the profession.

However, much is needed in the way of rigorous scholarship about how young adults engage with their libraries, what they need for current and future endeavors, and critical analysis of how youth are being served in libraries. Learning sciences has a demonstrated range of approach to research. Information science could greatly benefit by incorporating current learning sciences methodology with existing methodology.

Closing Reflections

Not to sound overly passionate and nonacademic, this is an exciting time to be researching libraries, learning, and serving youth in the library. I am inspired by the creation of a learning sciences SIG within Association of Information Science and Technology (ASIS&T) and the enthusiastic response during the first meeting during ASIS&T's Annual Conference 2017. The collaborations taking place between colleges of education and schools of information/information science across the United States indicate a mutual respect.

The new partnership between these fields, including a new journal, *Information and Learning Sciences*, offers hope for advancing and strengthening both fields. This essay presented a few of my reflections on opportunities for partnership and shared learning experiences. However, there is much room for additional conversation, collaboration, and share learning.

References

American Association of School Librarians. (2014). *AASL Strategic Plan*. Retrieved from www.ala.org/aasl/about/governing-docs/strategic-plan

American Association of School Librarians. (2017). *National School Library Standards*. Retrieved from http://standards.aasl.org/

Audunson, R., Essmat, S., & Aabø, S. (2011). Public libraries: A meeting place for immigrant women? *Library & Information Science Research, 33*(3), 220–227.

Braun, L., Hartman, M. L., Hughes-Hassell, S., Kumasi, K., & Yoke, B. (2014). *The Future of Library Services for and with Teens: A Call to Action*. Chicago, IL: Young Adults Library Services Association.

Design Based Research Collection. (2003). Design-based research: An emerging paradigm for educational inquiry. *Educational Researcher, 32*(1), 5–8.

Fishman, B., & Davis, E. A. (2006). Teacher learning research and the learning sciences. In R. K. Sawyer (Ed.), *Cambridge Handbook of the Learning Sciences* (pp. 535–550). New York, NY: Cambridge University Press.

Lankes, R. D. (2012). *Expect More: Demanding Better Libraries for Today's Complex World*. North Charleston, SC: CreateSpace.

Lee, V. R., Lewis, W., Searle, K. A., Recker, M., Hansen, J., & Phillips, A. (2017). Supporting interactive youth maker programs in public and school libraries: Design hypotheses and first implementations. In P. Blikstein & D. Abrahamson (Eds.), *Proceedings of Interaction Design and Children (IDC) 2017*. Stanford, CA: ACM.

Limberg, L., & Alexandersson, M. (2003). The school library as a space for learning. *School Libraries Worldwide, 9*(1), 1–15.

Penuel, W. R., Fishman, B. J., Haugan Cheng, B., & Sabelli, N. (2011). Organizing research and development at the intersection of learning, implementation, and design. *Educational Researcher*, *40*(7), 331–337. doi:https://doi.org/10.3102/0013189X11421826

Phillips, A. L. (2016). *The Empathetic Librarian: Rural Librarians as a Source of Support for Rural Cyberbullied Young Adults* (Order No. 10120555). Available from ProQuest Dissertations & Theses Global.

Phillips, A. L. (2017). Understanding empathetic services: The role of empathy in everyday library work. *Journal of Research on Libraries and Young Adults*, *8*(1).

Sommerhoff, D., Szameitat, A., Vogel, F., Chernikova, O., Loderer, K., & Fischer, F. (2018). What do we teach when we teach the learning sciences? A Document analysis of 75 graduate programs. *Journal of the Learning Sciences*, *null-null*. doi:10.1080/10508406.2018.1440353

LOOKING BACK TO SEE FORWARD

Beth Yoke

In thinking about the future of library services for and with youth, it may be helpful to first look at where we've been, as some of what we are dealing with today has been carried forward from the past. In *The Fair Garden and the Swarm of Beasts: The Library and the Young Adult*, by Margaret Edwards, which was first published in 1969, Edwards identifies five ways the public library has failed young people:

1. *It has failed in the relationship of the majority of the staff to adolescents.* Edwards points to a 1967 report that described the negative attitudes many library staff have toward teens and how this negativity turns youth away from libraries.
2. *The urban public library is off balance. Its concern is with its informational services to the neglect of other needs of its patrons.* Here Edwards talks about the fact that libraries focus much of their efforts toward youth around helping them with school assignments and neglect to provide any services or resources for their developmental or recreational needs, hobbies, or personal interests.
3. *The public library is passive rather than active.* Edwards compares libraries to grocery stores, where the customer is simply there to pick up some items and leave with them. She bemoans the fact that library staff are focused on collecting and organizing materials and don't interact much with patrons beyond checking materials in or out or answering questions if asked.
4. *Our obsession with the catalog is a boomerang that has sailed back to harm our relations with the teenager and to diminish his joy in reading.* Edwards sees the most important role of library staff as that of helping patrons rather than forcing the patrons to learn library systems and processes.
5. *We are not meeting new challenges with new ideas.* Edwards discusses the changing demographics of the youth in her community and decries the fact that many libraries see no need to evolve so they are better positioned to meet the needs of this new generation.

In reviewing her list, many would agree that the challenges libraries faced half a century ago mirror the ones many libraries are still struggling with now, and if we fail to address them, we will continue to struggle with in the future. It's worth it, then, to take a closer look at these challenges and how libraries might act to overcome them.

1. Library Staff Attitudes

Libraries need to be a place—both physical and virtual—where youth are welcomed. Unfortunately, it also needs to be stated that libraries must be a place where ALL youth are welcomed. Too many of today's libraries serve only those who they feel comfortable serving. These are often youth who are willing and able to come to the physical library space. Yet even those young people who do go to a public or school library often feel unwelcome. A survey of high school students done in 2013 found that about a quarter of the students' perceived libraries as having uninviting atmospheres and staffs.[1] For libraries to remain relevant into the future, they must appeal to young people and embrace ways to engage them in codesigning a library experience that meets their needs and interests.

It's also worth remembering that young people most in need of library services are often those who, for whatever reason(s), never come through the door and do not receive any services. Libraries cannot afford to turn a blind eye to them if they are going to remain relevant into the future. In the last century, Margaret Edwards resorted to loading up a horse-drawn vegetable cart with books and driving it through low-income neighborhoods to reach underserved youth. With the resources and technology we have today, libraries have absolutely no excuse for failing to serve those who traditionally have been underserved in their community. It is imperative that public libraries stop paying lip service to the notion of serving everyone from cradle to grave and start acting on it.

2. Services for and With Youth

In Margaret Edwards's time, she lamented the fact that most libraries focused only on helping youth with school assignments and neglected to address other needs and interests of youth. Many of today's libraries have made strides in this area and do provide services beyond homework help. In particular, most offer summer programming and recreational activities outside of school hours. However, the majority of libraries take a backward approach to planning and delivering these services and programs. Too often, library staff work in isolation to plan programs and then wonder why few or no young people show up. To be successful, the library worker must first find out the needs and interests of the youth in their community and then engage them and their families in planning and carrying out the program. Older youth in particular do not want something done *to* them. They want to have ownership in the activity and a chance to share their interests, knowledge, and skills.

3. Responsive Libraries

Margaret Edwards wanted libraries to focus on the individual, not on the materials. She did not believe that libraries were warehouses for storing books. Instead, she felt that libraries had the power to transform lives through the learning opportunities they provided. Still today, libraries are much too focused on what is housed in them, whether it's books or 3D printers. Library staff must stop thinking first about the materials and then about the community members as an afterthought. To succeed into the future, libraries must put young people first. Because most of today's library staff are white and female, while the majority of today's youth are not, putting young people first means library staff must build cultural competence skills. Cultural competency and a commitment to equity, diversity, and inclusion are necessary for library staff if libraries are going to survive into the future.

4. Library Processes and Policies

In Margaret Edwards's time, the card catalog was one of the most prominent features in the library. In her opinion, library staff placed too much emphasis on young people learning how to use this tool and as a result failed to adequately serve youth and address their needs. While the tools in twenty-first-century libraries are different from those in Edwards's time, libraries that focus too much on things like tools and policies over providing effective service do so at their own peril. For example, library policies that create barriers to access for young people, such as requiring an ID or signing a behavior contract, put libraries first and young people second. Doing so signals to young people that they are not valued or particularly welcome at the library, which is a perception that they can carry with them into adulthood, when they will be expected to vote for levies that support libraries. By focusing first on young people, libraries can create a welcoming, inclusive space that not only meets the needs of youth but cultivates future library advocates. This infographic from the Young Adult Library Services Association illustrates what youth-centered library services and programs looks like.

5. Recognizing the Need for Change

Edwards saw the world changing around her and felt that libraries would only be successful if they changed along with it. Her sentiment rings true today more than ever. Today, rapid and significant change is a fact of life, and accepting that our environment is in a constant state of flux is necessary if libraries are to survive. Yet acceptance is not enough. Libraries also must find creative solutions to problems. Albert Einstein is broadly credited with saying that "the definition of insanity is doing the same thing over and over again but expecting different results." Libraries must heed this warning and recognize that strategies that may have been adequate in the past are failing today's young people. For example, public libraries have been offering summer reading programs for youth for decades. Yet standardized

REIMAGINED LIBRARY SERVICES FOR AND WITH TEENS

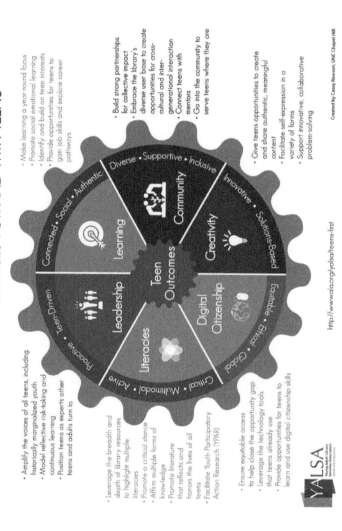

- Amplify the voices of all teens, including historically marginalized youth
- Model reflective risk-taking and continuous learning
- Position teens as experts other teens and adults turn to

- Make learning a year-round focus
- Promote social emotional learning
- Identify and build on teen interests
- Provide opportunities for teens to gain job skills and explore career pathways

- Build strong partnerships for collective impact
- Embrace the library's diverse user base to create opportunities for cross-cultural and inter-generational interaction
- Connect teens with mentors
- Go into the community to serve teens where they are

- Give teens opportunities to create and share authentic, meaningful content
- Facilitate self-expression in a variety of forms
- Support innovative, collaborative problem-solving

- Ensure equitable access to help close the opportunity gap
- Leverage the technology tools that teens already use
- Provide opportunities for teens to learn and use digital citizenship skills

- Leverage the breadth and depth of library resources to highlight multiple literacies
- Promote a critical stance
- Affirm multiple forms of knowledge
- Promote literature that reflects and honors the lives of all teens
- Facilitate Youth Participatory Action Research (YPAR)

(Wheel labels: Connected · Social · Authentic — Diverse · Supportive · Inclusive — Innovative · Solutions-based — Equitable · Ethical · Global — Critical · Multimodal · Active — Proactive · Teen-Driven)

(Wheel segments: Learning, Community, Creativity, Digital Citizenship, Literacies, Leadership, Teen Outcomes)

YALSA
Young Adult Library Services Association

http://www.ala.org/yalsa/teens-first

Created by Casey Rawson, UNC Chapel Hill

FIGURE 15.1   An infographic from the Young Adult Library Services Association that illustrates features of effective youth-centered library services and programs.

reading test scores are virtually flat. Worse, persistent gaps exist between reading achievement of white students and those of their peers of color.[2] Public libraries must stop offering the same summer reading programs and expecting that they are going to increase the literacy achievement of today's youth. Letting go of what is not working any longer as well as looking outward to find new ideas and models that work for today's youth is essential to libraries' survival into the future.

I. Future of Youth

To speculate with any accuracy as to the future of youth services through libraries, a reasonable approach is to examine trends and demographics of youth. Statistical resources, such as census information, provide reliable information about what the youth of the future will probably look like. Here are some quick estimates from the U.S. Census:

- By 2020, youth of color will comprise the majority of the youth population.
- By 2050, there is expected to be 45 million adolescents in the U.S.
- By 2060, the percentage of Hispanic youth is expected to reach 34%, while the percentage of white, non-Hispanic youth will drop to 36%; together, youth who belong to ethnic/racial "minority" groups will comprise 64% of the youth population.

In addition to demographics, it's important to examine the environment in which our nation's youth are growing up. Unfortunately, it seems very likely that systemic societal problems impacting youth now will continue into the future. A study released in February 2018 entitled "Healing Our Divided Society: Investing in America Fifty Years After the Kerner Report" says the percentage of people living in deep poverty has increased since 1975 by 16%, from 30% in 1975 to 46% today. Furthermore, gains to ending school segregation have been reversed because of a lack of court oversight and housing discrimination. Over the past fifty years, school districts were able to move away from desegregation plans, while at the same time, housing discrimination forced black and Latino families to move into largely minority neighborhoods. In 1988, about 44% of black students went to majority-white schools nationally. Only 20% of black students do so today, according to the report. "The result of these gaps means that people of color and those struggling with poverty are confined to poor areas with inadequate housing, underfunded schools and law enforcement that views those residents with suspicion."[3]

Another area of concern that will likely have an impact on youth is growing inequality and the opportunity gap it creates for young people. Multiple reports, including the 2018 World Inequality Report, have shone a light on the increasing inequality between the wealthy and the poor, including the fact that income inequality in the U.S. has been growing the past few decades. This has contributed to a widening opportunity gap for low-income youth and their families. As a result, "children's social class is one of the most significant predictors—if not the single most significant predictor—of their educational success."[4] With no strong indicators that this inequality trend will reverse any time soon, we must consider it when thinking about the future of our nation's youth.

Keeping these trends in mind when thinking about the future of library services for and with youth can help ensure that libraries are meeting critical needs in their community.

II. Future of Youth Services

With half of today's teens reporting that they leave high school unprepared for college or careers,[5] and standardized test scores that show persistent gaps between white students and their peers of color, it is clear that libraries need to rethink what they do and how they do it to better meet the needs of today's youth.[6] Luckily, how they can do that is not a mystery.

In 2014, the Young Adult Library Services Association (YALSA), with funding from the Institute of Museum and Library Services, published the report, "The Future of Library Services for and with Teens: A Call to Action." The report provided pages of recommendations for how libraries needed to evolve to meet the needs of twenty-first-century youth. Yet four years later, the recommendations have not seen widespread adoption. YALSA member surveys conducted in 2016 and 2017 showed that the majority of members had not moved forward with key recommendations and, in addition, showed little or no progress between 2016 and 2017. For example:

TABLE 15.1 Responses to a survey of Young Adult Library Services Association (YALSA) members in 2016 and 2017 showing limited adoption of YALSA's 2014 recommendations for youth programs and services in libraries.

Recommendation	% of survey respondents who implemented recommendation in 2016[1]	% of survey respondents who implemented recommendation in 2017[2]
Incorporated connected learning principles into programs	33.6%	34.0%
Adopted an outcomes focused approach to programs and services	24.6%	22.8%
Built my own cultural competence skills	52.8%	51.1%
Embedded youth voice into programs and services	45.9%	41.2%

1 Responses to a survey of Young Adult Library Services Association (YALSA) members in 2016.
2 Responses to a survey of Young Adult Library Services Association (YALSA) members in 2017.

The report's recommendations have relevance today and will likely continue to be relevant into the near future. Libraries that make a commitment to embracing the recommendations will be well-positioned to meet the needs of twenty-first-century youth. Revisiting the report and unpacking the recommendations can help libraries reenvision their youth services with a forward-thinking mindset. As a follow-up to the report, the book *Putting Teens First in Library Services: A Road Map* (YALSA, 2017), takes an in-depth approach to operationalizing the recommendations at the building level.

YALSA's report and book are by no means the only resources libraries have when creating a plan for meeting the needs of today's and tomorrow's youth. The Aspen Institute's 2014 report, "Rising to the Challenge: Re-Envisioning Public Libraries," lays out a clear plan for moving libraries forward, much of which is relevant and adaptable for youth services. As a sort of companion to the report and published in the same year by the Aspen Institute is "Learner at the Center of a Networked World." This youth-focused document provides a wealth of information for libraries regarding how to support the learning needs of youth.

Other key documents that are informing the future of youth services include:

- ASTC & ULC (2014, October). Learning Labs in Libraries and Museums: Transformative Spaces for Teens. Retrieved March 5, 2018, from www.urbanlibraries.org/filebin/pdfs/Learning_Labs_in_Libraries_and_Museums_2014.pdf
- Ito, M., et al. (2009). *Hanging Out, Messing Around, and Geeking Out: Kids Living and Learning with New Media*. Cambridge, MA: MIT Press.

Libraries that engage staff in reading these reports and exploring how the recommendations can help youth in their community will not only remain relevant into the future but increase their position in the community as a vital institution.

III. Positioning Ourselves For the Future

We cannot afford to value the past more than the future. Libraries must embrace a forward-focused approach to planning and delivering impactful library services for and with youth and reject past practices and mindsets that are holding us back. In no particular order, the following is an incomplete list of changes to embrace. Library staff can view the list as a starting point and no doubt identify other priorities for themselves and their libraries, based on the particular needs of their community.

Advocate

Libraries need funds in order to effectively serve their communities. Too often, we have been timid and willing to settle for crumbs that barely enable libraries to keep the doors open, let alone provide effective services and purchase needed resources.

To truly have a transformative impact on our communities, libraries need robust funding, which we will not get if we do not ask for it loudly and often. It's worth noting that the Institute of Museum and Library Services regularly requests about $230 million for the Library Services Technology Act, which goes to support the nation's 119,000+ libraries. On the other hand, there are multiple federal funding sources for after-school programs, just one of which provides over $1.2 billion annually for after-school programs. Compared to libraries, there are just over 4,000 Boys and Girls Clubs of America and just 2,700 YMCAs in the U.S. Why are we complacent about libraries getting so much less funding than other informal learning providers like after-school programs? Our hesitancy to speak up for robust funding is hurting our nation's youth. To reverse this, we need to be active at the local, state, and federal levels and engage others in advocacy work as well.

Rethink the Curriculum for Preprofessionals

The notion that the curriculum for preprofessionals in libraries is increasingly out of line with the knowledge and skills library staff need to be successful on the front line is fairly common throughout the profession. If schools continue to adhere to an antiquated curriculum, the future of libraries is in peril. For youth services, curricular content should focus on topics such as youth development, cultural competence, connected learning, multiple literacies, community and family engagement, collective impact, and more. By better preparing the next generation of library staff, we will position libraries to thrive in the future.

Reflect on What It Means to be a Librarian

Librarians have traditionally prided themselves on being the expert in all things; however, this mindset is not conducive to the future success of libraries. In today's rapidly changing environment, it is not realistic to think that any one individual can be an expert in everything. Librarians must abandon this idea and instead leverage community members' expertise whenever possible. For example, library staff should not avoid teaching youth how to code simply because staff are not confident coders. Libraries can connect with local businesses and colleges to identify coders who can host a program for youth. As noted in "The Future of Library Services for and with Teens: A Call to Action," "library staff have traditionally been information keepers; as young people and their learning expectations change, it will be critical for library staff to establish themselves in a role of co-learner and be comfortable working alongside young people to learn together."[7]

Prioritize Research

Unfortunately, much of the research that is done within the library community, especially when related to youth services, does little to advance libraries or the profession of librarianship. For example, determining the number of children's or young adult publications in a given year that are written by an author from a diverse background does not directly help libraries (nor is it truly research). However, determining the degree to which youth participation in summer learning programs prevents summer learning loss not only yields information that libraries can use to improve their programs but can be leveraged as an advocacy tool to show the positive impact libraries have on youth. As of spring 2018, the Association for Library Service to Children is in the process of developing a research agenda. The Young Adult Library Services Association's *National Research Agenda on Libraries, Learning and Teens 2017–2021* can be found online: www.ala.org/yalsa/guidelines/research/researchagenda. These agendas can help researchers home in on the research questions that are the most pressing to the profession.

Act With a Sense of Urgency

The world is changing around us and without us. Institutions that succeed are those that are flexible and responsive and can quickly adjust to a changing environment. Doing away with or modifying policies and practices that slow down decision making is vital if libraries are going to succeed in the future.

Embrace Equity, Diversity, and Inclusion

Libraries must do more than pay lip service to equity, diversity, and inclusion. As stated in YALSA's Teen Services Competencies for Library Staff, it's vital that library staff "recognizes barriers such as racism, ethnocentrism, classism, heterosexism, genderism, ableism, and other systems of discrimination and exclusion in the community and its institutions, including the library, and interrupts them by way of culturally competent services."[8] Additionally, recruiting to the profession must focus on individuals from diverse backgrounds to reverse the trend of library staff who are primarily white and female. As noted earlier, census data shows that youth of color will constitute the majority of youth by 2020. They want and deserve to be served by library staff who are both culturally competent and reflect the increasingly diverse population.

Look Beyond the Profession for Solutions

While it's natural to look within the profession for answers, it's also important to look to other education or youth-serving institutions, or even beyond those, for fresh solutions to challenges. The burgeoning after-school community is one example of a place library staff can look to for innovation and a different perspective.

Stop Feeding Stereotypes and Misperceptions

Multiple studies, including *Perceptions of Libraries, 2010: Context and Community*,[9] show that the vast majority of the general public, including youth, equate libraries only with books. As a result, they see libraries as antiquated places that have limited or no use for them. As noted in *The Library Quarterly* article "Teens, Technology, and Libraries: An Uncertain Relationship,"

> This limited perception meant they [youth] would mainly think to use a library when looking for a paper book, not for socializing or for entertainment opportunities or to take advantage of the many other services libraries offer. And since most of the participants expressed a preference for technology over paper books, they tended to view technology as more appealing than libraries. As one of the 18-year-old girls said, she didn't use libraries because "I'm not a book person."[10]

When we focus our library messaging and imagery primarily on paper books in our newsletters, signage, fliers, annual reports, social media, and so on, we are perpetuating the misperception that most of the general public has that libraries are primarily dusty old repositories for books. As a result, many thousands of people are not using or supporting libraries. Libraries must create and promote a fuller picture of what a twenty-first-century library has to offer, or future generations of Americans are going to continue to see them as irrelevant.

While today's libraries are facing many challenges, they have a window of opportunity to reinvent themselves. The amount of goodwill the general public feels toward libraries and library staff is significant. Leveraging this sentiment as well as embracing a commitment to change can help libraries shed outdated mindsets and methods and, as a result, increase their impact on the community by helping young people overcome societal challenges to succeed in school and prepare for college, careers, and life.

Notes

1 Agosto, D. E., & Abbas, J. (2017). "Don't Be Dumb—That's the Rule I Try to Live By": A Closer Look at Older Teens' Online Privacy and Safety Attitudes. *New Media & Society*, *19*(3), 347–365.

2 National Assessment of Educational Progress. (2015, September 22). *Achievement Gaps*. Retrieved March 5, 2018, from https://nces.ed.gov/nationsreportcard/studies/gaps/

3 Contreras, R. (2018, February 27). *Study: US Inequality Persists 50 Years After Landmark Report*. Retrieved March 5, 2018, from www.apnews.com/5b86a6a0b24a42dfa832103 e686144c0/Report:-Inequality-remains-50-years-after-Kerner-Report

4 Gauder, B. (2011). Perceptions of Libraries, 2010: Context and Community. A Report to the OCLC Membership. OCLC Online Computer Library Center, Inc.

5 Ito, M., Baumer, S., Bittanti, M., boyd, d., Cody, R., Herr-Stephenson, B., Horst, H. A., Lange, P. G., Mahendran, D., Martínez, K. Z., Pascoe, C. J., Perkel, D., Robinson, L., Sims, C., & Tripp, L. (2009). *Hanging out, Messing Around, and Geeking out: Kids Living and Learning with New Media*. Cambridge, MA: MIT Press.

   youthtruth.org. (2017). *Learning from Student Voice: How Prepared do Students Feel for College and Career?* Retrieved March 5, 2018, from www.youthtruthsurvey.org/college-career-readiness-2017/

6 National Assessment of Educational Progress. Achievement Gaps. (2015, September 22). Retrieved March 5, 2018, from https://nces.ed.gov/nationsreportcard/studies/gaps/

7 YALSA. (2014). *The Future of Library Services for and with Teens: A Call to Action*, p. 21. Retrieved March 6, 2018, from www.ala.org/yaforum/sites/ala.org.yaforum/files/content/YALSA_nationalforum_Final_web_0.pdf

8 YALSA. (2017). *Teen Services Competencies for Library Staff*. Retrieved March 6, 2018, from www.ala.org/yalsa/guidelines/yacompetencies2010

9 De Rosa, C., et al. (2011). *Perceptions of Libraries, 2010: Context and Community*. Dublin, OH: OCLC Online Computer Library Center. Retrieved March 6, 2018, from www.oclc.org/en/reports/2010perceptions.html

10 Agosto, D., et al. (2016). Teens, Technology, and Libraries: An Uncertain Relationship. *The Library Quarterly, 86*(3), 248–269.

INDEX

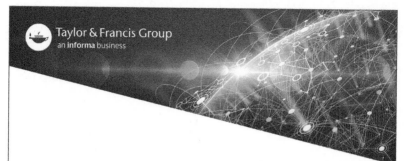